RUNNING DIALOGUE

Running Dialogue

A Coach's Story

Harry Wilson
with Angela Patmore
with a foreword by Steve Ovett

STANLEY PAUL
London Melbourne Sydney Auckland Johannesburg

Stanley Paul & Co. Ltd

An imprint of the Hutchinson Publishing Group

17–21 Conway Street, London W1P 6JD

Hutchinson Group (Australia) Pty Ltd
30–32 Cremorne Street, Richmond South, Victoria 3121
PO Box 151, Broadway, New South Wales 2007

Hutchinson Group (NZ) Ltd
32–34 View Road, PO Box 40-086, Glenfield, Auckland 10

Hutchinson Group (SA) Pty Ltd
PO Box 337, Bergvlei 2012, South Africa

First published 1982

Set in Baskerville by Computape (Pickering) Ltd,
Pickering, North Yorkshire

Printed in Great Britain by The Anchor Press Ltd
and bound by Wm Brendon & Son Ltd,
both of Tiptree, Essex

British Library Cataloguing in Publication Data
Wilson, Harry
    Running Dialogue
    1. Ovett, Steve 2. Runners (Sports) – England –
Biography
    I. Title
    796.4'26'0924   GV697.0/

To Ann, Delyse, Gloria, Janet, Josephine, Lesley, Margaret, Marion, Mary, Pat, Pauline, Sue, Wendy, Andy, Archie, Bill, Bob, Chris, Dave, Donald, Denver, Eddie, Henk, Hugh, Ian, Jim, John, Julian, Kirk, Mike, Pete, Richard, Roger, Tony and the many other athletes that I've coached but who have taught me so much – and of course Mr O. himself

Contents

Acknowledgements

I am eternally grateful for the extraordinary and unique assistance that came from Angela Patmore during the preparation of this book.

Photographic acknowledgements

The publishers and the author wish to thank the following for permission to use copyright photographs: George Herringshaw, Knut Ed. Holm, Mark Shearman, Mike Street, Bob Benn.

Foreword
Steve Ovett

I have hated Harry Wilson – have done on many
occasions ever since I've known him, and that's the best
compliment I can give him. Harry's diminutive figure,
increasing waistline and decreasing stride length belie
his ability to evoke this emotion, but instilled in his
psychological make-up and honed to cynical perfection
over the years of his involvement with athletics and
athletes is Harry's complete understanding of what not
to say at the right moment.

In various states of exhaustion and nausea I have lain
twitching on the track after a particularly gruelling
session, gazed up at Harry's smiling face and been
subjected to various statements such as, 'Did you have
one or two fried eggs for breakfast this morning Steve?' or
'Don't lie there too long: the sprinters have just come out
onto the track!' Hate is a great motivator.

I am a great believer in fate and I know that Harry is
too, so I suppose that looking back it should have been
no surprise to us both that we were fated to meet and
spend some of the most enjoyable, satisfying and sometimes splendidly humorous moments of our lives
together.

Harry has strength of character that I have heavily
relied upon on many occasions; he is decisive, humorous,
extremely emotive, fairly cunning and sometimes down-
right objectionable.

This is Harry's book, his thoughts, his views and his
reactions to some of the events in his career as an athlete

and coach. I am pleased to say that we differ on certain points, agree on many and laugh at a few. But I hope you enjoy the book as much as we had experiencing it. As to Harry all I can say is, I've had two eggs, I'm still exhausted and I still hate you – but it's been great fun hasn't it, Tiger?

Introduction

A bird's-eye view of Sydney appeared through the window. I was on the plane to Brisbane to coach on a young athletes course. Seeing the terrain down there, I started reminiscing about running round a rough old field, years ago and miles away, with a few friends. Just a bit of fun really: I never imagined that because of running round that field I'd one day be flying round the world to talk on athletics. Even when I began my coaching career, I never dreamt I'd coach a genius, or the greatest runner in the world, yet I came to regard Steve Ovett as both of those. And now I'm writing this book, which is another thing I never dreamt of. My publisher has been sticking pins in me for two years trying to get me to do it. I've only agreed in order to dispel one or two illusions about Steve, and before I tell you about him, I ought to tell you something about myself, and something about the middle distance scene he was to steal.

I played football in the Air Training Corps and in the summer our sports officer, an ex-professional sprinter by the name of Harry Morris, organized an athletics team in Welwyn Garden City. A group of us used to do what we fondly imagined was training around this old field, near what is now Gosling stadium. It was decided that as I'd played on the wing at football, I should be a sprinter, and that as I wasn't big enough to be a real 100 metres sprinter, I should do 200 and 400 metres (220 and 440 yards in those days).

Later, on my father's advice, I joined St Albans Athletics Club and won the Hertfordshire County Championship at 400 metres. For 400 metres I trained two or three times a week, sprinting and doing time trials mainly (though I recall doing a colossal 2×300 metres in an evening once) with a lot of talking and playing about. My best 400 time was around 51.5 seconds representing the Southern Counties. Running with me, against Oxford University, were Harold Parlett, who won the European 800-metres championship in 1958, and Arthur Wint, who became Olympic 400-metres champion in 1948. As an afterthought I tried a couple of 800 metres (best time around 1:58), and I kept going in these events for a long while without really knowing what I was doing.

In 1948 I had a glimpse of another side of athletics. I went on a week's summer school for prospective athletes at Loughborough. The Chief National Coach to the Amateur Athletics Association then was a former army major and PT instructor, Geoff Dyson. A self-made class hurdler, Dyson chose to coach the most technical events such as pole vault, shot and steeplechase. Recently some coaches have criticized him for concentrating on technique, but he did a great deal to bring the UK up to date in the world and travelled the length and breadth of what he called 'the athletic wilderness' lecturing and coining phrases that were to become part of the coaching patois.

As a talker Dyson was very straightforward, very open: even a bit theatrical. He knew how to hold an audience, and studied his delivery as well as his subject. I was impressed by this man's ability to direct and motivate people, and even now I'd say it's important, particularly with youngsters, to make an impact as he did, to capture their imagination. So although I'd gone on the course looking for tips on training, I was suddenly intrigued at the possibility of inspiring other people, like Geoff Dyson did. In the back of my mind even then I suppose I knew I'd never be a great athlete, that perhaps my true vocation was coaching.

14

In 1955, when I was twenty-nine, I switched to long distance. I had been knocked out in the heats of a 220 yards handicap race at Kempston Open sports meeting in Bedfordshire and I was persuaded to make up a team for St Albans AC in the 10-mile road race – using another runner's name. I finished the distance in 57.30 and I was given a gold medal – well, to me it was gold – for being in the winning team. 'This is a piece of cake,' I thought. 'If I can run ten miles in fifty-seven minutes on two to four hundred metre training I ought to amount to something at this.' True, the last two miles were an ordeal and my legs were solid, but never mind. I immediately changed my training habits. A little group of us would set out from the clubroom to go round the city roads, initially with the others going away from me and later with me going away from them.

Within twelve months I was tackling 20-milers and marathons. I ran 29:30 for 6 miles, 49:40 for 10 miles and 2 hours 35 minutes for the marathon – all on a training mileage of about forty miles a week. I found myself running quite fast sub-distance times too, which set me thinking. Altogether, I ran for Hertfordshire at every distance from 100 yards to 20 miles, with 440 yards hurdles and the triple jump thrown in. I represented Wales a couple of times on the track and several times in the International cross-country championships, and I was Welsh 6-mile (10,000 metres) champion in 1958. That was the zenith of my active career. The nadir came in the annual Poly Marathon from Windsor Castle to Chiswick.

The previous year I'd started much too fast, crawling home after being among the leaders at 10 miles. This year, I thought, I'll do the opposite: I'll start off gently and try to hang on better. At the 20-mile mark I was fortieth, with everybody going very painfully, when I heard somebody shout out that I was twenty something, from which I inferred that I must be twentieth, too near the front. I thought I'd better slow down. I reached Chiswick roundabout and a woman pushing a pram

15

along the pavement accelerated past, glancing back at me pityingly. I didn't realize how slowly I had been going. In my defence, I must add that the temperature was in the nineties and I did manage to finish in the first twenty-five.

More important than my long-distance efforts, I was reading all the great authorities on running: Gerschler, the German coach who developed Josy Barthel, the 1952 Olympic 1500 metres champion; Igloi, the Hungarian whose athletes once held every world record from 800 metres to 10,000 metres; Franz Stampfl who had coached the Oxbridge trio of Bannister, Chataway and Brasher; Lydiard, the New Zealander coach to Olympic champions Peter Snell and Murray Halberg; Cerutty the eccentric Australian, mentor to the great Herb Elliott. I met the great Percy Wells Cerutty at the Commonwealth Games in Cardiff in 1958. I also met Arthur Lydiard very briefly, and I was struck by the contrast between them. Lydiard seemed to have little time for discussing running with someone not well established, whereas Cerutty was willing to talk, and he made an indelible impression on me. He was a man of great charisma, capable of investing even batty ideas with the strength of his personality. Of course, I wasn't even a proper coach in those days, and even when I was and I visited Percy at his famous camp in Portsea, Victoria, he insisted I sit on the ground like a small boy while he delivered an oration from his legendary pulpit. He was incomparable.

I didn't have a coach during my athletic years: very few people did. The closest approximation was Stan Tomlin, an ex-Commonwealth Games 3-mile champion who was St Albans AC chairman. His main advice was not to overdo things. In the evolutionary chain, athletes came before coaches, and even today you occasionally find a successful athlete without a coach, though never the other way around. I often think athletes are ahead of us coaches in many ways, though our knowledge is pooled from both sides, of course. I continued running races until 1963 but I gave up competing seriously in 1959 because by then I had started coaching and I was more concerned with the performance of my athletes than I was with my own. One of my first 'pupils' was a boy called Richard Jones. In a year he went from running 4:24 for the mile to winning the AAA junior championship in 4:10, a new UK junior record.

Like all the best children from the previous year's championships Richard went on the annual English Schools course at Lilleshall in 1959. I think he must have talked to Geoff Dyson about me, because the following year when Jim Alford retired as national middle-distance coach, Dyson asked me to take over. I had done the odd weekend course at Lilleshall for him, but never anything as important as this. It was my first real break.

In 1961 Dyson unhappily tendered his resignation. I led a movement to try to get him to stay, but he had been a thorn in the side of some of the Amateur Athletics Association team officials who constantly overruled his authority even on technical matters, and at that time the status of a coach was very low: he was to be tolerated rather than respected. Those officials would be glad to see the back of him. Welwyn AC, the club I belonged to, mounted a big publicity campaign, forcing through a resolution of support for Geoff at the AAA annual general meeting, but by then he was committed to take up a post in Canada as director of the Royal Canadian Legion's national sports training plan. It was a shame and an outrage that the greatest impetus to the coaching scheme in Britain should feel obliged to leave us. Dyson was eventually to return to England in 1968, though in nothing like his former glory, as physical education director at Winchester College. Before he died in 1981 he had been awarded the OBE for his services to athletics. I know I should never have become a coach but for Geoff Dyson.

One of the repercussions of all this was the formation of the British Athletics Union, mainly for coaches dissatisfied with the status they were afforded in the UK. At an international match in those days there might be a single coach in attendance, or perhaps two, whereas now a British team will go abroad for the same meeting with four trained people and for the Olympics with eight to ten. In the early 1960s there were about the same number of professional coaches as there are at present, but nowadays there is a specialist called an event coach for each event as well: I am event coach for the 800 and 1500 metres; Ron Holman is in charge of long distance, and so on. In Britain the idea of event specialization developed partly from the UK coaching scheme. Gradually the coach became recognized as somebody to be taken a bit of notice of, though even today there are people who regard all coaches as parasites, and who think winter training abroad is actually a fortnight's holiday. About all the places I've visited with athletes on these excursions I can tell you four things: where the hotel is, where the running track is, where the woods are (for *fartlek* – a Swedish term to describe the form of training where an athlete runs through the woods or over golf courses, alternating varying lengths and intensities of fast running with jogging) and where the airport is. I've not the slightest idea how they rate as tourist resorts.

Another popular misconception is that all coaches like myself command whacking great salaries from the British Amateur Athletic board. In fact I'm not a coach by occupation at all; I give my services gratis but can claim expenses for travelling, telephone etc. This is partly of my own choosing because it at least enables me to study my own priorities. But I don't think there is anybody in Britain who earns a living coaching athletes. There *are* full-time salaried national coaches, but much of their time is spent coaching PE teachers and coaching coaches. In Finland, the top dozen athletes get an annual stipendiary, and the coach of each such athlete receives about half that sum, so if he's coaching three or four good athletes he earns enough to devote his time exclusively to athletics. Here, we generally have to make a living. I'm a marketing executive with the Engineering Industry

Training Board at Watford, with special responsibility for sales promotion of our training publications. I organize a lot of exhibitions, usually during the athletics off-peak season, and the long hours I put in then enable me to have extra time off in the summer. I'm lucky to have sympathetic employers. I find time for coaching in the same way that athletes find time for training: we concentrate on essentials, and in my case these are my home, my job, and the success of the athletes I coach.

As you'll see, the people I coach have taught me a great deal, both by their successes and by their failures. I've never imprinted any of them with a rubber stamp in the manner of 'Igloi runners' or 'Cerutty boys'. My idea of success in coaching is to produce satisfied athletes. When an athlete comes off the track after a race with 'Didn't he do well!' written all over his face, that makes it all worthwhile. The objectives of athletes vary. Satisfaction to Steve is winning a struggle to the line with a tremendous last-minute burst, whereas to Julian Goater it would be building a big lead and winning by a street. There's no one optimum performance. Sometimes a runner will finish second and yet feel inwardly pleased because he has done his best, and been beaten by a better man on the day. On the other hand, if he comes second because he's run badly, then he has really come nowhere because he should have won. A great athlete like Steve will not be satisfied even with winning if he feels he hasn't fulfilled his own potential.

There aren't any secrets in this business. There are no magic formulae for producing successful athletes. The key to middle-distance coaching is to get the mixture right for each individual. I think most coaches in the world now know the basic ingredients of a runner's training programme. What they then have to do is to get to know their own athletes so well that they know the right recipe for them. It's a bit like making a Christmas cake: a question of individual taste. A lot of coaches talk to their athletes without ever actually listening to them, which is strange, because they can give more information about themselves than anyone else can. I don't know very much about Sebastian Coe or Brendan Foster, but I *do* know a lot about the people I coach because I listen to what they tell me.

Until comparatively recently in the UK, there was nobody of any stature to guide us in our training: we had no schools, no camps and very little documentation as to what great runners of the past had done for training. So we struggled and, who knows, some fine runners may have been ruined along the way while others benefited. Sadly, athletes are the guinea pigs in training experiments.

If I had a method – which I don't – in the tradition of great coaching theorists, the Harry Wilson method would be to treat each athlete individually. You see, the technique of running itself is fairly easy: anybody can become a runner. You can make somebody a better sprinter or a better stylist, for the actual technique is basically simple and often monotonous. The individuals are the unknown variable: they are different both physically and psychologically. The difficult part of middle-distance coaching is making sure that technique and training are adapted to suit the individual. In this respect our event is quite different from field events, where the chief difficulty is one of moulding the athlete to fit the technique. Of course, even in a simple activity like running, a form of automatic natural selection takes place, depending on whether the runner is better endowed with fast-twitch muscle for sprinting or slow-twitch muscle for endurance. But after that, it is a question of individuality.

There have been a number of worldwide trends in middle- and long-distance training, but one theory that has definitely gone out of vogue now is the notion that there is one right way to do it. The old approach, whereby the athletics world switched from copying Igloi to copying Cerutty, and from following Cerutty to following Lydiard – I think that's over. We are all realizing these days, though we may have arrived at the same conclusion by different routes, that this old approach fostered an image of the coach as more important than the athlete, when in fact it's the talent that counts. A coach's job is to make the most of the material he is given to work with, whether it's a rough diamond or a lump of granite. He has to try to get the best out of the athletes in his care. So the concept of a universal method is gone, and I hope that I may have been instrumental in sending it on its way because I've tried to get other coaches in this country to think for themselves and develop along with their athletes rather than insist on a 'British method'. Even in an enlightened athletic nation like Finland, where I gave a seminar on these lines, the idea seemed to come as a welcome revelation. Most Finnish coaches had evidently been governed by the training manual, and any imaginative coach finds this restrictive.

The Russians too are realizing now that middle- and long-distance are *individual* events. The Russians used to operate a system whereby one coach would be responsible for all the top people in an event. I was talking to a Russian coach in Moscow about one of their 800 metres girls and I asked him what system they had been using. To my surprise he answered, 'We use the British system.'

'That's a new one on me,' I said. 'You tell me what the British system is!'

'The British system,' said the coach, 'is no system. We now have each coach trying to develop each girl to the best of her ability. We've learned that from you.'

They've learned it not only from the successful example of middle-distance runners like Steve Ovett and Seb Coe, but from long-distance men like Bedford and Stewart, each one of whom developed individually.

Middle-distance and long-distance running can't be reduced, as can field events, to mechanics. There are emotional factors involved. A coach has to try to harness these emotions. Steve Ovett is a case in point. As I once tried to explain to a journalist, you have to remember Ovett is a genius, and that no genius can be categorized. He relies so very much on his feelings.

1

Meeting Steve

Steve thinks perhaps fate played a hand in our getting together. Two years ago he told Mel Watman of *Athletics Weekly*, 'Harry's a friend really, a great help – and a laugh. We get on well as people; I couldn't do without Harry. His temperament and attitude towards things are so similar to mine that it's almost as though we were destined to meet.'*

It all began very simply.

In the late sixties and seventies the Southern Counties AAA used to hold training camps once a month at Crystal Palace, inviting along leading athletes and a few top juniors who would be likely to benefit. It was a very good and successful system because by paying all their expenses we were able to give valuable help to some remarkable young people. One Saturday afternoon in the autumn of 1972 we were about to jump into our convoy of three or four cars to drive the boys to a circuit three miles away at Shirley Hills, when I was approached by a tall, rather gaunt-looking lad whom I knew to be one of our sprinters. He was sixteen and his name was Steve Ovett.

'Can I join your group this afternoon?' he asked. This was rather strange.

'What about the sprinting group,' I said. 'Don't you want to be with them?'

'Well,' he explained in a manner older than his years,

Athletics Weekly, 14 April 1979.

'they muck about. They don't seem to train hard enough for my liking. I can join you.'

He could, could he? We were running four repetitions round a mile circuit; I pointed out, 'That'll be quite a tough programme.'

'OK,' he said. So off we went.

To my astonishment he not only did the repetitions but led on practically all of them, recording times worthy of a class distance runner. Julian Goater, whom I was later to coach, was reckoned to be a very good middle- and long-distance man, yet this sprinter was matching Julian without any apparent discomfort, though he had never done this sort of work before. I knew he was looking for a coach, though he may have had somebody helping him out at his club, Brighton and Hove AC. 'I'd like to coach him,' I thought. 'He's talented. I'm talented. The two ought to go together!'

Of course, it would be quite a responsibility. When I first started in on the project, a prominent coach who shall remain nameless remarked, 'You're a brave fellah. That lad's got so much talent I'd be afraid to coach him in case it went wrong.' I suppose my past experiences in coaching, including a few failures, had made me more intrepid.

Steve and I would see each other once a month on these camps and discuss training methods. I would give him a suggested schedule for the following weeks and Steve would take the plan away and do the training. I assume he did it. I never checked up. Right from the beginning I realized that because of the distance between Welwyn and Brighton it would be vital that he could be relied on to train on his own, and already I sensed that this young man was so committed in his approach that I wouldn't have to keep tabs on him. In the early summer of 1973 I had to go to Australia. When I came back I asked him how he'd been getting on. 'Great', he said. 'When I did my track sessions I could hear your voice reminding me to make sure of this, that and the other point. It was like being able to switch on a tape-

24

recorder.' In those days I was apt to push the message home by saying things over and over again – which you do with any athlete at the outset. He might think, 'Oh, I've heard all this before, Harry!' but I was conditioning automatic responses: to run the session a bit harder, use the arms a bit more, finish fast, and so on.

Everything seemed to come remarkably easy to Steve. Whenever he ran he was relaxed and natural. Having seen him take in his stride mile repetitions that any sixteen-year-old would normally be hard put to manage at all, I was in no doubt about his physical attributes. If he had the dedication and concentration to go with them, we were definitely on to something. In his junior school days he had done high jump, long jump, hurdles and sprinting. In 1972 before I knew him, he had not only distinguished himself at 400 metres but won the ESAA boys intermediate 800 metres at Washington, County Durham, by over 20 metres in 1:55.0. He'd taken the AAA youth 400-metres title in 49.1, and he had won an invitational youth event at 400 metres in the London v. Rest of the South match at Crystal Palace. On holiday in Germany with a Southend club team he had lowered his 400 metres best to 48.9 and run 800 metres in 1:53.6 after being up all night playing cards. Even earlier, in 1969 while still thirteen, he was running 400 metres in 53.7. He won the 1970 English Schools junior title at the same distance in 51.6 seconds and he followed this up in 1971 by taking the AAA Youth title in 49.8. He also set a British record for his age in the 800 metres in 1:55.3 at Crystal Palace.

While at school at Varndean Grammar, he was a good all-round athlete who naturally wanted to concentrate on his athletics rather than play soccer and cricket, where he would be consigned to the wing or boundary because of his speed. He says he didn't like team sports very much. This didn't go down too well with some of the school staff, particularly the headmaster, who felt Ovett wasn't playing his full part in school activities. I should have thought the talent in the lad might have been recognized and encouraged rather than criticized, but then people often found him precocious and wanted him to behave like other boys of his age. This was ironic. He was noticeably better than most seniors, so age didn't enter into it.

'At school,' Steve says, 'I was forced to make a decision between athletics or football or cricket. If you didn't want to play football or cricket then the school wasn't really interested and you were left to your own devices. It was really an academically minded school so the concept of being a serious sportsman ·rather went against the grain.'

During Easter 1973, Steve was one of sixty-six promising youngsters who attended an Esso-sponsored young athletes course at Lilleshall. Seeing him at close quarters for a week I began to realize just how easily athletics came to him. He would do repetitions and talk at the same time. It wasn't cockiness: he was just enjoying himself, having a laugh and a joke, and for heaven's sake, why not? There would have been no point in my telling him to grit his teeth and concentrate: he was simply training while others were straining. Some of the boys resented this but the more sensible ones took a philosophical view. I was coaching a boy in the same group, Kirk Dumpleton, when he said, 'It must be annoying for you, Harry. Here are we, struggling, and there's Steve so far ahead of us. If *I* could talk while I did the sessions, though, I would.' Young Dumpleton, in addition to sagacity, held the very rare distinction of having beaten both Steve and Seb Coe in the same race.

I remember the occasion quite clearly, though I was coaching Kirk rather than Steve at the time. The race was the English Schools intermediate cross-country championship which took place at Hillingdon in March 1972. Fifteen-year-old Steve finished second to Kirk in 21:42, whilst fifteen-year-old Seb was tenth in 22:05. But Kirk was so excited at having beaten Steve that it rather set a pattern of expectations for me in the future. Here was a boy who was basically a cross-country and long-distance runner, thrilled to bits at beating a 400 metres cum 800 metres runner. Whatever the distance, I thought, this Ovett is evidently going to excel.

Even in those early days Steve had read a lot about athletics and studied the form, so to speak, of some of his contemporaries. He had no heroes as such, but I think he was a closet admirer of a big fellow called Andy Barnett, who was held in awe by most of the youngsters in Britain at that time. I think his style was basically to run flat out from start to finish, and he held all the world records for his age group. Steve also admired David Hemery and Ian Stewart. Hemery because 'he was a gentleman as well as an athlete – we do not often come across men of his integrity in the sport'. Stewart 'because of his uncompromising character and blatant honesty'. For a teenager he knew quite a lot about training and was able to differentiate between the various schools of thought on the subject. He had already made up his mind what type of coach he wanted, and evidently sussed me out as the sort he would require. One important consideration would be that he didn't want anybody constantly ordering him about. Academically he was busying himself with his A levels and toying with the idea of accepting a place at Loughborough College of Design – though I rather think he was just flying a kite in that direction because he was already so serious about athletics.

Steve's parents were quick to recognize that they had a prodigy of some sort on their hands. When a child is gifted – whether at athletics or ballet or music – some families will adopt the approach: OK, we'll leave him to his own devices and if he gets on, he gets on; if he doesn't, hard luck. Other parents will go out of their way to give this talent some financial backing, sacrificing other things, and this is what Steve's parents did. They were prepared to do whatever was necessary to allow their son to develop his athletic potential. His father Mick worked long hours at his farm produce stall in Brighton market, and his mother Gay ran a catering business. Their support has been invaluable; right from the start Steve always knew that he would never have to worry about sponsorship, that at the back of him was their firm financial support. Steve feels that this support would have been there whatever he had set out to do. It was his parents' approach to all their children and they have treated his sister Sue and brother Nicky in the same manner.

One day early in 1973, he was training round a 600-metre grass track at a Brighton cycle stadium with his dad holding the stopwatch, when he was asked for an interview. In reply to a question about his parents, Steve explained, 'They were athletics fans before I came about, but having a family totally involved can have its drawbacks, especially after a bad race.' I would think that Steve's parents have probably been his sternest critics – a cliché but true. They have occasionally been very critical of his performances, and at times it seemed to me they almost expected him to be perfect. I can understand parents not wanting a budding athlete to become complacent, but there are inevitably going to be occasions when he doesn't turn in 100 per cent performances. As a coach you learn to live with this. Training doesn't always go well; there are good days and bad days, and days when races prove disappointing. You have to accept a degree of imperfection sometimes.

One weekend Steve and I were at Crystal Palace and on the Sunday morning he had a phone call to say his father, at thirty-seven, had suffered a heart attack. I immediately drove Steve to the station (he had no car in those days), and he turned to me and said quietly, 'Well, Harry, this might be the end of it. If my dad is that bad and they can't do anything for him, I'd have to take over his side of the business. I'd either have to finish with athletics altogether or pick it up when I could. After all, athletics is pretty insignificant in comparison to the people you love. I love my father and no matter how important athletics is to me, if the illness is as bad as they fear then athletics will have to give way.' It struck me as very mature for a lad of seventeen immediately to know his priorities and put his family before himself. In addition to his parents, there were his younger brother Nick and his younger sister Sue to think of. As it turned out the rest of the family rallied round, and Steve's father wasn't quite as bad as had been feared, so Steve was able to settle back into his routine.

An easy time of it

This is not to say I gave Steve an easy time of it. In those early days I used to push him, if not to the limit, certainly very hard in training. I think we were virtually pioneers of the type of interval work we were doing, tackling track training sessions of much higher quality than anybody else at that time. The standard type of interval training in those days was to run something like 8 × 200 metres fast with a jog in between each 200 metres or perhaps 6 × 300 metres fast, again with a jog as a recovery between each fast stretch. But early on, Steve and I developed a more intensive version of this type of training. Steve would run a very fast 200 or 300 metres, have just 30 seconds for recovery, then run another fast stretch. He would then have five or six minutes' rest then repeat the set of two again. His session would consist of three or four sets of these high-intensity runs. At times he would have a pulse rate of well over 200 beats per minute at the end of each set. It took some doing. Steve would often collapse on the track with his eyeballs rolling up in his head, gasping and groaning, 'I can't do another one!' He generally overdid the method acting, and I'd say casually, 'Well, let's think about it in five minutes' time then.' And in five minutes' time, of course, he'd get up and do another burst. I think the paroxysms were more a gesture of protest at doing what Harry told him, and of course a bit of showmanship, than a sign of utter depletion.

Steve's early training sessions made up in quality for what they lacked in quantity; they were in the nature of a short sharp shock rather than a long sentence. He might

29

run just 2 × 600 metres and that would constitute an evening's training. It didn't sound much, and we would never correct people who remarked that the training was light. What they didn't know was how fast and intensive those 600-metre bursts were. We also used to do what are called differential runs (to accustom the body to speeding up when tired). These were usually 400 metres, taking the first 200 fairly steadily and the last 200 flat out.

I think I was pretty tough with him, too, especially in the spring and summer of 1973. He was beginning to develop the dreaded Ovett kick. He had the essential requirements for this: a lot of natural speed and the ability to sprint, as well as some experience of high jump and long jump, which put a spring in his stride. But a kicker, no matter what his powers of acceleration, also has to have endurance to be able to arrive at the end of a race fresh enough to sprint. At middle distance, it's no good having the sprint ability of an Alan Wells, without endurance. Steve's training was designed to enhance his abilities in both departments.

In the spring and early summer of 1973, we were meeting once or twice a week to do these high-quality track sessions, and at home Steve would be doing longish runs, *fartlek* or perhaps interval work on grass. The actual volume of work was still rather modest. Later that season, after he'd won the European junior 800 metres championship, I was asked by a German magazine for an article detailing a typical week's training programme for Steve. I tried to be as objective as possible, but the article was returned unused. The editors said there was no point in publishing it as I was obviously trying to mislead them. They evidently thought Steve's workload derisory. So did European silver-medallist Willi Wulbeck. Willi laughed out loud when Steve talked in public about his daily schedule of 'five minutes' warm-up, twenty minutes' hard running and five minutes' warm down'. Actually his warm-up was a bit longer than five minutes: he was playing it down there.

Steve recollects, 'At the time, our after-training chats

about everything except athletics took up more time than the actual training itself. In fact we laughed a lot at the people who couldn't think about anything other than athletics.' Steve's concentration was there when it was required – during the intensive intervals in the training sessions – but once these had been accomplished then it was 'switch off and have a laugh'.

There are really three training periods in the year for a middle-distance runner. The first, from October to about the middle of March, is almost 100 per cent strength and endurance training – aerobic work to improve general fitness and oxygen exchange. A simple definition of aerobic work would be 'training at a pace where the oxygen you can extract from the air you breathe in roughly equals the amount of oxygen required to prevent the buildup of the waste products which appear in the muscles during exercise'. When the oxygen uptake is insufficient, lactic acid accumulates in the muscles and the activity becomes anaerobic. So the middle-distance runner must practise both energy processes, and obviously the shorter the event, the more anaerobic the activity. This would consist of a mixture of steady-state runs, either long easy runs or shorter brisk ones, all at a regular pace. The work might include some long repetitions, though not too fast. Even during this endurance period though, I like to maintain one session per week of sprinting and technique training (improving a runner's style), so that these abilities are kept primed. (I can recall much later on in our partnership when Steve was in the middle of a 100 mile-a-week schedule, he was still running repetitions of 60 metres indoors in about 7.2 or 7.3 seconds from a standing start.) Provided you keep the speed work going and do about 10 per cent anaerobic work, you don't necessarily lose your speed during heavy mileage. If a runner does cross-country races during the winter, this in itself will provide the necessary proportion of anaerobic work because cross-country racers do run into oxygen debt and develop tolerance to it.

The second training period, from about mid-March to

May, includes more of this anaerobic or oxygen-debt work. This is when it becomes vital to tailor the training to fit the individual athlete, because the transition period is both mentally distressing and physically painful. I regard it as the hardest part of the year for both coach and athlete; after all the winter donkey work, pressure is being applied, recovery times are cut down and speeds are stepped up. Understandably, this is when the athlete may become querulous and question the coach's judgement. During this period it is quite useful to get away from the athlete's normal environment and do the training in different surroundings. A change is as good as a rest. The weather in Britain tends to do the unexpected in springtime so it's quite useful to have a few days in the sun in somewhere like Portugal where the climate is usually reliable. I think the value of the training camp comes from the change in surroundings and it's wrong for athletes to use camps as a way of making up for time lost in the winter. Large groups of athletes in training camps are not generally a good thing. Steve doesn't like such camps as they usually become very competitive and the athletes find they need a rest after the camp. Steve is lucky that in the Brighton area he can find all the different running areas he needs to give variety to his training and only rarely feels the need to train elsewhere.

The final training period is from May to competition time. Mentally and physically the races become the focal point, and training is structured around them. Even in those early days of our partnership, it seemed to me pointless to try to tell Steve how actually to run his races. When you're a youngster racing abroad you don't know much about the opposition anyway, so to see you through you rely very much on fitness, and the ability to size up a situation and react very quickly. These qualities are generally much more useful on the day than any preconceived idea about how the race will go. At 800 metres, which was Steve's chief distance at the time, we knew that he would have to have his wits about him tactically; there was always the risk of getting boxed in or shoved about, and he knew that he needed to be able to respond and change pace very quickly in order to survive. So although Steve was criticized early on for lack of tactical shrewdness, I think this was a bit unfair. He knew well enough what his powers of acceleration were, and if he hung back in a race, there was invariably a good reason for it.

The 1973 season

The 1973 race season was our first as a team. Steve's first major race was when he represented Sussex in the Inter-Counties 400 metres at Warley in May. He was still a junior and we were aiming for two good-quality races in two days against senior fields. He was fourth in his heat with 48.0 seconds (European junior championship qualifying mark) and sixth in the final in 48.4 seconds. Despite the result, he was pleased at having made the final of a senior inter-counties race, which had been our main objective. Next, he ran in the National League for Brighton and Hove, winning the 200 metres in 22.8 seconds and the 800 metres in 1:54.4. Then came the Southern 800 metres championships at Crystal Palace. I'd gone to Australia on a business trip that week and Steve rang me at about 3 a.m. to tell me the result. He had run 1:48.4 and come second to Pete Browne, but he had knocked nearly 4 seconds off his previous best of 1:52.5 and shattered all previous records by any UK seventeen- or eighteen-year-old. Still, there was a note of disappointment in his voice over the phone; I think he felt, as he was coming up very strongly at the finish, that if he'd had a bit more confidence and broken a little earlier he could have won it. He had closed to within a stride of Browne as they came off the turn and challenged him persistently to the line. To me it was a marvellous performance for a seventeen-year-old schoolboy. Besides, this was only June; by the European junior championships he'd probably be favourite for the 800 metres.

Right from the start of the season he had made up his

mind that the European Junior Games were to be the thing. To give him more experience at his distance in a class field, he entered the 800 metres (senior) AAA championship at Crystal Palace. He finished sixth, again behind Pete Browne, in 1:47.3, which was one second below his previous best and a world best for a seventeen-year-old. Steve had recorded a seventeen-year-old world best of 1:47.5 in the heats on the Friday night, but the result was a disappointment to him. I thought it an exceptionally good run myself; he simply hadn't had the strength in the final 100 metres. He was positioned well throughout the race, but his legs hadn't the running in them then to be able to cope with a fast finish. On the Monday after the race, John Rodda of the *Guardian* gave Steve a mention. It was nice to know that somebody from the newspapers was aware that you could finish sixth and still produce a very good performance. Steve knew that the experience would benefit him; on the other hand, he never enters a race *just* for the experience. So he was a little crestfallen.

At this point I judged from his training that he was about ready for the mile. A race where there was likely to be a bit of pacemaking would give Steve a time of around 4 minutes, and there was no reason why he couldn't break the mark. So this was his aim. The race, the BMC City Mile at Motspur Park, went very much as we'd anticipated, with a reasonably fast start, a slight lull, then a quick last lap. Steve, who was amongst the pack, went through the bell in 3:02.5, passing the 1500-metre mark in 3:44.8. In the last 150 metres Steve kicked, passing four men along the straight for second. He ended up with 4 minutes dead, which was really infuriating to him, and he considered he had run 'brainlessly'. He thought it uncanny that he'd gone through the bell in the time I'd predicted, though in fact a coach ought to know, roughly. I shouldn't think he was unconsciously obeying me but it may well be that he was holding back a bit for the last lap. This was a new area for him; his three-quarter time was a personal best and his 4:00.0 was a

UK junior record and 9 seconds faster than ever before, bettered internationally at that age only by Jim Ryan. I do think, though, that there was a doubt in his mind in his first few mile and 1500 metres races about saving something for the finish, with the result that he was sometimes a little too far back at the bell.

I can remember looking at my watch, standing over by the 200-metre mark, and shouting, 'You'll need a twenty-six!' After the race Steve said, 'I just speeded up, passed four people and ran a twenty-six to finish in four dead. If I'd been nearer Nick Rose at the end I'd have won, in about 3:58.' In fact I was on the side of the track going a bit berserk because I'd made it about 3:59.8 – coaches usually tend to be optimistic – and I was shouting, 'You've done it!' When 'Four minutes dead' was announced, our hearts sank. Afterwards Steve assured me, 'Well if you'd *told* me "You need a twenty-five," I'd have done 3:59!'

It was a pretty good finish for all that. Passing four runners you have to go wide, which means the real time was a little less than 26 seconds for the last 200 metres. And he wasn't tired. He continued jogging round the track to look at my stopwatch. I don't think Steve's dad was very pleased with his performance, though; Steve later told a reporter his father said it was 'bloody awful'. I don't think you should dent a youngster's pleasure in a race like that. *I* was very pleased with it.

Steve says, 'Obviously I was thrilled – a four-minute mile in my first race and on a cinder track. Some athletes have struggled for most of their careers to run such a time.' What a debut!

After this came Steve's first international vest. He was selected for a British 'A' team for a match in Sotteville against a French 'A' side. He ran reasonably well, coming third in the 800 metres in 1:49.6, behind the increasingly familiar back of Pete Browne. I know he was disappointed. He'd had a difficult journey getting to Sotteville and the arrangements for what was an international meeting weren't quite what he had looked forward to. Over and above the transport problems, for some reason he wasn't even given a British vest. When young athletes are starting their UK careers, their first priority is to get a British vest, so this was a pretty sad state of affairs. Steve was very grateful to Pete Browne during this trip. 'He was one of my rivals yet still took the trouble to cheer me up in the warm-up. He loaned me a spare GB vest and tracksuit and made the trip a lot more enjoyable.' The situation, I know, has improved and nowadays we welcome new team members with their first international issue and make a bit of a song and dance about it, as well we should. But this was the sort of early experience that can influence an athlete's whole future attitude. Steve was a case in point, perhaps. One day he ran particularly well in a red Russian vest, which has now become a sort of mascot cum protest shirt. He favours it regularly. Just prior to the European junior championships in Duisburg there was the London Fire Brigade meeting at Crystal Palace. Steve set a UK junior best, winning the 1000 metres in 2:20.0.

We'd gone over Steve's training before Duisburg and discussed the prospects for the 800 metres; we knew that Steve would probably be favourite and that some of the other competitors, notably the West German Willi Wulbeck and the East German Gohlke, had produced fast times. We also knew that the way Steve was running, he had only to match his current form to put the others out of contention. But there was nothing I could tell him on how to run the race. I wasn't going to be there, so it was up to Steve to conduct himself responsibly in the matters of transport, accommodation and race tactics. Even when he became very experienced, we wouldn't plan race tactics: it would really be up to him to size up the field when the gun went. With another athlete I might have acted differently. Some want to be given exact instructions. Even then, though, I would emphasize their own running strengths rather than worry too much about their opponents.

In the Duisburg 800 metres Steve won his heat fairly

easily and won his semifinal in 1:49.6, moving up from fifth. In the final, everyone considered he left his kick a bit late. 'OK,' he told me, 'it was a bit close, but it never entered my head that I wouldn't win it. I knew how much I could make up at the finish.'

I think you have to recognize the maturity of a seventeen-year-old who can make an assessment like that. You don't criticize a fellow for it. If he wins by a few hundredths, so what? He's won. The first lap was very fast: 52.6 seconds, so he wasn't too worried at not being right at the front because these fellows weren't going to be able to continue at that pace. Eventually the leaders were going to fade, and it was his job to pick them off. Steve says he let Wulbeck and Gohlke go, easing into third down the back straight and then going as they came off the last bend. In fact he had to move out past the dying Germans, both of whom cluttered him up. Steve took the gold in 1:47.5, from Wulbeck in second place with 1:47.6.

Steve hadn't been bothered by the travel, the food or the hotel arrangements, having shared rooms as necessary. The only thing that worried him was a forty-five minute delay between the warm-up and the race. This does sometimes happen at big championships where competitors are asked to report long before the gun, and unless the runner is careful he or she can go off the boil. However Steve showed he could manage perfectly well on his own. His parents usually travelled to see him race but they were holidaying in Spain during the European Games. 'Mum said Duisburg was my holiday,' said Steve to a *World Sports* reporter. 'I ask you – lousy food, no sleep and sick twice. Some holiday.'

The following Wednesday at Crystal Palace, it took me some persuading to get Steve to pull his gold medal out of his bag. Obviously he was pleased, but I think his attitude was, 'Well, I've done what was expected of me.' He sets such high targets for himself, he doesn't see any reason to make a fuss if he succeeds. At the time, though, we thought that his European junior win would be sufficient to justify selection for the Commonwealth Games. There was a bit of an anticlimax after Duisburg and Steve's training eased up accordingly. We intended to build up again for the Commonwealth Games trials and the games themselves. He finished ninth, in 4:09.2, in the IAC/Coca-Cola Mile at Crystal Palace. He just went through the motions really. He wasn't fit physically, and mentally I don't think he was in it. The fitness achieved by our style of high-intensity training wore off very quickly the minute he slackened, and in future we would remember this lesson.

Personally, I feel that with intelligent selection and management it shouldn't have been necessary for Steve to run in the Commonwealth trials. He had had three good races in a short space of time, and the selectors should have had enough belief in his ability to include him as the third team member. What happened in the 800 metres trial was that he faded slightly down the straight to finish third in 1:48.4. The winning time was 1:48.0 (by Colin Campbell) and the second was 1:48.2 (by Tony Settle). I still thought Steve would make the team, but in fact they picked Pete Browne, Colin Campbell and Andy Carter. Carter was number one in the country and Browne had beaten Steve several times that year, so we weren't upset about their selection. But Campbell we weren't so happy about. He'd had an up-and-down season and there were doubts about his fitness.

I think, had Steve gone, he'd have been determined to run faster than ever before – it wasn't simply that he wanted the experience. However Campbell went instead, and went out in the semifinals with 1:51.6, 'troubled by injury'. A letter from Arthur Gold to *Athletics Weekly* explained that the Commonwealth Games were regarded as a family gathering rather than an airing of potential talent. This seemed to me a failure to understand any good competitor's approach. As it happened, fate intervened. The very week that the Commonwealth Games were taking place, Steve was diagnosed as suffering from glandular fever.

This whole affair had a most profound effect on him. 'Well, that's it, Harry,' he told me. 'I'm never again going to leave myself in a position where I've got to rely on somebody doing me a favour for selection. I'm going to make myself so good that it will be my right to be in the team.' And that's what he did. Selection isn't an honour bestowed on the leading athletes. It's not a privilege. If you're good enough you've earned the selection anyway.

Right from the early days, Steve had an underlying belief that he was fated to be a champion. Champion athletes must have this belief, whatever their current state of development. A lot of people dream of achieving something and then sit back and hope that by some magical chance it's going to happen. Whereas a Steve Ovett will actually go out and do everything necessary to *make* it happen, by dedication, concentration, sacrifice and sheer hard work. I used to coach a girl sprinter, Ann Jenner. She ran in the Olympic 100 metres in 1960 and she was an extraordinary girl. She taught me that you don't necessarily have to know everything about an event to do well in it. When she lined up in her heat in Rome against Olympic champion Wilma Rudolph, Ann didn't even know who she was. All she knew was that she wanted to run in the Olympics, and she was prepared to do anything to get there.

She was a very attractive girl who later became a model, but at the time I coached her she was a hair-dresser, working a six-day week. Her only time to train on Saturday was in the evening, but she'd come down to Gosling Stadium on winter Saturdays and sweep the snow off the track in order to train. I learned from her, even before Steve came along, that if an athlete wants to do something badly enough, then the least a coach can do is to harness that energy, to make the dream come true. Champions must have this powerful inner motivation, because it can't be taught. By pushing and pulling and prodding, a coach may get some results, but in the end it's up to the athlete. Ann intended to retire after the Olympics, but I managed to persuade her to run one 400 metres before she said goodbye to her sport. Her farewell 400 metres set the best time of the year by any British athlete.

The day of the Commonwealth Games trials was very sad for me, and not only because Steve failed to make the team. I was also coaching two girl competitors, Lesley Kiernan and Gloria O'Leary (later Mrs David Hemery). Neither ran well in the trials, and neither qualified. Quite often people see me at big international matches and think, 'My word, this coaching business must be a plum job!' Well, coaching has its miserable days too, when everything goes wrong, when your athletes all seem to lose and turn to you for help and consolation. You have to cope with those days too.

2

No Room in Rome

It was the end of a bleak period that had begun late in December 1973. While the Commonwealth Games were taking place in New Zealand, Steve, perhaps inwardly thinking he'd show the selectors a thing or two, decided to do some really fast running indoors. He ran at an indoor meeting at Cosford, recording 1:52.8 for 800 metres, but after a very fast first lap he suddenly found himself barely able to finish the race. We knew there must be something seriously wrong. Injuries cause pain and restrict movement, and it's up to a coach to judge how serious they are, but the onset of an illness is different: it tends to creep up on you. You have to distinguish between staleness or depletion from heavy training and the symptoms of a disease. If training is going downhill and the athlete is not recovering from day to day, you begin to suspect some illness, possible anaemia, a fairly common runners' complaint. What Steve had, though, was more drastic than that. One day he abandoned a training run and actually had to stop and walk home because he felt so dreadful. After the Cosford race he went straight to a doctor who immediately diagnosed glandular fever.

Glandular fever? We consulted a medical friend, a doctor of exercise physiology at Chelsea College in Eastbourne, Ray Watson. Ray explained that the disease was an infection of the entire lymphatic system. Physical exercise of any kind came to a halt. No training, no walks, no football, no anything. Compared with even a non-athlete Steve was about 10 per cent fit. Not until about the beginning of April did he start running again, and then only in tiny amounts every other day, building up very gradually. We wanted to make sure, after such a long lay-off, that he was really 100 per cent fit. This was the reason for the Merthyr Mawr trip.

Merthyr Mawr in South Wales is a very tough place to train. Not just because of the sand dunes the athletes have to run on, or the distances they run, but because our training weekends there are highly competitive. There's very little opportunity for anyone to take things easy, and the only respite is jogging to and from the dunes. Each spring we perform the annual ritual of going to Merthyr Mawr to test our athletes for fitness and compare it with the previous year's performance, because that's nearly always a good guide.

Merthyr Mawr is tough, but toughest of all is the Big Dipper. The Dipper is a horrendous hill, a diabolical dune capable of testing the most seasoned athlete. These days, I walk up it. I remember one stupid occasion when Denis Watts and I were coaching on a course down there and for some reason I decided to see how far I could run up the Dipper without taking a breath. I collapsed. Not to be outdone, Denis took a deep breath and started up the foothills. *He* collapsed. In fact we were rather worried because he didn't revive for quite some time.

When we felt Steve was on the road to recovery from glandular fever we decided to try out his fitness by the Merthyr Mawr test, and down we went for a training weekend. The first session we did was a series of repetitions up the Big Dipper. 'Somehow I got to the top,' Steve recalls, 'but I just lay there, feeling like death and being sick all over the place. I couldn't do anything for the rest of the day. But after that I felt better, and everything started to click into place.'

So here he was, green and gasping on top of the Dipper like a fish out of water, with the other lads poking fun at him. This may seem cruel, but normally, you see, Steve would be in a position to make merry at *their* expense if they wilted. It was a very competitive atmosphere. Only newcomers to the camp, for example, had a full breakfast on their first morning. The rest would have toast, or go without, and sit there squirming with laughter and nudging one another. We knew we'd all see that breakfast later on, distributed over the Welsh countryside. Accepting pain and a measure of cruel humour, learning to live with insult on top of injury, is part of the general toughening-up process our lads go through. Most middle- and long-distance training has to do with overcoming yourself and the little voice inside that says, 'Oh this one doesn't matter: ease off.' The vital character training you need to conquer that voice occurs in training sessions rather than in the races themselves. Steve could have just sprawled there on that hill and said, 'That's it, I'm finished,' and been laid low again for a long time. Instead he picked himself up, told me, 'OK, I'll try again,' and off he went. He was responding to a bit of a talk from me and a bit of leg-pulling from the others.

1974: the races

Steve's first major race in 1974 was in the Southern junior championships at Crystal Palace on 15 June: the 400 metres. He ran in the heats on the Friday night and felt rotten afterwards, which raised the spectre of glandular fever all over again as he was still having to have monthly check-ups. But the next day he managed to pull himself together, and in winning the final produced his best 400 metres time ever – 47.5 seconds – half a second inside his previous best and in only his second 400 metres in over a year. He had beaten two members of the Duisburg 4 × 400 metres squad, Bob Benn and Chris Van Rees, regarded then as probably the best 400 metres juniors around. At the time, Bob was a bearded, barrel-chested rival and an associate of Steve's in the GB junior team. Later he was to become one of Steve's close friends and a collaborator in several of Steve's fastest races.

Steve was really thrilled about that race; after feeling
so ill in the heats, it bucked him up no end. He took the
lead barely 12 metres out after hanging back and being
well adrift at the 200-metre mark and won actually
going away from Benn in second and Van Rees in third
place. The splits were almost dead even (23.6 and 23.9
seconds), and he had had enough belief in himself to let
the others go and then cut them down at the finish.

A few days later came the Southern senior championships, also at Crystal Palace. With all the training time
he had lost, Steve was thinking now about the European
championships in Rome, knowing he hadn't many races
left in which to qualify. So though he hadn't tackled an
800 metres for a long time, he decided he had better try
one now. With 800 metres races, anyway, you're very
dependent on weather conditions and it's sometimes
quite late in the season before you make the mark. At the
bell Steve kicked past John Greatrex who had led from
the gun, taking Pete Browne and Colin Campbell with
him, and on the final straight Campbell faded but
Browne gave him a tussle. Steve won by a metre, 0.5
seconds inside the European qualifying mark with
1:47.6. He said he'd found it a hard race but it was great
to know that he'd qualified in his first 800 metres of the
season, and that *en route* he'd beaten Browne, who'd
always been one of his main rivals. Browne in fact
equalled the Rome qualifying mark in second place.

Steve was a little surprised to be selected for the
Poland v. UK v. Canada match in Warsaw on 30 June
and I wasn't there for his 800 metres at that meeting.
Evidently Dave McMeekin did himself a bit of good
making the early pace because he too qualified for Rome.
Steve, though, came wide off the last bend to win in a
new personal best of 1:46.8. In doing so he apparently
made athletics correspondent Neil Allen 'blush'. by
waving to the British supporters in the crowd as he
strode home. This was to be the first of many such
adverse reactions to Steve showing his pleasure in this
way.

44

The AAA 800 metres championship at Crystal Palace in July was a very important race. It was going to be Steve's attempt to establish himself as the number one 800 metres runner in Britain. Since Munich 1972, Andy Carter had been regarded as the UK number one, and Carter had the times to warrant it. This was to be their first meeting of 1974 and they were both a little short of training, Steve because of his illness and Andy because of a foot injury, which meant that they were in comparable condition. The 800 metres final started quite fast, with Mark Winzenried of the USA leading at the 200-metre mark. McMeekin went in front as they completed the first lap, but then Winzenried challenged again and at 550 metres it was the American ahead of Byron Dyce of Jamaica, Campbell, Carter – and Steve way back in seventh place, thinking 'I've had it!' Jockeying for position Steve did tend to get himself pushed around rather more in those days and he was fairly well jostled back now – being seventh out of eight doesn't leave many people behind you. It must have struck the opposition with some surprise when suddenly, coming out of the turn, Steve moved out and accelerated gracefully past six men to win in 1:46.9, covering the last 200 metres in about 26 seconds. On the straight he'd had to dig very deeply into his physical reserves to overhaul Carter, the title-holder, by a stride at the finish. Steve said it was 'a bit of a struggle', but beating the reputed number one in the country and passing six people in the process was a big psychological boost. He'd had the nerve to wait until precisely the right moment before kicking for home. If you're not careful you tend to panic and push yourself out of position too soon, so you have to gamble and hold on to your trump card until you know you can make the trick with it. Then, even if you only win by an inch, you still gambled right. At 1500 metres there may well be a few more opportunities, but in the 800 metres little openings occur that you must grab immediately or you'll never see them – or the race – again.

The siege of Carter's number one status continued in

the UK v. Czechoslovakia match at Meadowbank
stadium, Edinburgh, on 26 July. Some time had elapsed
between the AAA 800 metres and this 800 metres race
and if Carter was better, here was his chance to show it.
There was another of Steve's main rivals in the field too:
Jozef Plachy, the 1969 European silver-medallist, who
led at the bell, going quite slowly, with the others
apparently content to string along behind. Plachy made
the running until 50 metres from home, at which point
Carter took off. Steve watched and waited, then making
up 0.4 seconds in the last 30 or 40 yards he surged past
Plachy and Carter to win in 1:48.8. Up to then, this was
the best race I'd seen Steve run. Perfect positioning, the
nerve to bide his time, and a late kick so decisive that in
the end the win looked comfortable. To me it was
conclusive proof that Steve was now the number one in
the country.

He was in training for Rome, using basically the same
system as the previous year, but with a few more
repetitions. Instead of doing 2×600 metres, he might do
the two 600s and then some 150s on top. Or else perhaps
three sets of 3×200, moving up to four sets of 3×200.
The quality and regularity of training determines the
performances and unless training is important to an
athlete, the racing results won't come. It's a reflection of
attitude. But the actual volume of work was still comparatively light by most standards. Apart from training
once a day after school (where he'd been studying for his
A levels) he was doing very little; I doubt that he had
been logging 50 miles a week.

Just how much training is right for each athlete a
coach can only really discover by experience. One year,
at the annual Lilleshall course for the English Schools
champions, I met two young runners, Andy Green and
Mary Tagg. Andy may be remembered for winning the
AAA mile championship; Mary was a very good 400
metres runner. Later they married. Their big year should
have been 1968, in the Mexico Games, and Mary
actually ran extremely well. She was knocked out in the

semi-finals, but she got just about everything out of herself as a 400 metres runner that she could. Andy, though, didn't even make the team. I believe this was my fault. The previous year he'd won the AAA championship mile and I thought he could afford to step up his training quite considerably. We did an enormous workload that winter, and by the time the race season began I think he was overtrained. I'd worked him too hard and his freshness was gone. Mary was getting better and better, and poor Andy was getting worse and worse, and in the end he wasn't selected. Definitely my mistake.

Another athlete I coached, Roger Matthews from Bournemouth, seemed to lap up the training and look round for more. Roger was an incredible fellow, and one of my favourite pupils. To begin with, he could never break 60 seconds for 400 metres, but by sheer bulk of training and hard work he ended up running about 28.40 minutes for 10,000 metres and finished fourth in the Commonwealth Games. I'd say that's one of the best coaching jobs I've ever done. He gave up soon after those games, though, because he felt he'd screwed absolutely everything out of himself that he could. He realized then that although he'd done marvellously well on very little natural speed, he'd never be involved in a major title at the finish because of his lack of pace. He was limited in the tactics he could employ; there have been quite a lot of runners with Roger's problem, though perhaps none of them worked quite so hard to overcome it. At one stage he was running 160 miles a week, and developed a mild liver complaint. That was one of his reasons for packing up.

17 July 1974, was another milestone in the Ovett career: a sub-4-minute milestone, to be exact. At eighteen Steve actually equalled Roger Bannister's historic mile breakthrough time, achieved in 1954, of 3:59.4, when he won the Brigg Mile at the Beverley Baxter Trophy meeting in Harringay. In so doing Steve became Britain's youngest ever 4-minute miler. The pace was pretty slow at the bell (3:04.3), with the field bunched,

when Steve opened up with a 55.1 second final lap, to finish 20 metres clear of Chris Barber in second place. Steve commented afterwards that it had felt 'a bit like a training spin', and we soon realized that four-minute miles weren't all they were cracked up to be because shortly before the Rome championships, Steve and Tony Simmons ran a mile time trial in training on this same track in Harringay. The plan was for Tony and Steve to alternate laps but in fact Tony led only on the first lap, in 60 seconds. Steve then took over, running so fast that Tony could only hang on like grim death. Steve ended up with 4 minutes exactly while Tony got a personal best of 4 minutes 2 seconds. If Steve could run 4 minutes for the mile in training, with no crowd and no adrenalin flowing, we knew that if he were fit he could run much faster in a race. Steve realized then that there was no mystique about running a mile in 4 minutes – if you were fit enough you could do it. A far cry from Roger Bannister's response to me after I'd said at a training weekend that we would soon see athletes doing 4 minutes in training. He didn't think it was possible without the stimulus of rivals and a big occasion.

Tony and Steve helped each other on that time trial: it's not often that this happens in training, which is usually very competitive. For Steve it was an over-distance run; for Tony it was under distance, and he recorded his best ever time. I'd known Tony for several years because he lives near me, in Luton. He always struck me as somebody who had a lot of talent yet didn't quite know what to do with it. He didn't do very well in the Christchurch Commonwealth Games and he rang me when he came back to ask if I'd like to coach him. In February 1974 we met and talked over his training, and his rather slaphappy attitude towards running. He'd held the mile record for a fourteen-year-old, yet for the last few years he'd been content to make the cross-country team and, occasionally, the track team. He'd never really thought of himself as a potential world-class athlete, and I realized that what he needed was a sense of direction and discipline in his training, preparation for key races, and some clear objectives. Within a week he had started to train with me and by luck or good judgement we seemed to click. Tony was selected for the Rome 10,000 metres team.

Tony was small, at 5 feet 5 inches, and his stride was a bit tight. He overcame these disadvantages by intense and regular training. What had seemed a handicap actually became useful to him because he could use his short stride for acceleration. Retrospectively, though, I don't think I've ever managed to get 100 per cent out of Tony. There is still a little corner of doubt in his mind that has not been reached and somehow he can't quite believe he might be number one in the world. Steve believed in himself; Tony has reservations.

The last meeting before Rome was the British International Games at Crystal Palace. Steve ran in the Emsley Carr Mile and came fifth. He may have been unconsciously saving himself for the European championships, but at the time it seemed that whenever he ran a mile or 1500 metres he tended either to lose concentration or nerve on the third lap. In this mile he was at least 30 yards down going into the bell, though he pulled up some ground over the last 200 metres to finish in 4:03.5. He certainly wasn't seeing how far he could let the race go before hauling it in: that exercise is strictly a luxury and depends on the people you're running against. With good opposition you'd generally want to be poised on the leader's shoulder, ready to kick. He hadn't physically prepared, really, for a 1500 or mile race at any great pace: he was concentrating on 800 metres. He could finish fast off a nice easy mile, but he wasn't quite ready yet for the concentration needed in the middle of the fast longer races. Still, we got this Emsley Carr Mile out of his system with a weekend on the Merthyr Mawr sand dunes. Like hanging, it concentrates the mind wonderfully.

Rome

Our accommodation in Rome was rather strange to say the least. A few of the team whose events were coming up early went out a week ahead of the rest. Steve's 800 metres heats were scheduled for the first day, and so was Tony's 10,000 metres, so those two were in the advance party, getting used to the heat and humidity. The hotel seemed spacious, about two to a room, and nice and comfortable. Then the rest of us arrived and it was instantly transformed into the Black Hole of Calcutta.

Perhaps I should mention here that this was the first time I'd ever accompanied the team in an official capacity. I felt pretty sore in 1972 that Dr Ray Watson and myself were not invited to join the official Olympic squad, considering we had gone to St Moritz for three weeks beforehand to prepare the team for Munich. When we arrived in Germany we were found dismal lodgings and left to forage each day for tickets to see the games. In Rome I think it was appreciated that I had three people in the team: Steve, Tony and Lesley Kiernan, who'd qualified at the last minute as the youngest squad member.

In Steve's room, after the rest of us arrived, there were six athletes. I was on the top floor, sharing one room with five coaches and a physiotherapist. Athletes, particularly, do need a lot of space because they're going out training all the time and coming back to dry their wet kit. With one shower and one toilet between six in hot, humid conditions, it wasn't exactly pleasant. A number of the lads made complaints because apart from being steamed and pressed by day, they were also being disturbed at night by the staggered late arrivals, and it's imperative for an athlete to get the right amount of sleep before a race.

Help came in the shape of Eddie Kulukundis, a millionaire of Greek descent who in addition to being part owner of a shipping line is also a theatrical impresario, and later married Susan Hampshire. Eddie was an

athletics nut, helping out with the lads' training expenses
without ever seeking recognition for his generosity,
extremely patriotic, and keen to see the Union Jack
flying on the victory rostrum. I ran into him in Rome;
he'd read in the newspapers about the crowded hotel
conditions, and said he'd be prepared to foot the bill if we
wanted to move some of the team across the road to
another hotel. Well, four in particular said they wanted
to move: Steve, Brendan Foster, David Black and David
Jenkins, so I put Eddie's offer to the Board. I consulted
the other coaches, and they were a bit concerned about
splitting the team, but agreed that it would relieve the
general congestion. Team manager Jim Biddle told me
he would mention iit to Arthur Gold, the *chef de mission*.
Imagine my astonishment when Arthur Gold opened
that night's team meeting by announcing that anyone
who was discontented or disruptive at these games, be he
athlete or coach, would be likely to find himself going
home.

I protested that I didn't think I was being disruptive. I
was just trying to help some of the athletes who had
approached me, as a coach, about their accommodation.
Unfortunately hardly any of the other coaches supported
me, except for Tom McNab, who argued strongly that
something should be done on the athletes' behalf. After
much ado something *was* done. The Board declined
Eddie's offer, but took a few single rooms in another
hotel to allow competitors to get at least one good night's
sleep before their races.

Having surmounted these problems, we came to the
games themselves. I was very excited on the first day,
because all three people I coached were running. Steve
got through his heat very comfortably. Lesley struggled
through hers in a personal best of 2:02.8. And at the end
of the afternoon came the very dramatic 10,000 metres.
It was so hot that by the end of the race the inside lane
had changed colour because of all the sweat dripping off
the runners. With about three laps to go, Tony made a
bid for the lead but couldn't quite break away, and at the

bell it was the East German Kuschman who led by 10 or
15 metres. It looked all over, but then with about 200
metres to go Tony suddenly went berserk and closed the
gap, sprinting into a neck-and-neck finish. In fact he
recorded the same time as the winner, 28:25.8, which
after 10,000 metres is ridiculously unlikely. Tony was
rather pleased at first, but by the next day it had begun
to gnaw at his insides: if only I'd done this or that, he
seemed to be thinking, I'd have won it. To me, there
were no physical factors involved, just a lack of belief in
himself. Two or three inches: it's an opportunity that
may never come again. At least he'd handled the conditions well.

In Steve's 800 metres semifinal he had to contend with
the overall race favourite: Yugoslav Luciano Susanj.
Coming up the back straight Steve was positioned quite
well: runners often neglect to watch the inside very
carefully and if the field opens out wide you can sometimes move through on the inside. This Steve did,
comfortably and without anyone touching him, tucking
in behind Susanj and dipping in front at the line to win in
1:47.1. In the other semi, world record holder Marcello
Fiasconaro had qualified quite easily and we knew that
in the final it would be Fiasco who would have to do all
the work. Though raised and trained in South Africa he
was an Italian by birth and he would therefore be
obliged to put on a show for the crowd. And because he
had come up to 800 metres from 400 metres, he would
probably choose to lead. We wondered how far he was
going to blaze it.

It was fairly late on the evening of the 800 metres final
when a minor disaster struck. I had only the one race to
attend to that day, which was Steve's, so all the rest of
the team had gone to the stadium. Steve and I were the
only ones left in the hotel, waiting for a car to take us. I
was in my room and there was a knock on the door. It
was Steve.

'I'm a bit worried,' he said. 'I can't find my running
shoes.'

'Are you *sure*?'

'Yes.' We went down to his room and there – as you can imagine with six of them sharing — was a mountain of athletic kit, some wet, some dry, some dirty, and shoes of all shapes and sizes, spares and spikes. We delved down in the heap but couldn't find Steve's anywhere. Although we didn't know it at the time, Steve's shoes were buried under a pile of kit in Tony's bag. There was nothing for it but to look for another pair the same size, and the nearest we could find were a pair of Bernie Ford's spikes, which were actually half a size too large for Steve. This was the one race Steve had been looking forward to, and training for, over months and years, and he didn't even have the right shoes.

'It's a shame,' I said, commiserating.

'Oh well,' said Steve, 'half a size isn't going to make all that much difference. If I can win, I'll win.' So away he went to his race with Bernie's shoes and never mentioned it again. People have often talked about Steve being immature. Not in my experience.

We didn't discuss race tactics: it was fairly certain that Fiasconaro would lead and it was up to Steve to position himself as best he could and use his finish at the right moment. The danger man was Susanj, but Steve had sized him up in their semifinal and he felt he stood a good chance against the man he'd beaten there. The big crowd gave Fiasco a tremendous reception and he was so high that when the gun went you knew he would fly away. Setting off incredibly fast, he went through 200 in 24.5 and through the bell in 50.1. Steve was lying some way back in fifth (51.5 seconds). His positioning had obviously gone astray because he was still fifth as they entered the back straight, one place behind Susanj. Suddenly Susanj struck out for home. Within the space of 50 metres he had opened a yawning gap. Steve, who had moved inside, was so badly positioned that he couldn't cover the break. Indeed he couldn't move at all until they rounded the turn into the finishing straight and by then he must have known his chance had gone because he could see Susanj howling away in front. At last he burst through to daylight, and, in a vain bid to catch the disappearing figure of the Yugoslav, finished second in a personal best and European junior record of 1:45.8. He was desperately disappointed.

The race had been over so quickly. After all those months of preparation and pain and being sick on the Big Dipper, the race was decided with almost 200 metres to go. What made it even worse was the fact that Steve had come through so well at the finish that he was now haunted by possibilities: supposing he had been better positioned, supposing he could have gone with Susanj, supposing he could have pipped him. As Steve's coach I'm not saying he *could* have beaten 1:44.1 (which was Susanj's time); I don't think he was quite ready for that. However I think he could have given Susanj a very good run for his money.

After the race Steve talked to the press. 'I was so disgusted with myself that the feeling carried over into the press conference later and stayed with me all evening. I'm afraid I was a bit abrupt with the British press boys and probably gave them the impression that I'm an arrogant young upstart who should have accepted defeat gracefully and been satisfied with the silver medal, but there you are. At the time, I just wanted to see my parents and talk the race over with Harry, and see how he felt about it, and I knew the press were likely to keep the athletes hanging around for hours at these major meetings. Then I just wanted to go away and be alone and work out my feelings. What I was trying to say that night was that I know I could have done a lot better than I did, not necessarily that I felt I could have beaten Susanj. I didn't get a clear run at him, so I'll never know and no one else will ever know if I could have beaten him now. I'm not really worried what the press and people think of me. If you start to worry about what the press think and write about you, you're in a bad way, because they change their editorial opinions as quickly as the wind changes direction. I felt I'd let a lot of people down.

My family because they had made sacrifices for me, Harry because of all the help and encouragement he'd been to me and above all I'd let myself down because I finished without having run myself out.'*

This is Steve's own account of the race: 'It wasn't a good run. They went out fast, really fast. I didn't know how fast until we broke from lanes and then it was too late to catch up quickly because you run into anaerobic debt if you try that. So I took it fairly steadily and did my moving through on the inside. This was my first mistake, because they boxed me in and kept slowing it down. I saw Susanj move through them very fast at about 250 metres but the two East Germans were ahead of me then, walling me in, and I had to barge my way through. Then on the final bend I reached out and shoved Fromm and moved outside him. They slowed me up again in the straight so that I had to push again and move right out, and all the time I felt I was gaining on Susanj, even when we were slowing and shoving each other. When I did get a clear run at him it was too late.'

I think the press could have been kinder to Steve, considering how in April we had still been wondering if he was well enough to race that season at all. The newspapermen were carping at somebody who was technically a junior, running in his first major senior games, yet he had beaten the world record holder Fiasconaro, run a personal best time that was also a European junior record, and won the silver medal. Criticize him by all means for his mistakes, but at least give him credit for pulling out the silver. This was one occasion when Britain was doing quite well for medals, so maybe Steve's was rather devalued. But if you're hurt and annoyed with yourself for your incompetence and then you find there's very little praise even for what you did right, it can be very hurtful indeed.

John Rodda wrote, 'Frankly, I was surprised that he was not disqualified for the tactics he used,' and scoffed

* *Athletics Weekly*, 14 December 1974.

at Steve's suggestion that he might have won, given a clear run. He said it 'seemed, from a seat in the stand, to be at the least an optimistic forecast against a man of Susanj's quality'. A newspaper reporter views everything, as Rodda says, from his seat in the press box. That's quite *different* from being down in the fight below. Athletes are, on the whole, an honest lot when it comes to assessing a race very carefully. If they genuinely feel that they could have challenged somebody, they're not saying that out of bravado, but because they know their strengths and they know their opposition. Usually, as Steve was later to show, a runner will be the first to admit it if he is beaten by a better man on the night. Well, Steve felt he hadn't given himself a chance to pull Susanj back, as he never had a clear shot at him – for which he blamed no one but himself.

I don't think he was in any danger of disqualification. It was a rough race, with a lot of pushing, and I don't know of anybody that has been disqualified in any 800 metres race I've seen, because when everyone's jostling, you have to jostle, and just as hard. There are a number of qualities that determine whether an athlete is going to become a champion runner at middle distance. For a start, he has to love running, so much that he will run of his own accord and get a thrill out of it, and actually dislike resting. Next, a potential champion has to really want to excel and *be* a champion, and will be prepared to do whatever is necessary to fulfil that potential. Middle-distance running is unique: it's the only track or field event where competitors actually compete *against each other*. In all the other events you are competing principally against distance, time, height, oxygen debt or the elements; even in sprinting you run in your own lane. But in middle-distance running more than anywhere else you're actually coming in contact with other people and jockeying for position to beat them, so it's very much a combative sport. You have to push and shove, and be jostled yourself. Occasionally you have to be prepared to struggle and scramble at the finish, no matter what it looks like. A champion will want to win so badly that he'll do all these things.

After Steve won the 1980 Olympic 800 metres, many newspapermen attacked him for his aggression. Had he allowed himself to be pushed around and lost the race, the same writers would no doubt have criticized him for lack of initiative. On one occasion Colin Hart of the *Sun* confronted me about Steve using his elbows and said, 'You're teaching your fellow to be a dirty runner.' I answered, 'No, but what do you want me to teach him? To let somebody else win?' In his spare time from criticizing Steve, the man was a boxing correspondent, always expounding on the lack of killer instinct in British boxers. Well, in middle distance, if you reach a situation where you either push or you've lost the race, what's your alternative? There's a great deal of physical contact anyway. When you have eight people in the space of five or six yards and they're moving at a lick, it's inevitable that they will touch each other, and a good runner or coach accepts that pushing is an essential part of the race. I like 800 metres and 1500 metres precisely because they *are* aggressive races. A runner has to learn to survive. There are no excuses afterwards if somebody knocks you and you go flying off the track. It's no good complaining, 'I was a bit shocked, because so-and-so dug his elbow in me.' You have to expect that and be alert enough to look after yourself. Apart from anything else, it's very dangerous to be trodden on because the runners are wearing spikes and it's also dangerous to tread on anybody else because you are liable to stumble. In fast 800 and 1500 metres races the danger is less of abrasions from spikes than of having your rhythm and concentration severely impaired. So the runners are trying to keep out of one another's way. Steve doesn't regard himself as a 'hard man' – certainly no different from many others – and feels that it's strange that the press never criticize other British athletes for being over-physical. There are quite a few other runners who take good care of themselves and these characters are usually patted on the back and praised for being so positive.

Chris Brasher thought Steve's Rome race was a 'tactically stupid' run and, true, he did show his inexperience. But I think Brasher may well have been influenced in his comments on other people's races by what happened to him in the Melbourne Olympics. He went out as the third steeplechaser in the team and by dint of a lot of intelligent training he had made himself extremely fit. He ran a very good, positive race. He ran so positively, in fact, that he was disqualified for allegedly interfering with other competitors as they went over the last barrier. Our team manager put in a protest and eventually, after several agonizing hours, Brasher was reinstated. All credit to him, but I always think it only right and proper that this should have happened to him: he's such a dramatic individual, and so full of stories, it wouldn't do for him *just* to win the gold medal straight off, without something to flesh out the tale.

Steve didn't have the qualifying time to enter the Rome 1500 metres, but that turned out to be such a pathetic race, with such stereotype tactics (three and a half laps slow followed by a sprint) that Steve could have bided his time and kicked past the best of them. The winning time of 3:40.6 was about the equivalent of a 3:59 mile, which anyone of Steve's pace would have found congenial. Mel Watman in *Athletics Weekly* described the race appositely as 'instantly forgettable'. It's easy to be wise after the event, of course; we could never have known the race would be run to Steve's strengths.

I was in Rome in the capacity of event coach along with Denis Watts, responsible mainly for the middle- and long-distance runners. The job entails looking after their training facilities and transport, seeing they have their numbers on and being on hand if they need somebody to chat to during warm-up, to discuss tactics, or to advise them after a race. In other words, you make yourself available as required. When I'm selected as part of the official British squad, I assume responsibility not only for my own athletes but others too. I didn't spend too much

time with the other coaches, though I was rooming with
them, because I consider my job to be with the athletes
themselves, talking to them and finding out how they feel
about things rather than just popping up two minutes
before the gun and then washing my hands of them. The
day before the 5000 metres I spent a long time talking to
Brendan Foster, mainly about tactics. I think runners
like to have a sounding board: you don't even necessarily
have to voice an opinion as to whether they're right or
wrong. In Rome I don't think I showed favouritism
towards Steve, or Tony or Lesley either. I shared myself
out. On the last day I missed the finish of the 1500
metres in the stadium because I'd promised to tell Ian
Thompson, at the marathon 25-mile mark, how far he
was in front. I watched part of the 1500 metres, jogged a
mile or so in my tracksuit to tell Ian there was no one in
sight, then jogged back to the stadium, by which time I'd
missed the 1500 and the relays as well.

My 'disruptive' behaviour in Rome, trying to improve
the accommodation and hobnobbing with the athletes,
was undoubtedly the reason for my being excluded from
the official party for Montreal in 1976. It couldn't have
helped my cause, either, that at the end of the games,
when Eddie Kulukundis threw a party for the athletes
and anybody else who wanted to come along, at the
Hilton, I went along. The traditional view of coaches was
that they should place certain limits on their fraterniza-
tion with the athletes. Well, I did the best job I could,
and most of the athletes were appreciative. My own three
didn't do too badly either. Steve and Tony won silver
medals and Lesley got a new UK junior record. Perhaps
the most disappointed was Steve. He admitted later that
he had had to push himself to go for the silver after the
gold had gone.

In this strange animal called a 'winner' there is always
this slight temptation not to bother too much if he or she
can't actually *win*. It's very hard for an onlooker to
understand and sometimes I can't believe it myself. I
couldn't figure out why Lynn Davies seemed to give up

after Bob Beamon's incredible jump in Mexico, but then I'd never coached one of these 'winners' in those days. Now, I think I see it more clearly. I don't agree, and neither does Steve, that 'first is first and second is nowhere', but these thoughts may cross a runner's mind as he actually sees a race slipping away from him. *After* the race, all that matters is whether or not he has performed to his own satisfaction, and that will be the measure of his success. You see, it's like boxing. If a fighter gets beaten by a better man, fair enough, but if he lets his guard down for a second to hitch up his shorts and the other boxer knocks him out, he feels aggrieved because he's let himself down. That's roughly how Steve felt about Rome.

Steve had made up his mind before he went to the championships that afterwards he was going on a hiking holiday around Italy. The Coke meeting back home was Andy Norman's first major promotion and he badly wanted Steve, so I felt quite sorry for Andy, though Steve has more than compensated since then with appearances at Andy's meetings. But Steve was quite adamant about this hiking tour. So far as races were concerned, he felt he had had enough. I looked after his luggage with typical efficiency – I managed to leave his case behind. I don't think it was loaded on the wagon when we left the hotel, and when we arrived at Heathrow, S. Ovett's bag was nowhere to be seen. I felt pretty sick. Thank goodness he hadn't left his medal in his case. Steve toured northern Italy, stopping off at Florence; he's always been interested in art and he wanted to see some of Europe's great art treasures in their natural setting. Later, that autumn he began studying at Brighton College of Art, though I think he was half in and half out of academia and only stayed there for two terms. Apart from running, he was a typical teenager, enjoying the Brighton social life, a laugh, and a few beers with his friends.

All in all, it wasn't a bad year. Steve won the Pepsi-Cola award for the best athlete under twenty-one in the AAA: he forgave me for losing his suitcase, and he forgave Tony for making it necessary for Bernie Ford's shoes to tear round 800 metres in Rome. 'One thing's for sure, Bernie,' he said, reuniting the Ford footwear with its rightful owner, 'those shoes will never run as fast as that again!'

3

Row over Nice

Steve had decided on Brighton art college despite a flood of scholarship offers, both American and British. He saw no reason to rock the boat by going to the United States: he loved his home, and Brighton, close to the Downs and with its Stanmer and Preston parks, was a congenial base from which to study and train. He had the support of his parents and he was happy with his coach, so though it might have been prestigious for the American college concerned to have somebody like Steve on the campus, it wouldn't have been particularly beneficial to him. One of my earlier athletes, Richard Jones, had chosen less happily. Inundated like Steve with American scholarship offers after his European junior mile record he asked, 'Well, what do you think, Harry?' It turned out later that he had wanted me to say, 'Stay here, and you'll be a world-class athlete,' though I hadn't the confidence or experience in those days to try to influence him. He went to America and his running seemed to suffer.

Many British runners who are attracted by American college scholarships find that they are expected to turn in high-quality performances week after week (sometimes three races in one afternoon) in inter-college track matches, often travelling considerable distances to the meetings. It's not surprising that by the time the American season finishes at the end of June, they are often in no condition to perform well in the major European meetings.

Winter work

Steve began 1975 by winning the Sussex junior cross-country championships in January by the huge margin, in race terms, of two minutes. We also did some early season training abroad. We'd gone to St Moritz for altitude work, but we picked a week that was cold and wet, which meant that we didn't achieve very much. The body adapts to the 'thin' air at high altitudes by producing more red blood cells in order to pick up what oxygen is available, and the red-cell level stays high for several days upon returning to sea level. Obviously the more haemoglobin present, the more oxygen is extracted and in an earlier chapter I explained how oxygen cleans away the waste products of exercise. I'm not sure, now, that St Moritz is actually high enough for altitude training anyway; because of the cold too (nearly all altitude spots are cold) you tend to find that you're doing endurance work rather than speed work unless you're lucky enough to catch seasonable weather. Ideally such a trip should be left until July or August – just prior to major games. I've done more altitude work, with more athletes, than any other coach in Britain, but I'm not sure of the benefits to 800 metres runners. I think the training may well be of more value for 1500 metres and longer distances. As with everything in athletics, it depends on the individual. With the benefit of hindsight, I don't think you profit by taking whole teams to altitude, as we did in 1972: adaptation and readaptation on returning to sea level vary from runner to runner. Some individuals benefit enormously. Julian Goater, who is an extraordinary athlete anyway, is not blessed with great natural speed, yet he can run 13:15.6 for 5000 metres, less than a second behind Brendan Foster. Julian thrives on altitude work. So does Ian Stewart. 'It's a ruddy sight harder at 8000 feet, so it must be better for me,' Ian assured me.

I wish more were known in this country about the effects of blood-packing. There's a strong case for specialist research centres to investigate both the benefits and dangers of retransfusing some of an athlete's own blood before an event, to increase the haemoglobin-bearing red cells. If it were to prove safe and beneficial, blood-packing could be offered to athletes under medical supervision who wished to take advantage of it, pointing out the risks of any possible side effects such as infection or increased blood pressure. Not all athletes or their coaches would *wish* to take advantage of such a service: I'm not sure that I would myself, because of all the moral implications involved. But I think it should at least be offered. I don't think blood-doping, as it is called, is actually comparable with doping or taking anabolic steroids. All retransfusion does is to increase the oxygen-bearing capacity of the blood, which is what you are trying to achieve at altitude. If you can produce this effect without harm to the athlete by means of a re-transfusion, you could save the incredible expense of three or four weeks at a mountain resort. In other words you'd have internal altitude training. Quite recently, Dr Peltokalli, the official team doctor to the Finns, made disclosures to the press that certain members of the Finnish team have indeed benefited from red cell packing. He mentioned as an example Leppilampi, who broke the world steeplechase record, and implied that he wasn't the only one.

Another training trip in early 1975 was to Torremolinos in Spain. We went, perhaps misguidedly, the week before the AAA indoor championships. We'd been given some misleading advice about the place and we arrived to find it totally unsuitable. The sand on the beaches was so soft you couldn't run on it, so we had to do our repetitions round the municipal rubbish tip, with lean and hungry dogs prowling about. Then we had to make an hour-and-a-half long bus journey to a rotten old track in Malaga, where the toilet smelt so foul that people were going in with towels wrapped round their heads.

A couple of days after our return the indoor championships were upon us. Steve wanted just to go out and run fast in the 1500 metres, to see what happened, and he ran through the heats very smoothly. In the final, Walter Wilkinson took the field through the first 200 metres quite quickly, then Steve went in front and kept up a brisk pace. Between 1000 and 1100 metres, though, he started to tie up and the race was won by Phil Banning in a new British indoor record of 3:42.4. Steve finished fifth in 3:45.9. Phil Banning had been to Spain with us, but he had cunningly used the week as a build-up for these championships instead of flogging himself every day like the others. Phil eased off and only did about half the training sessions, so he was refreshed and fit. That race taught Steve that if you're going to lead in a 1500 metres and push the pace along, you really have to be quite a bit better than the opposition, because unless you can break clear, they will just hang on and pick you off when you start to fade. He also learned how *not* to prepare for a 1500 metres race.

He was now building up for the 6-mile national junior cross-country championships. He had a fine run in Dieppe just two weeks before it, on 16 February, finishing joint first with Pete Standing, a senior cross-country international, in a 10,200 metres cross-country race ahead of several good Continental runners. I don't think that result had penetrated the British press box, because on the morning of the national junior race at Luton, nobody dreamed of tipping Steve to win. Yet he made it all look so easy, trotting along briefly with the field and then, without any apparent distortion of style, launching off over the mud and hills to win by a considerable margin. Everyone was rather shocked. The same afternoon, Tony Simmons won the coveted national senior title on his home ground, so I was doubly delighted. Coaching really is a carefree job on days like that.

Steve attributed his Luton win to daily training in Brighton with a Scots schoolteacher, Matt Paterson, who helped him a great deal. 'I'm really enjoying distance running,' Steve said. He was now doing forty to fifty miles of quite hard endurance work each week. The 1500 metres is a fifty-fifty event – 50 per cent anaerobic and 50 per cent aerobic – so even in the summer, although the training emphasis might shift towards speed, Steve would still be keeping these long runs going. As we've seen, endurance work is vital to a middle-distance man like Steve; he can't live by his kick alone. To do those long, steady-state runs, where oxygen uptake matches oxygen requirements, though, you generally need company, and an integral part of his training now was Matt.

Matt was quite happy to join Steve, not only on the long easy-pace runs but on the shorter, steady-state runs as well. In fact Steve fits in the morning runs to suit Matt and at times has difficulty in holding him on these runs. Matt is also good on hill work and when he goes down to Merthyr Mawr he can train faster than many athletes who have superior track times. Matt isn't really built for speed, so he couldn't do all the intensive track repetitions, but on the aerobic side his help made a huge difference to Steve, for which he'll always be grateful. It has often puzzled both Steve and myself that Matt doesn't *race* better. The day Steve won the junior national, for instance, Matt came about 180th in the senior event – not bad in a 1000-strong field, but not what you'd expect after all this training. I think a lot of the running that Steve finds easy is actually quite hard going for Matt, and it's difficult to say whether he has improved as a result or sacrificed some of his own form to help Steve. But Matt loves steady-state running anyway, and I think his commitments to his family and his job prevent him from travelling extensively to races. Matt's contribution is vital, providing both companionship in training and a constant stimulation.

Typically, a few days after Steve's marvellous win in Luton, a letter appeared in *Athletics Weekly* from a reader complaining that Steve should have been disqualified for failing to wear his Brighton and Hove club vest. There were probably hundreds of runners sporting eccentric vests that day, but this chap had to pick on Steve. Great running was evidently the next most important thing after singlets.

Steve rounded off the cross-country season with a very fast leg in a road relay race on 5 April, in which he finished just a few seconds behind Bernie Ford, one of our top long-distance men. It was a very good winter's work, but unfortunately Steve now had a debilitating throat infection that refused to clear up. Fitness and training are related by a sort of knock-on effect: the faster you train, the fitter you become, and the fitter you get the harder you train, because you are benefiting physically and mentally from the improvement. But certain areas of fitness are outside the control of either the coach or the athlete. You do your best to train heart, lungs, circulation, and get the body into superb condition, and then suddenly fate intervenes and the athlete gets a cold, or a throat virus. According to one theory he is actually more prone to infection because he is stressing his body to the limit and he is only specifically fit. But it's like a blow beneath the belt. The kind of fitness problems Steve had been having were no fault of his own, and all he could do was to try to get over them as quickly as possible.

Summer season

Steve had had a couple of easy league races to start off that summer, but his first important run was a tough outing at Crystal Palace on 31 May – the Emsley Carr Mile, staged early that year, and with a field that included the new world record holder for the mile, in a time of 3:51.0, Filbert Bayi of Tanzania. It turned out to be a typical Bayi race, with the Tanzanian pushing off right from the start and leading all the way to win in 3:55.5, a good time for so early in the season. Steve flopped out on the ground afterwards looking rather ill, and for a moment we thought perhaps his glandular fever had come back to plague us. The one good thing about the race was that Steve had been the only competitor who'd had the nerve to go with Bayi – faster than Steve had ever gone before – and for two and a half laps at least, he hung on at hair-raising speed. The others had merely waited for the pickings.

Filbert is a very quiet sort of fellow, who in those days must have had great confidence in his fitness because he'd just run a whole string of fast times close together. Going into a race against Bayi has always been a supreme test of anybody's preparation, because his style is to run you into the ground, to pre-empt any last-lap attack. He has run for most of his career like this, right up to the Moscow steeplechase where Poland's Malinowski took him apart on the final lap despite the big safety margin Bayi had put between them. Bayi tends to run all his races in the same way: extravagantly hard from the start, burn everybody off and then hang on tight. His worst disappointment, I've no doubt, was to be withdrawn from Montreal in the African walkout. It would have been his biggest season, I think, and in the Olympics he would have had a great battle with New Zealander John Walker.

Feeling none too happy or healthy, Steve went with a British team to Dresden next, to meet the mighty East Germans. On the first day he was down as reserve in the 800 metres but Tony Settle pulled out at the last minute, so in went Steve to come third in 1:47.6, 'eyeballs out', as he said later. But he felt a bit better the next day and asked to run in the 1500 metres as a non-scorer. He ran a more contained race and was the first British finisher, coming second in 3:43.3 behind Hans-Henning Ohlert, who also won the 800 metres. In fact Steve was dead last at the bell but came through fast at the finish. This annual UK v. East Germany match is apt to be a dispiriting affair because Britain usually gets crushed by the Germans. I believe they may be taking us for a ride, as early each season before we're half into our speed work, they seem to come out of their winter traps and seize on the UK as a team to hammer the life out of early

in the year. I don't think it does our morale a power of
good.

On 30 June a group of us went to Stockholm for an
extraordinary mile race in which five different national
records were broken. It was won in 3:52.2 by John
Walker. Steve was lying a very strong third at 1500
metres, and watching his progress I thought, 'Now, he's
beautifully positioned here; if he finishes well it'll be a
fantastic time.' Instead, on the last 100 metres, his legs
turned to mush and he finished ninth in 3:57 dead. It was
a new European junior record, but the tantalizing thing
was that Frank Clement had scraped home in seventh
place in 3:55.0, which was a new UK record. This wasn't
all. At 1500 metres Steve had actually been 2 seconds
ahead of Frank, so he'd actually lost 4 seconds to Frank
over the last 100 metres. This was a real blow to Steve,
and he was very cut up about that race for quite some
while afterwards, despite the record and the personal
best of 3:57. 'Well what's *wrong*, Harry? What have I got
to *do*? What have I got to *get*?' As I tried to explain, all he
needed was time. It was just a case of waiting until he
had the mileage and training behind him that these other
people had. That's the trouble with strength and endurance events of 1500 metres and up: it may take years for
the results to come. It's not like teaching somebody a
technique, where you see almost immediate results. With
Steve it was fully two years before he was really getting
the benefit of his 1500 metres training, and long-distance
men like Foster and Simmons have achieved best performances at the age of around twenty-eight, after
perhaps fourteen or fifteen years of work. During all that
time they had to believe in themselves, and that the
results would eventually come.

On 4 July, Steve ran third (in a time of 1:49.3) in an
800 metres race at Crystal Palace in the Philips Golden
International, behind Mike Boit of Kenya (in 1:48.6)
and Rick Wohluter of the USA (in 1:48.7). It was pretty
slow and Steve wasn't lively enough to make much of a
challenge. So when he ran in the Europa Cup semifinal

at Crystal Palace the following week, although his training was going well there were still some doubts in his mind about his fitness, and he wanted the reassurance of racing results. The Europa Cup semifinal 800 metres was just what he needed, and actually turned out to be a bit of a doddle for him. Third at the bell, which was reached by race leader Ake Svenson of Sweden in 52.2 seconds, Steve waited until the 600 metres mark and then in a flash opened a 5-metre gap, striding round the last 150 metres majestically, to finish first in 1:46.7. It was quite a surprise – and a relief – because there was nothing in his recent form to indicate that he was ready to run like that. The race was perhaps a sign that his fitness troubles were over, and that he was ready to roll.

It was a lovely run, but unfortunately Steve's comments afterwards sparked off a controversy that was to lead to Steve's well-known disillusionment with the press. When asked about the Europa Cup final to be held in Nice, Steve replied that he wasn't sure that he'd even be running in it, because he wasn't yet satisfied with his fitness and he'd just have to wait and see. If he did decide that he wasn't ready, it would be no great loss so far as he was concerned as he didn't regard the race as a very high priority. He said he'd rather hitch to Athens and then build up for the Montreal Olympics. Steve was just trying to convey the feelings of somebody who didn't want to run in a race where he might not do himself justice. You wouldn't tell a boxer in doubt about his fitness, 'Well, get in the ring anyway and have a go.'

A hue and cry followed in which Steve's comments were completely misconstrued and he was accused of arrogance, high treason and not wanting to run for his country. I think the manner in which he was attacked by the press on this occasion turned him against newspapermen once and for all. He said later, 'Who am I to criticize the press? I respect their opinions; they obviously know more about athletics than I do. Some of them put in a lot of work in the bar lifting glasses, and then they stagger up to the press box to regale us with their opinions. I got very fed up with the British press. They have this lazy, imperious attitude to the athletes. We run our guts out on the track and if we've pleased them enough for them to want to talk to us, we get this summons to attend the press interview room like some sort of Royal Command. Then we have to sit there like good little boys and say what they expect us to say. If we don't say what they want, or if we offend their sense of patriotism, we get branded as arrogant, immature upstarts, or there's something terribly wrong with us. I got the impression in '75 that because I wasn't talking as they had me programmed to talk they'd be better off interviewing an empty chair and making up their own answers.'*

You have to understand that what happened in those days when a runner had just finished a race was that he'd be trying to warm down on the track, or perhaps talking to somebody, and over would come a steward with a court summons to the press box. Steve found that when he went up there, instead of him talking to the press, *they* were talking to him, making suggestions as to how he should perform and being decidedly rude about it. Steve wanted no part of this. It's a sensitive time to catch an athlete, just after a race, particularly if you're going to lambast him with your opinions instead of listening to him. So in future when these press summonses came, Steve exercised the right of every individual to say 'No, thanks.' There is after all no God-given right to interviews. I think the job of athletics reporters is primarily to report what they see – or what they think they see – not to pry out quotes and juicy bits from the athletes.

Steve has often adopted a policy of 'I'll wait and see how I'm running' before he decides on a particular race. Throughout his career, this attitude has infuriated many people, but Steve doesn't like to commit himself too far

* *Athletics Weekly*, 22 January 1977.

ahead. He may deep down inside know that he wants to run, but because he doesn't know what form he'll be in, and because he doesn't like to run substandard races, there's always a proviso, and sometimes he leaves his decision until the last minute. He might say something like, 'Well, I'll see how I run in the AAA championships and if they don't go too well, I'll call it a day for this season and start preparing for Montreal. But if I run well in the AAA, I'll carry on with the season.'

I thought it most unfair, and far outside normal editorial protocol, that in the middle of Steve's impasse with the press, *Athletics Weekly* should print an open letter from Jimmy Green, the magazine's business manager, to Steve Ovett, telling him he should run for Queen and country. I was so incensed by the contents of this screed that although Steve wanted me to ignore it, I replied. I hope that my own letter may have cleared up one or two fanciful notions about international runners.

Open Letter to Steve Ovett*

Dear Steve,

I listened to the radio, and read the newspaper report of your comments and intention to miss the European Cup Final in Nice almost with disbelief.

You may be obsessed with the idea of a gold medal in the Montreal Olympics, but on reflection I am sure you will realise that there *are* other important things in life. Being a great athlete also brings responsibilities, to your team and to the supporters of the team.

Perhaps you think the fans don't matter, but without them –the people who packed the Crystal Palace and 'lifted' you and the other members of the team to such heights last weekend – there would be no spectators, no atmosphere, and no trips to Montreal.

These supporters of the British team would give their right arm to be in your position, to have the talent (and the guts and determination) which you are fortunate enough to be endowed with. They and others who could not get to the Crystal Palace

* *Athletics Weekly*, 19 July 1975.

72

but probably watched it all on their TV screens, are the people who provide most of the money to send athletes like you on glamorous trips abroad. People like Alf Mignot, an ordinary working chap from Custom House, who travels to all the major events he can afford to go to and supports all the fund-raising efforts which pay for the athletes who are privileged – yes, privileged – to compete for Britain. . . .

Jimmy Green

*Harry Wilson – Steve Ovett's Coach – Replies**

Dear Sir,

I would like to write a few words in answer to Jimmy Green's open letter to Steve Ovett. Not that Steve needs anyone to act on his behalf – he is well capable of taking care of himself on the track or verbally.

Steve's reasons for his comments after his fine win in the European Cup semi-final are complicated, but in the main are due to a lack of understanding by some of our senior officials. There are many very young people coming into the international team at the moment and there is no doubt in my mind that the older generation of officials have very little in common with the ideas and aims of these young people. They have a different set of values and a different life style to that which was in vogue 20, 30 or even 40 years ago. It's no good officials making such remarks as 'none of the boys will wear a tie' or 'why must all the girls wear jeans', and complaining that athletes areeen't what they used to be. They aren't what they used to be (in many ways, thank goodness), but very quickly the establishment has to develop a good relationship with the younger element and above all not talk down to them.

Jimmy says that Steve is very fortunate to have so much talent. OK, but so have many other young athletes. It needs a lot more than natural talent to reach the very top in athletics. It calls for a lot of hard work, careful planning and much sacrifice in terms of time, money and career advancement. It's not luck; it's determination and single-mindedness, and Steve possesses these vital assets.

As regards glamorous trips – well, a typical trip entails several hours hanging around at airports, a couple of sleepless

* *Athletics Weekly*, 2 August 1975.

nights in a strange hotel bed, a good chance of picking up some obscure stomach bug, a nerve-racking day waiting for a race, then a channelling of several months preparation into less than two minutes of running. If the race goes well then you can have a good night out – providing you haven't got to get up early to catch a plane. This is the sort of trip that a businessman would flinch at. However, it's what an athlete knows he must face and what he prepares for. But glamorous –no!

I agree that Steve is privileged to compete for Great Britain – perhaps honoured is a better word – but if he's the best in the country then it's his right to compete or not. If an athlete is the number one in a country then surely he has earned the right to be selected; his selection isn't a favour that has to be granted.

Regarding priorities and responsibilities, Steve knows where these lie and I hope that his future races will provide ample evidence of this. Remember that he supported the BAAB's British Games meet despite a badly infected throat and that he was getting a hammering in Dresden along with the rest of the team when several other notabilities were missing.

What I must stress is that he has a right to say what he thinks regardless of whether I, Jimmy Green or Uncle Tom Cobley and all agree with what he says. I can do no more than to quote Voltaire: 'I disapprove of what you say, but I will defend to the death your right to say it.'

Harry Wilson

The week before the AAA Championship, Steve ran four races in one afternoon. It was down in Barking, in a league match. He ran a personal best 200 metres of 21.7 seconds, a 400 metres, and two legs in relays of 4 × 100 metres and 4 × 400 metres. It was a reasonable after-noon's work, but it may have had a carry-over effect with all the rest of his training and when the AAA champion-ships began, he was still unsure about his form. In the 800 metres he found himself baulked near the end of the first lap and had to manoeuvre out of a poor position. Pete Browne, who had gone in front at the break from lanes, passed 400 metres in 51.8 seconds. Just before the 600-metre mark, Steve challenged for the lead, but had some trouble getting past Browne when he couldn't find his usual quick burst of acceleration and was obliged to cut in rather sharply. He had to fight hard all the way down the straight to edge home first in 1:46.1, to retain the title in his second fastest time ever after Rome. Steve was worried at this; without any intended disrespect to Pete, who ran his best time for two years, Steve would normally have expected to go out at 200 metres and pile on the power for a big winning margin. He felt guilty, too, about bumping Pete on the bend, and he admitted afterwards that he wouldn't have been too upset to have been disqualified. There are some people of whom it *might* be true to say that Steve wouldn't mind shutting their whiskers in the door, but Pete had been a good chum for a long time, and Steve felt he'd been unfair to cut him up.

What seemed to anger the press immensely in those days was Steve's habit of turning down the power a couple of strides out in his 800 metres races. He would do most of the damage at the 600-metre mark, open up a gap very quickly, and then settle back into his long, loping stride for the rest of the race. He usually had races won by the time he entered the finishing straight so it was his custom to ease in. There was really no need for him to come hammering through the finishing tape, because these races weren't at world-record pace anyway. And if you're winning 15-nil in the last minute of a football match you aren't generally expected to go charging all over the field after the ball.

Though Steve was still voicing doubts about his fitness, his training was going well and the racing results were beginning to come, so he decided to run in Nice. Having made up his mind to run, he was quite looking forward to it. His morale had been boosted slightly by an impromptu 800 metres win in a Southern Counties AAA open race at Crystal Palace in 1:47.7, an hour or so after a training session there. The Europa Cup final 800 metres in Nice was a tough race. It opened up quite fast but then slowed between 300 and 550 metres, with Steve lying fourth, and at the end of the back straight, I recall very clearly, the whole field was bunched and looking very tentative as to who should make a move. Somebody, I think it was Wulbeck, suddenly stretched out a hand and planted it in the middle of Steve's back. This seemed to set Steve in motion. Bursting his way through the pack that immediately cleared a path for him, Steve surged through the 600-metre mark, opening a gap so decisive that by the start of the finishing straight the race was won. He coasted in in 1:46.6. But it was a very physical race and at one stage, halfway down that back straight, the whole field could have gone tumbling over, punching and shoving. Fortunately Steve looked after himself; that little push in the back seemed to cue him to clear out, and away he went.

I ran into Ron Pickering behind the stands after the race, and he made a comment about Steve 'giving those lads a rough time this afternoon'. You can't win. Before Steve came along, Britain used to be regularly filing official protests about our runners being bumped and nudged by everybody else. Steve has never, ever, protested after a race about anyone or anything; he has always regarded it as inevitable that you get elbowed or sloshed, or that somebody will grab your shorts. He doesn't mind: he can look after himself. After the Nice 800 metres he said, 'I wouldn't have been surprised to have been disqualified, no.' He explained, 'It's not the accolade or the spoils of the race that interest me. It's man versus man. A 800 metres final is a battlefield: you expect to take knocks. I've taken knocks and I've given as good as I've got. You don't run in your own private world down there. You can't say, "Excuse me, I'm going to move out now, is that OK?" Things happen spontaneously.'

Steve *still* didn't think the Europa Cup meeting was a high priority. The races are, after all, one-offs with no heats or semifinals, so they're a bit of a gamble and nearly always tactical contests. They haven't the same individual appeal to an athlete as the European championships or the Olympics, because the Europa Cup is more of a team event. The most important thing about Steve's 800 metres race to us was that he won it convincingly, whereas a few weeks previously he had been struggling.

End of an Era

Steve missed the UK v. USSR match at Crystal Palace on August Bank Holiday, side-lined with gastro-enteritis. It had been a season of steady progress, interrupted by illness and setbacks outside our control. It ended rather sadly, as an era ended, with the death of Percy Wells Cerutty, aged eighty. I wrote an obituary for *Athletics Weekly*, part of which said:

As I was probably the last British coach to spend some time with Percy (I had a great day at Portsea in the summer of 1973) I'd like to pay a tribute to a man who became a legend in his own lifetime and who well and truly lived up to the legend.... When I met him in 1973 he was a very lively 78. He did little running but was ever anxious to demonstrate his four basic running techniques: the jog trot, the lope, the gallop and the drop in order to accelerate. However, he was still great with the weights – he 'cleaned' 120 lb and did half-squats with 200 lb. He talked incessantly while I sat on the grass beneath his rostrum, entitled 'Percy's Pulpit'. Much of what he said I'd heard before but every now and then he came up with some gems, e.g. 'Whatever you do son – don't do it in moderation.' ... He was pleased when I asked him to become an honorary member of the British Milers Club (Steve is also an honoured member) and promptly used the club tie that I gave him as a belt to hold up his brief sun-bleached shorts.

So we are now without one of the great characters of our sport and I for one feel richer for having known him. Percy was a great motivator. He was a runner's coach for he knew about feelings and emotions – he loved triers. He had more genuine feeling for athletes in his big toe than many of those so-called sophisticated coaches who derided him have in their whole bodies. Of course some of their criticisms were valid – what man worthy of his salt is perfect? – and he made mistakes, but much of the criticism levelled against him was prompted by jealousy of his results and his relationship with athletes. He

77

leaves behind him many athletes and coaches who are better men for having met him and the films of Elliott in action are a monument to his teaching. He was a 'one-off' and Shakespeare might well have had Percy in mind when he wrote, 'He was a man, take him for all in all, I shall not look upon his like again.' I'm sure I won't.*

Steve was preparing for 1976 and the Montreal Olympics, but although we had a training plan, this was no inflexible, dogmatic programme that couldn't take account of changes in Steve's feelings or fitness requirements. This contrasts sharply with the precise, formula-type approach followed by Sebastian Coe, and may well reflect their different personalities. Steve is at his happiest in the unrehearsed situation where he has to improvise as the race unfolds; Seb seems to excel in the races which proceed according to a pre-set plan without any unexpected incidents. I feel you have to keep a fairly open mind because if you say, 'This is the schedule and we're not going to budge from it,' then if you have a setback, an illness or even a slight injury, the plan is disrupted for a couple of weeks and this throws the whole thing out of kilter. Which means that you start worrying about it, and it becomes a bad omen. I'm not superstitious at all. If I were I should be a bit doubtful about Steve because I was always told to be wary of left-handed people! I think Steve is slightly superstitious though. I don't know when he first wore that red Russian vest of his, but it must have been a very good race because he stuck to that vest until it practically dropped off him. Of course there was a bit of devilment in it too: Steve always had a streak of fiendish humour. 'You can't come in here,' he tells the other runners trying to get into the dressing room, 'this is for the *bad* guys. Yours is along the corridor.' Remarks like that probably make people want to beat him all the more.

Steve and I share a rather sardonic sense of fun that brings us down to earth and keeps athletics in proportion. Anyway, he says he wouldn't throw himself off

* *Athletics Weekly*, 13 September 1975.

Beachy Head if his racing career ended tomorrow. Our mutual humour has been part of any formula we may have as a team. We've always respected each other's ability. I never kid Steve about his training; I always tell him the bitter truth if it doesn't come up to standard, and he will always be prepared to argue with me on the finer points. There was never any question of his doing anything simply because Harry said so: it had to be a sensible idea. I have always been prepared to discuss training with him and I think that has made a lot of difference. What I wanted really was to develop Steve's own method of doing things to the best advantage. Very early on we realized that although athletics is a serious business, and although races are serious, and training is never to be taken lightly, there are many aspects of our sport – not excluding some of the people in it – that need debunking.

We have a rather peculiar brand of humour, laced with a good proportion of mickey-taking. Because I'm small, and accustomed to being told, 'Stand up Harry!' when I'm already standing up, I'm quite happy to enter into the spirit of things and take the rise out of other people. I think it's the same with Steve. People have often poked fun at him and tried to gee him up for his socalled cockiness and arrogance, so he likes to get his own back. A typical example of Steve's sardonic humour is the nickname 'Tiger', which he has used on me for several years. You'd need a vivid imagination to see any 'fearful symmetry' about me. Sensible onlookers like Rachel (Mrs Ovett) are often baffled at the pair of us doubled up with laughter over some silliness. One instance occurred in Prague, at the European Games. Geoff Capes, a friend of Steve, was involved in a thunderous row about not having the correct amount of numbers on his vest, the upshot of which was that the enormous Geoff came striding through the village, bag in hand and blazer on, on his way home with a worried team manager Doug Goodman. He was looking very fearsome and aggressive about having been disqualified, but Steve walked past with an air of indifference, smiled and said, 'Hear you had a spot of bother this afternoon, Geoff.' Geoff swallowed hard, while Doug winced and waited for the explosion that never came.

On another occasion, Steve was just stepping off the track after breaking the British mile record when he was approached by a rather rotund reporter in very high spirits, one of them scotch. Clasping Steve closely like a personal chum, the press person enthused, 'Great! Great run, Steve! Fantastic race!'

'Thanks,' said Steve, drawing back and then turning to indicate Frank Clement, who had finished second in the same race, 'but what about Frank here?'

'Frank?' questioned the obviously bewildered reporter.

'Yes,' says Steve, 'did you see his pole vault?'

'Great!'' said the reporter. 'A great vault. I knew you had it in you, Frank!' And this was poor Frank Clement, who'd run his heart out and seen his British record disappear to Steve that afternoon. Frank is one of the nicest fellows in athletics and you'd think anybody, even an athletics writer, might recognize Frank. He's not exactly a pretty runner, but he's very strong. He took the bronze in the Commonwealth Games in 1978, but I think he should really have won it because he came through so powerfully at the end. We've always felt that he never really made the best of himself because he seems to lose contact around the start of the last lap and then lets people go, before coming along like a train at the finish. These days he usually appears on the scene with his two daughters. Or is it three now, Frank?

The earliest recorded instance of Steve larking about was Christmas 1971, when he went on a Crystal Palace Southern Counties course for any budding middle-distance youngsters who'd like to pay for a training weekend. Steve was about sixteen then; this was before I met him. He apparently treated the course as an opportunity to train and have a laugh at the same time, and he was accused of being disorderly. On the final day, during one of coach Frank Horwill's talks, Steve blew a raspberry, and Frank immediately rounded on him with a piece of vituperation he now finds rather amusing. 'Ovett,' said Frank, 'you just haven't got what it takes to be a champion!'

As a youngster Steve used to race in a terrible pair of shorts in a fancy floral fabric, like something out of 'Hawaii 5-0'. This is part of a strange contradiction in his nature. He doesn't seek publicity, and away from the running track he tries to be fairly inconspicuous, dressing in dark, anonymous clothes. He's a very private person, and genuinely embarrassed to have people pointing at him in the street. At the same time, on the track he will do flamboyant things. I've seen him wear a cap like a Union Jack, a cap with a miniature umbrella on top, and even a Viking helmet complete with horns sticking out of the sides. He's very unpredictable in this regard. People have called him arrogant, but he's actually confident. He has great trust and belief in his ability: he knows that in athletics he's going a long way. Now, if you're better at something than other people and you seem to be superior, I suppose people are entitled to call you conceited, but Steve *isn't* superior in his attitude. He doesn't at all feel that because he's good at athletics he's a cut above other mortals. We're all good at some things rather than others and it behoves none of us to give ourselves airs and graces about it. Steve doesn't set himself apart. I've never known him turn down an autograph-hunter in his life. He's always patient. I've seen him standing with a queue of people in front of him, signing autographs for hours after a race. If kids approach him with their scraps of paper before his run, he'll say, 'I can't stop now, but if you wait after the race I'll get back to you.' And he goes back later. Many sportsmen would sweep them aside.

Steve has always had the same feeling that I have about athletics: that because we're lucky enough to be healthy, with all our limbs in roughly the right proportions, it's incumbent upon us to squeeze as much out of our abilities as we can. Near Welwyn Garden City where we train in the woods, there's a school for spastic children and some of them come out to watch us training. I tell all the lads I coach, 'Look, stop moaning, because those kids over there would give anything to be able to run like you.' Steve has always shared this attitude. He thinks he's lucky to be so fit and so fast, and he believes he ought to try to get the maximum out of his talent.

4

Blind Lane, Montreal
Blind Lane, Montreal

As a measure of greatness, the Olympic Games are rather artificial. A competition held once every four years is scarcely a test of whether a person is a great athlete or not. Steve and myself have known complete idiots who were Olympic champions, and extraordinary talents who never were. One of the greatest runners of all time and the British athlete I regard as the second greatest of all after Steve was Sydney Wooderson. He won the Commonwealth and European Games, broke the world 800 metres record and won the national cross-country championship but in 1936 he was injured, so he didn't win an Olympic title. It could well be that because of forces beyond an athlete's control – injury, illness, domestic problems, personal setbacks – he is simply not at his best in an Olympic year. This shouldn't detract from his performances in another year when he *is* at his best. Mel Lattany was to my mind the best sprinter in the world in 1981. By the time the Los Angeles Olympics come round he may have left college and given up sprinting. That doesn't alter the fact that he's a great athlete.

1976 was an Olympic year. Early on I'd heard rumours that the Board had selected the coaches for Montreal and that I wasn't one of them. They had chosen Stan Long, Brendan Foster's coach. Now, in the normal course of events, an area staff coach like Stan Long would actually report to a national event coach like myself, so for Montreal they had effectively appointed a coach subordinate to me to take overall charge of the event. They didn't have a Director of Coaching then but there were two Principal National Coaches, Denis Watts and John le Masurier. Denis Watts (who ran up the Big Dipper without taking a breath) was in overall charge of running events and middle-distance event coach. (In those days I was long-distance event coach.) So I asked these two about Long's selection and although they seemed very unhappy about it they confirmed that I wasn't appointed for Montreal. Somebody else had loaded the gun and they had the unenviable task of firing it at me. In Rome I had apparently favoured individual athletes, though this was news to me. Strangely, the 1974 men's team manager, Jim Biddle, was also dropped, though everyone, including the athletes, had thought he'd done a good job in Rome.

Stan Long was also asked to take charge of an altitude training trip to Colorado Springs two weeks before Montreal. Only a few of the squad chose to go on that trip, and in the event personal differences arose between Stan Long and some of those athletes. I think it was rather foolish to send somebody to train a group of international athletes at altitude who had had no previous experience of doing so, especially since some of them, like Ian Stewart, themselves had trained at altitude many times. His authority was inevitably going to be resented. As it transpired, immediately after Montreal Stan Long resigned. He didn't ever submit a report on Colorado, or correlate the training effects there with the athletes' performances in the games. Nothing was learned from that trip that might have been of benefit to future British squads, though of course it was financed by the British Amateur Athletic Board.

While all these plots were thickening, Steve was once again up to his knees in muck and snow, running cross-country. On 3 January he won the Sussex senior cross-country championship, though not without the usual controversy. These were the senior championships and he was still technically a junior. When he stepped up to collect the trophy, so did second-placed senior Peter Standing, another Brighton and Hove runner. Standing said he understood Steve was only running as a junior guest and that he was therefore not eligible to win, but the county association ruled in Steve's favour and he received the trophy after all. It was a strange complaint to come from an older runner, particularly as there was no rule to prevent a junior from running in the senior race, and as a result Pete Standing, a good class runner, left the club. It seemed that whatever Steve did caused a disturbance. He followed up his Sussex win with a victory in the South of the Thames cross-country championship, at Stanmer Park, on his own Brighton doorstep. Things seemed to be going well – too well. The next we knew, he had knee trouble.

With Matt Patterson, Steve had been doing much bigger mileage than before as part of his gradual training build-up. With roadwork of any intensity there's always the danger of niggling injuries, particularly while an athlete is still growing. Steve lost a valuable three months of winter endurance training, so the trip we had coming up in April became a gamble to see if the altitude effect would make up a little for the time he had lost. On 9 April a small group of us went to South Lake Tahoe, Nevada, to train. Steve, Tony Simmons, Lesley Kiernan and myself were joined by Mary and Ian Stewart, with whom I'd worked at altitude prior to the Munich Olympics. Our trip was financed privately and was nothing to do with the Board. We wanted to do some altitude work prior to the Olympic trials in reasonable weather; Colorado Springs sounded a bit inhospitable as the training site was apparently an airforce station, and St Moritz, another possibility, was under snow. South Lake Tahoe sounded ideal: 8000 feet up, but with good weather at this time of year, and even a tartan track to run on.

I couldn't manage a whole month off from work so we arranged that I'd fly out a week later and we'd meet up in this heavenly place. I took flights via New York, in baking heat, and San Francisco. Then, descending almost vertically through the clouds, my plane came in over a tiny landing strip amid the most beautiful scenery imaginable, bathed in sunlight. I was thinking, 'The others will be pleased to see me.'

I was met by cold, stony faces. 'What the hell have you sent us here for? This is a terrible place. We're clearing out to Mexico!' Apparently they'd had blizzards every other day, interspersed with light snowstorms. On long morning runs they'd taken turns sheltering behind one another to avoid crystallization. They'd already studied the timetables for flights to Mexico, and they were off. I managed to calm them down by saying, 'Well, it doesn't seem too bad today. Let's hang on here until tomorrow.' From then onwards, the weather magically improved and though it was always cold first thing and last, usually by about 11 a.m. it was quite sunny and warm.

All four chaps were in one room, which was a bit fraught at times. At night you were OK so long as you were asleep, but if you woke up, you had to lie there till morning listening to the unendurable levels of snoring. By day there was the usual problem of drying out wet towels and training kit, which upset the chambermaid and also the proprietor, who were unaccustomed to having the hotel used as a drying room. However we got on very well, considering the circumstances. There's always tension when athletes are in training together because it becomes competitive, and it's not surprising that some needle enters the conversation occasionally. Steve doesn't particularly like training in a group; he prefers just one other person, such as Matt, and he's none too happy when competitiveness creeps into the proceedings. The group developed a good routine though. The athletes would get up and do an hour's steady run between 8 a.m. and 9 a.m., have breakfast, sleep for another couple of hours, get up again, wander about, train around 3 or 4 p.m., and then have the evening free to go to the pictures or whoop it up on the pool table at Sharky's Pizza Parlour, which we did most nights.

One evening I remember particularly as it was the only occasion I've ever really lost my temper with Steve. We were playing doubles at pool, Steve and I versus Tony and Ian. Now, Steve has this annoying habit at times of giving gratuitous advice. You'd be about to play your shot and he would suck in his breath and say, 'Fffff. Not that one. Go for the six-ball!' I put up with this for quite a while but then it began to rile me. 'Look, Steve,' I said, 'if you do it once more I'll wrap this cue round your neck.' Sure enough, I was getting down to play the very next shot when I heard, 'No! Play it off the cushion!' Something snapped. Ovett (Brighton and Hove) tore through the parlour, closely pressed by Wilson (Welwyn GC) in second place, brandishing a pool cue. Steve's speed came in handy that night. Until the humour of it overtook me I came pretty close to braining him rather than training him. PS: I missed the six-ball!

South Lake Tahoe was probably the nicest training spot we've ever seen in the world: the surroundings were idyllic. On one training spin down the middle of the main street, the team ran into Tom Van Ruden, who ran for the USA in the 1968 Olympics ad now ran the local travel agency. He immediately befriended these Britishers and took them on a fifteen-mile run up the mountains to 9000 or 10,000 feet. They couldn't do much the following day, but they said the scenery was magnificent. It was difficult to do much pure speed work at Lake Tahoe because the weather wasn't really warm enough, but Steve did run a very good series on the track of 6 × 400 metres in 54.0, 53.8, 53.5, 53.8, 52.8 and 52.8, averaging 53.4 seconds. He was looking very smooth and strong. As I stood on the sidelines watching them all warming up round the track, a fellow came up and asked, 'Hey, do you know anything about those British guys training over there?' I said I did. 'Well! Are you their manager?'

'No, I'm a coach.'

'You're a *what*?' He looked puzzled. 'Out here a coach

has a cap on his head, a whistle, a clipboard round his neck, and right across his back it says COACH. You *sure* you're a coach?' It took me some time to convince him that I was the real McCoy.

Steve and the others were missing out on an early season match in Yugoslavia with the rest of the team, who were planning to stay on there for a few days' warm-weather training afterwards. The match didn't seem too important; the opposition wasn't too keen and it was early in the season for brilliant showings. Two or three days after we came home, on 12 May, Steve ran at Crystal Palace in an open meeting. It was a dreadfully cold evening, and he led all the way in the 600 metres race and won narrowly in 78.5 seconds from Peter Lewis, who finished strongly. Steve was obviously jetlagged and weary from training. Most of the Lake Tahoe work had been aerobic: long steady runs. Even on the track or in the woods there was very little real speed work because of the temperature and the need to make up for the lost three months of endurance running. So his first race back was a bit disappointing, but later that evening he ran a 48.9 for 400 metres which looked very smooth.

There was the inevitable controversy after the races. All the reporters were peeved at his failure to break the British 600 metres best and his refusal to tell them what his plans were. As soon as Steve's back was turned, these characters started to slate him. So I said, 'You people don't understand. You just won't recognize his talent. You think because Steve's young he's incapable of working things out for himself.'

At which Chris Brasher piped up, '*I* understand why he's behaving like this – it's because he hasn't won anything yet!'

'Well!' I said, warming slightly, 'he's *not very old* yet, is he? But he will win, just you wait and see.' I sensed I was up against the wall of frustration that the press build up towards anybody who hasn't yet shown them a world record or an Olympic gold. Such an athlete was scarcely even entitled to an opinion, let alone private plans.

The press had asked Steve why he had refused to run in a recent 800 metres at Gateshead, to which Steve replied that he hadn't wanted to. As usual this wasn't enough – there had to be some secret reason. The truth was simply that he wasn't ready yet. He'd lost twelve weeks of work because of injury and this threw his whole programme back, as he couldn't skimp on his endurance training. What was the point of trying to explain all this to reporters? Steve decided silence was best. He wasn't ready, either, for a match ten days later against the Russians in Kiev. The meeting produced some splendid performances, including a 13:21.2 5000 metres world best from Tony Simmons. He'd been refused entry to the race until the last minute, and was then allowed in only as a replacement, because the selectors would only offer him the 10,000 metres. In the 5000 metres race his finishing time was so superb he was assured it would stand him in good stead for Olympic selection. I knew that it wouldn't, of course. He would still have to qualify through the trials.

On 31 May Steve ran very nicely in the Inter-Counties 800 metres at Crystal Palace. There wasn't a great deal of opposition but he looked good tucking in behind the leaders, Clement and McMeekin, and kicking at 600 metres to open up a big gap. His time was 1:47.3 and the splits were even (53.5 and 53.8 seconds). He was pleased with this, as it was very windy. The following week saw the first of the Olympic Games trials: the Kraft meeting at Crystal Palace, on 4 and 5 June. In the 800 metres Steve used exactly the same tactics as in the Inter-Counties race, staying back until 600 metres and then putting in a decisive burst. I remember it very clearly because it was spectacular to watch: one moment there was quite a race going on, with several contenders bunched together; the next, Steve had disappeared to the tape leaving the others struggling for the remaining places and looking very tired and ragged. His winning time was 1:46.7, good in the conditions.

I was asked about Steve's 800 metres ranking: fifteenth

in the world last year. How did I feel about that going into the games? I replied, 'When Peter Snell went to Rome in 1960 he wasn't ranked in the first twenty, but he was a racer and he won.' Steve was again questioned about his plans before Montreal, and said that he preferred not to race against his main rivals. He explained, 'The actual advantage I've got is that they don't know what I'm like. They don't know my stride length, or what it's like to run behind me when I kick.' There's always a question as to whether to pit a young runner against his rivals to gain experience, or keep him back as a surprise package. Either way it's a calculated risk, but we settled on the latter so as to let everybody else worry about Steve, rather than the other way round. They had never matched him stride for stride in his finishing sprint and there was bound to be some doubt in their minds. We felt he was doing enough good-quality training to cope with even the power of a man like Rick Wohlhuter, who could burn off a kick by sheer strength. We weren't expecting the Montreal 800 metres to be slow, but we suspected it would be a tactical race in the tradition of big middle-distance battles.

The second part of the Kraft Games included the 1500 metres. Steve had decided the previous Wednesday night to double up – to enter the 800 metres and the 1500 metres. He ran comfortably in the heats, coming third and giving nothing away, and there was some confusion and disagreement among his rivals in the final who wondered what the devil he was doing in the 1500 metres trial, since he couldn't possibly be planning to attempt both distances in Montreal. As usual, Steve kept his own counsel. He had every intention both of winning the 1500 metres trial and doubling up in Montreal, particularly since his main event at that time, the 800 metres, would be run first. In fact he won the 1500 metres trial in a most extraordinary way. At one stage he was so badly boxed in that he was pushed off the inside of the track and took a few strides on the grass. He manoeuvred back in, and coming down the finishing straight he observed Moor-

croft and Clement battling strenuously for first place.
Seeing a chink between them, Steve twisted sideways
and slipped through 30 metres out to win, waving and
smiling, in 3:39.6. He so enjoyed catching people nap-
ping, and he was expressing his relief after having been
boxed in. He said afterwards that he'd run 'a bloody
awful race for about 1450 metres, and I was turning to
my mum and dad in the stands. You see, all the time
you're running the pressure builds up, especially if
you're boxed in.' It's true that early on he did seem to
bumble from one crisis to another, but when the crucial
gap opened he was ready. You have to be fit, and you
have to be quick.

Steve found he was having 'too much time to think in
the 1500'. He found 1500 metres races rather boring.
Between 600 and 1200 he would tell me 'I got fed up.'
He'd been used to the action on the shorter distance and
was having some difficulty adjusting to the lull mid-1500.
The first of the trials unfortunately bore out my suspicions concerning Tony Simmons' selection. He had a
cold, finished fifth in the 5000 metres trial and wasn't
picked despite his world best time. In the 10,000 metres
he came second, and was selected. Poor Lesley, who had
been running superbly, caught shingles the week we
came back from Lake Tahoe and was out for the season.

Immediately after the trials Steve and I did a couple of
days' training down at Merthyr Mawr, getting away
from the publicity. It was there that we learned of Steve's
selection for both events in Montreal. One press photographer found out where we were. He bought us a
modest lunch and took some pictures of Steve training
and running in the sea 'for his records'. We were to see
two of those photographs time and again in various
publications afterwards.

Steve went to Finland next for a significant 800 metres
in which he beat John Walker, the New Zealander. On
paper the race looks slow – 1:50.1, but the first lap was
outside 60 seconds, and Steve actually ran inside 50 for
the last 400 metres. He felt good. He'd beaten Walker, an

800 metres rival in Montreal and the favourite for the 1500 metres. The following week, on 3 July, Steve ran in a UK v. Poland v. Canada match at Crystal Palace, winning an 800 metres yet again in 1:46.7, and yet again by bursting away at 600 metres. He covered the last 200 in 25.2 seconds ahead of Marian Gesicki. The position going into Montreal, then, was that Steve was now ranked twenty-third in the world on times at 800 metres. His main rivals had all run under 1:46.0; Steve's fastest time was 1:46.7. Favourites were Wohlhuter of the USA and Susanj of Yugoslavia, with the Cuban Alberto Juantorena a dangerous outsider. He was reputed to be going for the 400 metres, but at 800 he had already clocked the odd fast time. Another threat, the Belgian Ivo Van Damme, was only a year older than Steve and had recorded 1:46.4 and 1:45.1. Surprisingly, Frank Clement had a 1:45.8 to his credit, having himself beaten John Walker. It seemed extraordinary, though, that while Steve was being written off by the press in terms of his lowly ranking, he was simultaneously being tipped as a possible medallist.

A big factor in Montreal in the 800 metres would be the lanes. There had been an almighty muddle during the past couple of years over the break from lanes (after the staggered start) in 800 metres races. Two years before the Montreal Olympics it was decided to run the first 300 metres of the Olympic race in lanes. During the intervening period you'd turn up at one meeting and run the first 100 metres in lanes, and at another it would be 300 metres in lanes or a free-for-all from the gun. Obviously in Montreal for anyone in the outside lanes there was going to be the problem after 300 metres of whether to cut in sharply and go straight across the track, losing three or four yards in the process, or to veer in on a diagonal towards the end of the straight. Either way, whoever drew the outside lanes would be at a great disadvantage, despite official reassurances, because it would be hard for them to evaluate their speed. Out on the 7 and 8 lanes you have no one to key your own pace

Above The finish I didn't see. Steve wins the Olympic 800 metres title in Moscow after a four-year wait

Below On the rostrum after the Olympic 1500 metres. Steve's mature manners made a deep impression on thousands of TV viewers

Opposite

Far left 'Just spinning along', and winning the 1975 national junior cross-country championship in the process

Near left June 1974. 'No bugles, no drums' — a four-minute mile in training. Steve leads from Tony Simmons, with myself as the only spectator

Below 'There was never any doubt!' Steve wins the 1973 European junior 800 metres from Willi Wulbeck with the late Ivo Van Damme (in the cap) fourth

This page

Left What Steve thought about coming second. The photographer lost his feet — Steve lost his shoes

Below 1974 European 800 metres in Rome. Susanj has gone, but Steve finally breaks clear of the rest to take the silver medal

Above The rest of the field are struggling after Steve breaks away at 600 metres in the 1975 Europa Cup 800 metres

Below 100 metres to go in the 1976 Olympic trial — how's he going to get through?

Above Could Steve possibly be giving advice to one of his greatest rivals — John Walker?

Below Staying cool and calm and waiting to collect the 1977 World Cup 1500 metres title at Düsseldorf. The perfect race

Above 'Suddenly this big guy came thundering past.' Olaf Beyer beat Steve and Seb Coe in the 1978 European 800 metres championship

Below After the 800 metres — 'Sorry, Harry, but you can't win 'em all'

Below First is first and second is first. Steve wins the Prague 1500 metres title while Eamonn Coghlan also celebrates

ove 'How many laps can I last?'
adowing Henry Rono during the
nile world record race

low A happy win for Steve over
rgen Straub, and the Crystal Palace
owd get a wave from their favourite

Below Steve with his friend and training companion
Matt Patterson

Above Oslo — and a new world record for the mile is within sight . . .

. . . and a salute to the press box after the world record is announced

'You devil' is the image the press would like the public to have of Steve

On the Pennine Way. It's a hard life but Rachel's fruit cake tastes good to Steve, Bob and myself

Opposite below 'Didn't he do well?' Arne Haukvik and myself also seem quite pleased with the world record

Below Steve with some of his many friends after a wheelchair race at the Chailey Heritage home for handicapped children. He didn't win this one

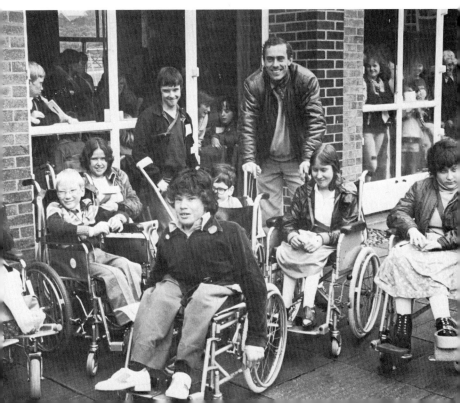

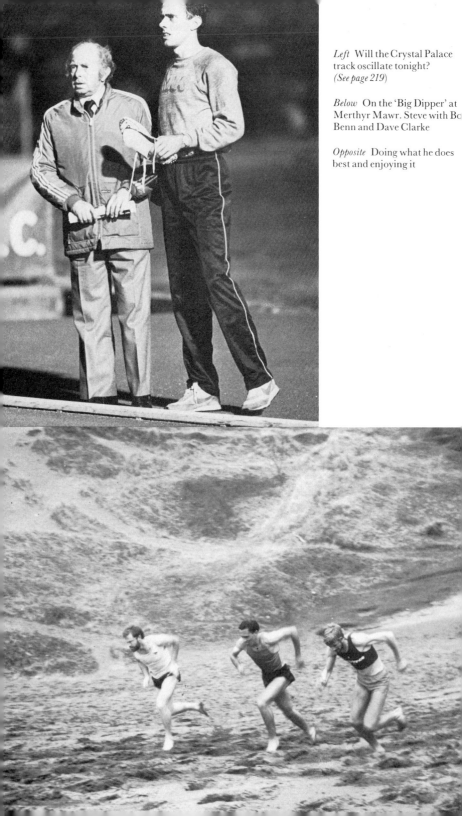

Left Will the Crystal Palace track oscillate tonight?
(See page 219)

Below On the 'Big Dipper' at Merthyr Mawr. Steve with Bo Benn and Dave Clarke

Opposite Doing what he does best and enjoying it

Two happy people — Rachel and Steve on
18 September 1981

on; you are in front, and everybody else is pacing against
you. You can't look behind, and it's not until the second
bend that you can make any comparison. If you notice
then that you're too slow, it's too late: the others are
coming through you.

The lane draw would be a mere lottery: there was no
seeding involved. It wouldn't even be useful to experiment in smaller races beforehand by taking the outside
lane, because there's a world of difference between that
and racing outside seven Olympic athletes. Steve did
run a 400 metres at Crystal Palace without blocks; we
were very pleased with the split times – 24.5 and 23.6
seconds. But there's really only one way to gain
Olympic 800 metres experience: to run in the Olympics.
As fate would have it, Montreal proved to be the first
and last Olympic 800 metres with a 300 lane break; after
that event it reverted inexplicably to 100 metres: the
International Amateur Athletic Federation changed
their minds.

Montreal: the 1976 Olympics

So off we went to Montreal. The team left and I was to
follow under my own steam four or five days later, in my
official capacity as uninvited coach. I was very lucky: it
was an expensive trip and Eddie Kulukundis came to my
rescue with a plane ticket. I boarded the plane with no
accommodation booked at the other end, but by great
good fortune a friend of mine, Alf Wilkins, was on the
same flight, and said I could sleep on the floor of his flat
outside the Olympic village that night. Next morning
Alf's landlady told me there was a flat down the block
that would be vacant while the girl who owned it was on
holiday. I looked it over, agreed terms with a lady who
said she was the girl's mother, and that was my accommodation settled. I was on my way to the track to meet
Steve and Tony when I spotted them zooming past in a
car. They saw me and stopped to pick me up.

It turned out that they were having problems at the

village. It was very noisy and they couldn't sleep. Here is Steve's description of the place. 'When you get to the Olympic village, you're essentially on your own. Don't kid yourself that anyone cares particularly about you. The village is a human zoo and no one is going to bother one way or the other if you win a gold medal or go out in the first round. This is when you are on your own, and those who can't adapt themselves to this are going to go under very quickly. Two things can combine to ruin your preparation: the boredom and the food. Now in Montreal the food was fantastic. You could have big juicy steaks for *breakfast*, and as much of anything you liked whenever you liked. The problem here is that if you stuff yourself with food at this period, when you are cutting down the training load in order to peak up, you're going to put on weight. The girls find this a big problem especially.

'Then there is the boredom. Athletes herded together in overcrowded conditions, on edge for the toughest competition of their lives, find the time just drags by. People do silly things. Some overtrain, and our marathon runners were a classic example of that. Others go for the big show bit. You know, flashing around the warm-up track in front of the public, signing autographs, showing off the suntan and generally acting at being Famous People. Some of our team really love all that kind of thing. The warm-up track was a place I avoided like the plague. Because of the crowding there and all this business going on, there was just no way you could get any decent tune-up sessions done.'

Steve and Tony had permission to move out of the village if they found somewhere suitable close by, so we decided they could share with me, paying out of their own pockets towards the rent. It seemed ideal – very quiet, convenient and comfortable. They would get up early and wander over to the village, where they would get their meals. We didn't realize until we'd been at this flat a couple of night what the occupation of the owner was. She had decided to go away that fortnight, which was rather strange as she could probably have done a lot of business in those two weeks. She was a – well, I don't know how to word it, but it seemed she made her living from her charms. The telephone would ring, usually late at night, and a man's voice would say, 'What's happened to Carmen? Oh, gee! Where am I going to get somebody else?' On close inspection, we found the flat to contain strange objects and florid literature scattered about. The night before the games opened Steve had a bright idea to prevent the phone from waking everybody up. He wrapped it in a towel and pushed it inside the refrigerator so that if anybody rang for Carmen, instead of a hot line he would get a frigid response. The situation invited comparison with Rome, where there had been a tremendous hoo-ha about letting the lads sleep in a hotel across the road.

The games got under way without the Africans. We'd heard rumours of a possible boycott but never took them seriously and though there was a flutter of relief it depressed us, more than anything else, that they had gone through with it. I thought, well, these people have trained so very hard. What if it were one of my athletes? On one of the rare occasions when I was allowed into the village, I was having lunch with Steve in one of the competitors' restaurants and Mike Boit of Kenya went past and tapped on the window. He looked at Steve and gave a sickly wave. 'Cheerio'. We felt very sad because there was nothing you could say to him through the glass. He had all his bags outside, and you knew that this would have been the greatest time of his life. Yet in the space of perhaps forty-eight hours people like him would all be forgotten and 'Juantorena' or some other name would be on everybody's lips. It's a very realistic sport, and a very cruel sport.

The day before the 800 metres heats one of the official team coaches came over to us and almost proudly announced that he'd seen Juantorena training and timed him running sub-75-second 2×600s – and 'he looked easy'. What delightful news. I should have thought a

95

coach might have known better than to impart such information in front of Steve at such a time. The ballad of Juantorena was already being sung in the newspapers, though the press were fools if they believed he was some sort of hard-done-by peasant from the Cuban jungle. Far from it. He was a student, already an Olympic athlete (400 metres semifinalist in 1972), and he'd been well looked after and properly trained. There was nothing of the sugar-cutting noble savage about him at all.

The heats went very comfortably for Steve; he won his, heat 3 in a drift round of 1:48.3, and though the winner had been fed into the computer as Steve O'Vett, it was none the less he. The second heat was a surprise because John Walker was knocked out in a very tight finish. The race was won by Frank Clement in 1:47.5. Juantorena's heat was very slow. He looked uncomfortable at one stage and almost tripped, but with 300 metres to go he opened up with awesome power. This was the danger man. I suppose I was hoping that he'd run as clumsily in the final as he had then. The fastest-looking man in the heats was actually Rick Wohlhuter, with 1:45.7. But the favourites had come through so comfortably apart from Walker that the heats didn't tell you very much. On the same day, Tony ran in the 10,000 metres heats. He sat in for a long while and then over the last 5000 metres ran extravagantly fast, it seemed to me, for 28:01.8.

Steve once described what it was like to be one of the competitors at round about this time: 'The tension mounts up when the time for the qualifying rounds comes up. You get your start lists, work out who you know in your heat, and then you just have to wait your turn. They kept the heats penned together in the tunnel in Montreal, and sometimes this meant a wait of half an hour or more if there was a big entry. So you sit in this tunnel, noting how all the others in your heat are looking, watching for signs of worry or nerves, and trying not to get drawn into any silly inane conversations.

'You watch the early heats on these little TV sets, and straight away the results get you feeling jumpy. Wohl-

huter won the first heat in 1:45.7 from Singh (1:45.9).
"Christ! Have we got to run *that* fast to QUALIFY?!
These other guys look mean. They might give me more
trouble than I expected. Maybe it won't be just between
three of us; perhaps there's some bimbo here who's going
to go out in fifty seconds and not come back!" The
temptation to give way to the surging adrenalin at this
point and blast off from the gun can become too much.
Then they call you out and suddenly you are out in the
bright sunshine and the rows of spectators just seem to
go up into the heavens and there is this horrible hushed
buzz of excitement everywhere, and you can feel millions
of eyes on you. That's how the Christians must have felt
when they were led out to the lions!

'Now is the time you have to concentrate totally on the
job in hand. Let your attention wander or get frightened
or overawed by the atmosphere and it's all over for you.
Don't kid yourself that this is any big deal, though. The
terrible thing is that no one cares. Your team mates are
too concerned with their own performance to spare any
time for your problems; you are cut off from friends and
family and things are usually just happening too fast for
the team managers to have more than a few seconds to
listen to you. So the first rule is: Look after number one.
If you don't; no one else will.'

Day two brought Steve's 800 metres semifinals. He ran
in the same half as Juantorena and Van Damme, but
looked well within himself. Juantorena took the lead at
200 metres and then cruised home in 1:45.9, with Van
Damme second in 1:46.0 and Steve a very comfortable
third in 1:46.1. This gave him confidence. He looked
smooth and contained, positioning nicely and showing
no signs of panic to win. The other semifinal was a
rough-and-tumble affair and quite a bit slower, won by
Wohlhuter in 1:46.7. Frank Clement was knocked about
and finished last in 1:48.3. Susanj was third and looking
good.

So now it was simply a question of sitting back and

waiting for the lane draw. Day three dawned, the day of the Olympic 800 metres final. Susanj and Steve, the two big kickers of this competition and the ones who would be hurt most by outside berths, drew lanes 7 and 8 respectively. There was nothing you could do. The gun went, and Singh of India led around the first turn. It was at the 150-metre mark when – to borrow David Coleman's immortal words – Juantorena 'opened up his legs and showed his class'. When they broke from lanes after the 300-metre mark, Steve and Susanj were a long way behind the inside-lane runners, and Steve fought to close this huge gap all the way to the bell; it took an awful lot out of him. He actually went through the bell sixth in 51.6 seconds, compared with Juantorena's leading time of 50.85 – already 0.8 seconds down and with a lot to do. Juantorena never faltered. The only development on the second lap was that Wohlhuter, who had chased the Cuban hard, now faded slightly nearing the tape and Van Damme came thundering in for second place. Wulbeck, who had never before beaten Steve, managed to hold on for fourth, although after Wohlhuter there was a big gap. But Steve came through strongly at the finish to produce a personal best time ahead of Susanj. So the result read: first Juantorena (Cuba) 1:43.5 (a new world and Olympic record), second Van Damme (Belgium) 1:43.9, third Wohlhuter (USA) 1:44.1, fourth Wulbeck (West Germany) 1:45.3, fifth O'Vett 1:45.4. Juantorena dedicated his gold medal to Castro and the Revolution to show his gratitude for state aid.

Steve said afterwards, 'I didn't see them till 300 metres and then I knew I couldn't catch them. My legs were dead on the back straight.' He explained, 'With this 300 in lanes business the guy in lane 8 has no real chance unless he's an athlete who liked to take it out really fast and keep going. I just went off too slowly in the first 200 and that was where I blew the race. I'm really glad they are doing away with the 300 stagger in international 800 metres races next season. We've got the women to thank for it. They got into so much trouble with running over each other in unstaggered races that the IAAF thought they'd sort it out by adopting this weird rule. Women, being frail and perhaps a little unsure of themselves, don't really know how to react in a contact situation'*

I really do think that the way the lanes were drawn was the most significant thing about the race. Steve was inexperienced, OK, but he was very fit, and with a good draw I think he'd have made an awful lot of distance. As with Susanj in Rome, I'm not saying he'd have beaten Juantorena. I'm saying he'd have put up one heck of a good show. Because the one thing that Steve enjoys more than anything else is being involved at the finish: with a chance of winning he'll pull out all the stops. But when you get to the bell and you're way adrift in sixth it does tend to dampen your enthusiasm. I think the best man probably won, and he won in record time – a rare achievement in a major race. But the other places would have been significantly different had the break from lanes come after the first hundred metres. Trying to avoid pile-ups by the prolonged stagger turns an 800 metres into a long 400 metres. As I've tried to explain earlier, at 800 metres you are inevitably going to have a pile-up somewhere: at the start, after 100 metres, coming into the back straight, but somewhere. If you don't want these fellows to touch each other, the ultimate answer would have to be running the whole two laps in lanes. Instead of that, why not accept the nature of the 800 metres, accept pile-ups as part of the race, and let the runners look after themselves?

By wearing a British tracksuit top and with a modicum of hassle, I was able to get onto the training track, but it was a terrible job getting from the warm-up track into the stadium. I managed it on the day of Steve's 800 metres final; it was ten minutes' walk across two fields and down some steps into a long tunnel, following a yellow dotted line all the way. It wasn't exactly Judy Garland's Yellow Brick Road either, as it didn't appear

* *Athletics Weekly*, 22 January 1977.

to lead to happiness. All the faces coming the other way seemed very downcast and sad. I met Steve at last back on the warm-up track after the race. He at least didn't look devastated. I think he was feeling rather philosophical. Once he'd drawn lane 8, he knew the cards were stacked pretty heavily against him. Besides, he hadn't done too badly. He was young, he had finished fifth in the Olympics, and he'd run a good time. The world hadn't come to an end. He still had to get out and do some training for the 1500 metres which under the circumstances was probably good for him. I think he felt a bit let down that I was going home before the 1500. I had to; my holiday entitlement had all gone. Luckily his father Mick saved the day by going out to join him, and actually took over the flat. It helped Steve a lot to have somebody there. Meanwhile, Tony ran in the 10,000 metres final. I think if he'd had the nerve and belief in himself he'd have won a silver or bronze, but he did the same as in Rome and allowed a big gap to appear before pulling a tremendous amount back and nearly catching Foster at the finish. He was fourth.

I watched Steve's 1500 metres heats on the telly back home. He looked comfortable from that distance, winning in 3:37.9, a personal best. There had been two days' rest between the 800 metres final and the 1500 metres heats, and he seemed to move up pretty smoothly to finish almost dead level with Thomas Wessinghage. Unfortunately, though, he was obviously very weary the next day, semifinal day. He was in Walker's half, and coming off the last turn into the straight, he was positioned so well that I thought, He's OK, he's going to come through here. But then the Canadian Dave Hill fell over just in front of him. Steve had to leap over him and he couldn't get his stride going again in time. Being tired, he lacked his normal finish anyway, and he slipped back finally to sixth. The winner was John Walker in 3:39.7. In second place three men were tied with 3:39.9 – Crouch of Australia, Zemen of Hungary, and Dave Moorcroft, who went past Steve at the finish.

Fifth was Wessinghage in 3:40.1; sixth was Steve in 3:40.3. Walker went on to win the final, for which Steve obviously didn't qualify. John must have been a very relieved man, because he'd gone through a bad patch that season and when he was knocked out in the first round of the 800 metres we used to see him every day practising his 150-metre sprints on the track. Even if Bayi had run, I'd still have backed Walker. He deserved to win.

I think the games did Steve good. He matured as a runner. He learned that life itself doesn't cease the minute you fail to win an Olympic gold, and this was to stand him in good stead four years later. It made him even more determined that when he was old enough and strong enough, he'd be there. Several months later, with the wisdom of hindsight, it might have been better had he concentrated on the 1500 metres, but that would have been an exceptionally difficult decision at the time. We'd have to have been clairvoyant. Anyway he'd run personal best times in both events: in the 800 final and the 1500 heats.

High-intensity racing

There was a big welcome back on 6 August at the Coca-Cola Meeting, held that year at Meadowbank stadium in Scotland. It was the proverbial cold, wet, windy night but a huge crowd turned out to give Steve and the others a terrific reception. Steve's 800 metres race was Mike Boit's first opportunity to run since the Olympic boycott and unfortunately it was a bit chilly for him. He has big teeth anyway but they were chattering noticeably, and he looked a bluish shade rather than black. Mike likes to run from the front, weather and fitness permitting, which is just as well because he has been one of the most dangerous runners for tripping other people up. He's all right when he does run from the front, as everybody can see where he is. But he's very tall and gangly, like a big praying mantis, so you like to keep an eye on his arms and legs. If he's in the middle of the pack and he decides to step out, he tends to do so without too much regard for his surroundings, and those arms and legs get involved with everything in the immediate vicinity. In the Coke race, Steve tucked in behind and took off down the straight, pulling away from Wulbeck who finished second ahead of Boit. It was a good win for Steve, in 1:46.9, because he'd beaten Boit – the unknown factor in Montreal – and he'd beaten Wulbeck, reversing their places there.

Then for the first time in his career Steve tried a period of high-intensity racing, as he was to do several times more. On 10 August he ran an 800 metres in Helsinki, finishing second to Boit (1:46.1 to 1:44.9). On 14 August he won the AAA 800 metres championship at Crystal Palace in 1:47.3. That was an interesting race because John Walker was in the field and Steve obviously wanted a crack at the Olympic champion, albeit at 1500 metres. We'd talked it over during the warm-up and decided that whatever happened he mustn't get into a position where Walker was behind him. John was no doubt thinking the same thing about *him*, but Steve kept his nerve, biding his time until 600 metres as first Pete Browne and then Dave McMeekin led the field, with Walker and Steve at a respectable distance in third and fourth. While McMeekin was building up his lead, Steve was watching Walker. The gap to the front grew larger and larger, and when it looked absolutely enormous Walker decided he could wait no longer: his nerve broke and off he went, scurrying to catch McMeekin with Steve poised quietly on his shoulder. Steve reeled him in at the finish to win in 1:47.3.

On 16 August, Steve finished second, in 2:19.2, in a 1000 metres race in Nice, again behind Mike Boit (who ran 2:19.0). Here the climate favoured Boit more than at Meadowbank. Then on 18 August Steve ran in Zürich in a very fast 800 metres, finishing behind Boit (whose time was 1:43.9) once again, this time in fifth place with a time of 1:45.5. His track season ended with a win on 21

August in the Highland Games 800 metres at Edinburgh, in 1:48.0, ahead of Frank Clement. Which meant that in the space of fifteen days between 6 August and 21 August he had run six races – eight including heats. It was a good spell, and saved him from brooding over Montreal. At the end of that track season Steve was ranked first in the UK at 800 metres and third at 1500 metres and the mile. Undoubtedly, though it's not the be-all and end-all, you *are* a bit disappointed not to win, but then you weigh the good against the bad and, taken all in all, I think he was reasonably satisfied.

During the season he had bought an old sports car cheap and decided to do it up himself, which took quite a bit of his time. It wasn't, as one interviewer inferred, occupational therapy to keep his mind off the tensions of the games: he just wanted something to get about in. He took a short break at the end of the summer and then the cross-country season rolled round again. He ran in his first big senior cross-country event, the Mike Sully cross-country race, down at Bristol on 7 November. It was won by Tony and Steve came eighth. He finished nineteenth in the International Invitation Race at Crystal Palace in December. It was a very good field, and Steve rushed out to the front – I think he led momentarily at the end of the first lap – but then he faded slightly. What I liked about that race was that there was no hanging back – 'just go out and have a go, and stay with them if you could'. He was back to his old self.

The year ended very sadly, with the death of Ivo Van Damme, in a car accident. The Belgian was just twenty-two when he died on 29 December, in France. Steve wrote a tribute to him in *Athletics Weekly*:

It was a terrible shock for me to hear of the tragic death of Ivo Van Damme.

Athletes are a strange breed who tend to have a certain disrespect of fate, believing that it plays little or no part in their lives or those of their fellow athletes. Only when something of this nature happens are we all shaken, and we take it hard.

To win two silver medals in any Olympics is a fabulous performance; to win them in only your first Games and at the age of 22 marks the greatness of the man, who surely must have gone on to greater honours.

I do not think the significance of the death of a friend or someone close is truly recognised immediately; it only comes with time and on odd occasions. As a friend I will miss him at the beginning of races when we used to worry and joke together, during them when we both raced hard, and then finally afterwards – the sharing of the joy and disappointment we both recognized in each other.

Now all I feel is a certain numbness at the loss of a friend and the emptiness that will be left when it goes.

My sympathy goes to his parents and friends.

5

Perfection in Düsseldorf

1977 was Steve's first senior cross-country season, and as with everything else he didn't want to do reasonably: he wanted to do very well. In particular he wanted to be among the first finishers in the National Championships, to qualify for selection in the International cross-country race. If anything, since the International was over a shorter distance (7 miles compared with 9) he could expect to do better there than in the National. We were hoping, too, that the extra endurance gained from cross-country would help with the other major development of that year: the step up to 1500 metres.

The cross-country season opened rather well. Steve did some extra mileage up to Christmas 1976; then he won the Sussex cross-country on 8 January, and raced in Belgium on 16 January, finishing just behind the renowned cross-country and long-distance runner Emil Puttemans of Belgium. A fortnight later came the Inter-Counties cross-country championships, his first major race as a senior over $7\frac{1}{2}$ miles (his previous maximum was 6 miles), and he rather astonished everybody by finishing second, just 10 seconds behind David Black. I wasn't there, but Steve told me afterwards what happened. It was quite a tough course and at one stage, just as Black was breaking away, Steve had an attack of stitch ('I could hardly breathe'), dropped back to fifth, but pulled out a storming finish to overhaul several of the leaders for his second place. He was a little disappointed that the course wasn't more hilly, as he was used to training round Stanmer Park in Brighton. I've run there myself and the hills are so appalling that if you're not going very well, you begin to doubt your sanity.

Just after the Inter-Counties race Steve's knee trouble began to recur, and it niggled away at his training. We had stepped up his mileage and he was knocking in eighty to ninety miles a week at the time. The injury wasn't serious, but then just before the all-important national cross-country championships he caught the mother and father of a cold as well, and couldn't make up his mind whether to race or not. There was a very close-knit little organization, comprising Steve's mum and dad, Steve and myself, which would deliberate on these things, and although Steve's parents were very know-ledgeable they would rely on me to gauge his fitness. His mother in particular also acted as a buffer between Steve and the press and promoters. He always felt strongly about giving a good account of himself and not letting people down in his races, and none of us wanted him to turn into the sort of athlete who just put in appearances and didn't bother about results. I think this is why he was sometimes selective in what he did, and though he would sound out opinions the final decision would be his – always. Sometimes he wouldn't decide whether to run until the morning of the race or even the warm-up, and he actually arrived at the National undecided either way. You see, there are no excuses in this business. It's no good saying, as some runners do after they've run badly, 'I wasn't in good shape.' If that's the case they shouldn't have competed. At this level they have a responsibility towards the spectators as well as to themselves to live up to their potential, and if these people had come to see the national cross-country championships, they didn't want to watch a three-legged race, any more than they would wish to see Lord Olivier stumble through a part. Steve was the first to admit that Arthur Gold and the BAAB had been fair to him in never putting any obstacles in his way when it came to choosing races, or competing abroad. They had a pretty good idea at the start of the season what his overall plans were, as I was one of their event coaches, and there were no problems, not in 1977 anyway. Steve took the view that he was an independent amateur, and therefore had a right to choose his races to suit himself.

The national cross-country was a big step to take – a very demanding 9-mile haul around Parliament Hill, with parts of the course a swamp. I've known people lose shoes in the mud and never find them again. I thought Steve would be ill-advised to attempt it with such a heavy cold, but he warmed up anyway and at the last minute decided to run. It was rather surprising, in the circumstances, to see him shoot out in front. When you start at Parliament Hill, you run up a steep incline for the first 800 metres, and Steve led to the top and for a 3-mile lap before fading. He dropped back among the thirties, but wouldn't give in and finally fought his way through the field to finish thirteenth. To him it was a disappointment; to me it was pretty good. In front of him in the results were quite a few of the best 10,000 metres men in the world; OK, they were all English, but at the time we were very strong at 10,000 metres. Not bad, at least, for a 9-mile debut.

Steve ran a couple of fast legs in road relay races shortly afterwards, so he was back in trim. This was just as well, as we were off to Merthyr Mawr for one of those weekend courses at the beginning of April. To give you some insight into this part of Steve's background, perhaps you'd like to know what a typical weekend schedule down there looks like. Usually, the lads arrive late on Friday night, and we put up in a school camp, five or six, on bunk beds, to each room. We get up early on Saturday morning and after a gentle talk from me which includes advice to the newcomers about not having breakfast, we start running at around 9.30 to 9.45, jogging from the camp to the dunes about five miles away. Then we see how many laps they can do in ten minutes round an up-and-down circuit in the sand, have ten minutes' rest, and follow this with repetition runs up various steep hills and sand dunes, culminating in the Big Dipper, which is about 100 metres from top to bottom. If you can run up it with a good action all the way, you're very lucky. Most runners come to a halt at the three-quarter mark and then stagger and scramble the last few metres. We do repetitions up a smaller hill, emphasizing all the time 'powerful lift and knees driving through straight'. Ten minutes' rest then, and we run the five miles back, which admittedly includes a stopover for a swift pint at the Pelican. Lunch next, followed by a talk and perhaps interviews, and then we run to a beach called Southerndown, two or three miles away in a beautiful setting amid rugged cliffs. The sand there is firm enough to run really fast on, either in spikes or bare feet. We do 300-metre repetitions of almost tartan track quality. I think Percy Cerutty pioneered the idea of sand-dune running, and when we first started the British training camps we used to spend most of the time on the dunes; now we prefer the beach for the fast work. In the early days we used to hold the camps at Braunton, North Devon, and we concentrated on quantity, screwing the fellows into the ground as hard as we could. Nowadays we're more concerned with quality. Those 300-metre repetitions are either done very fast or with fast recovery jogs in between, which is tough. Then we jog back to the school and have plates of bread, jam and cake – there are four meals a day on offer here and it's all good, nourishing food with extra carbohydrates included. The evening, after dinner and a shower, is generally spent in the village pub, as there's nothing much else to do down there.

We never have any problems getting our lot to bed early, as sometimes happens with the field events people; by 10.30 their heads are nodding and by 11 the place is in darkness, as they're all pretty shattered. At Merthyr Mawr there are no inscriptions on the bunks (like the famous 'John Landy slept here' bunk at Portsea): it would be tantamount to inviting our fellows to fill the bed with sand. Sunday morning we get up early, jog to the dunes, run eight half-mile circuits, run some repetitions up a switchback hill, up and down, quick as they can, then jog back to camp. After lunch, they run to the beach for 100-metre repetitions or shuttle relays, then run back to camp. It's quite a tough weekend and most people prefer to take it easy for a couple of days afterwards, yet these lads will travel miles and miles to do it. They're invariably very grateful. 'Fantastic!' they say. They've been punished from Friday night to Sunday night, and they go away saying, 'Thank you very much for doing it to us.'

Back to track

Steve started the track season in good physical shape. On 30 April in an inter-club match he ran 1:53.9 for 800 metres, 4:0.4 for 1500 metres and 8:18.8 for his first track 3000 metres – all in one afternoon. On 13 May Steve raced in Kingston, Jamaica, in an international 1500 metres. He was anticipating a fairly leisurely run but it proved to be a hard, tight race, in which he finished second to American Steve Scott (they both recorded 3:39.8, but Scott outdove him into the tape). One-tenth behind was Filbert Bayi. It was to be Steve's last defeat over 1500 metres or the mile for a very long time. Five days later he raced against Bayi again – this time at Crystal Palace in a 3000 metres on the Philips Silver Jubilee Night of Athletics. Steve was well positioned for three or four of the seven laps, but with 200 metres to go he slipped back to fourth, recovered to third and tackled Paul Lawther on the finishing straight for second, just too late to reel in the Tanzanian. Bayi won in 7:53.3, a whisker from Steve, who wasted a little distance going round two men on the last turn and recorded 7:53.4 in second place. A useful effort, I thought, for his first serious 3000 metres, as among the people behind him was Malinowski, the Polish Olympic steeplechaser. 'I got a bit fed up in the middle,' said Steve. The 3000 metres pace is slow to a runner coming up from 800 metres in his first 1500 metres season.

The next important run was in the Belfast Festival Meeting, on 28 May, where Steve produced a reasonably fast 3:56.2 to win the mile, with a 54 last lap – a good sign so early in the season. Then came an international match in St Maur, Paris. I wish we had more of these matches: six countries took part and the races were all middle and long distance, with no other events at all. Everyone enjoyed it, including the athletes, and with another good last lap Steve won the 1500 metres in 3:39.8 again, from Jim McGuinness in second place. It was hoped that this match would be held annually, but it proved to be a one-off. There was another new meeting on 12 June: the UK championships (called the Kraft Jubilee Games). The traditional AAA championships were open to all-comers, and these were to be the closed national championships, confined to British athletes. However it was adding another event to an already crowded season. The meeting was to be held in Cwmbran, South Wales.

I arrived on the Friday night; Steve, who was entering the 1500 metres, left his journey until the Saturday morning of the meeting, and I had arranged to pick him up at the station. That morning the phone rang; it was Steve. His train departure had been delayed, and it would be touch and go whether he could make it in time, so would I ask the organizers to give him ten minutes' grace by putting him in the last heat. I did; they agreed, but then by the time I picked Steve up from the station we were cutting it very fine indeed, and drove like maniacs to the stadium whilst Steve was changing in the back seat. We screeched to a halt outside the stadium and Steve rushed into the gents. While Steve was attending to the call of nature the rest of his rivals were being evil, shouting out such things as 'Better finish it off quick, Steve – they're on their marks.' In fact they knew that only twelve people had reported for the race so there was no necessity to have heats. We were early!

The race (the one on the track) was a pretty good one. Mike Downes set the pace for most of the way, with

Steve lying third behind Mike Kearns; with 200 to go Steve moved up into second. Then at the start of the back straight he roared past, opening up a 10-metre gap in the space of 50 metres, and with his usual wave to the crowd strode home in 3:37.5. Had he kicked at 200 metres instead of 150 metres, he would probably have broken Frank Clement's UK record of 3:37.4, and not by the odd tenth either, but comfortably. Still, you can't legislate for things like that. Steve would just run his best race, win, and leave the speculation to others. He was pleased with his 3:37.5 – it came so easily.

It was one of my good days as a coach. Lesley Kiernan won the 800 metres. Since she had been out of racing with shingles she had been demoted to a has-been, and she announced her return with a personal best of 2:01.5. Lesley's married now and has a baby. When she and Steve ran in the European Games as juniors, she was runner-up in the 800 metres, and set a new European junior record later on.

Musical chairs

Steve was very well prepared for the Debenham Games mile on 26 June, but not quite prepared for what preceded it. Both Juantorena and Boit had been invited to race at this meeting, but Mr Cuba refused to compete against Boit in the 800 metres. He had run in the 400 metres on the Saturday night; he wanted to run in the 800 metres and he did not want Boit in the race. The organizer, Brian Hewson of Debenhams, decided to let Boit run the mile instead, which was Steve's event. On Sunday morning, Steve rang me up. 'Have you heard? They're switching Boit to the mile. We don't want that, do we?' We didn't. Steve's preparation for that race had been built around the Olympic 1500 metres champion, John Walker. Walker would be in his element at this distance, and Steve wanted to test himself against the New Zealander. He had enough to worry about without the additional problem of someone like Boit coming into the race. There was also a matter of principle involved. It always seemed, and this was an instance of it, that the overseas athletes could come to Crystal Palace and virtually dictate terms about their races. So now it was a case of Steve digging in his heels and saying, 'OK, if Juantorena doesn't want Boit, neither do I. If Juantorena won't race against him in the 800 metres, I won't race against him in the mile.' And poor Brian of Debenhams, in his first major promotion, had the unfortunate job of sorting it all out. Andy Norman, himself by then an experienced promoter, warned Brian that Steve would pull out, and that he meant what he said.

In the end it was decided that Boit should run, as originally intended, in the 800 metres, but to keep Juantorena happy it would a second, quite separate 800 metres. We were, after all, trying to maintain good diplomatic relations with Cuba. The mile was a fabulous race, once it got under way. It set off at a fairly leisurely 60.0 for the first lap, with army international Glen Grant leading, through 59.0 for the second and 60.6 for lap 3. So far, the race looked nothing special: just outside 3 minutes at the bell, with Steve lying third behind Graeme Crouch of Australia. Then, with 250 metres to go, Walker hit the front and stepped up the pace several notches, and at 200 metres out it was Walker from Ari Paunonen of Finland and Steve in third place. Rounding the turn, Steve dropped Paunonen and struck out for home, surging past Walker with 70 metres to go, and finishing some 5 metres clear in a new British record of 3:54.7, which included a 55-second last lap. Walker faded to fourth in 3:56.0, Wilson Waigwa of Kenya was second in 3:55.2 and Paunonen was third in 3:55.7. The crowd went berserk, Steve went on a lap of honour, went home, and forgot all about it until the following morning when the newspapers came.

I personally thought that some of those newspaper reports were nothing short of shameful in their approach. Well – 'reports' – they didn't really describe the race at all. Instead they worked themselves into a lather about the administrative problems before the race. That they had watched a remarkable mile, and seen the British record broken, seemed to have dwindled into insignificance. In their anxiety to foster the images they had created of Ovett the villain and Ovett the upstart, they had evidently determined not to write about Ovett the athlete at all. David Miller, of the *Express*, thought Steve should have been disqualified – for what, we do not know. Colin Hart's article in the *Sun* was headlined 'Shameful Ovett'. The press in general and the tabloids in particular blamed Steve entirely for Boit's race switch; they appeared to ignore the fact that Juantorena had started the game of musical chairs in the first place, and to find nothing odd in watching two 800 metres races instead of one, to appease Juantorena. They didn't look into the background of these events, but concentrated on criticizing Steve and playing down his UK record. As Steve commented, 'Why weren't the press worked up about Juantorena avoiding Boit? After all this was advertised as the main event of the meeting – the big clash between the Olympic champion and the unfortunate Boit, who would have been his main rival.' There was one fair and interesting report on the race itself, by Roy Moor of the *Mail*, who watched the race carefully and pointed out that at 300 metres Steve was slightly boxed in. He quoted Steve as saying, 'I was worried; I couldn't move out to my right.' My suspicions about the British press in general were borne out later in the season, in Helsinki. Some Finnish reporters there told us that they had been in the press room when Steve finished, and that they themselves had immediately jumped to their feet and applauded, despite having come to see Paunonen, rather than Steve. All around them was stony silence. They asked the British reporters, 'Well, aren't you going to cheer him?' And the British press broke into polite applause.

What it takes to be a champion

After this little lot, Steve ran a 3:59.1 mile on a grass track in Cork, beating Eamonn Coghlan, and then came the 1500 metres in the Europa Cup semifinal at Crystal Palace – which was a procession really. Steve's winning time was 3:39.1, but if one looks at the splits he finished very strongly, running the last 200 metres in 26.1 seconds and his last 400 in 53.5 (his last 800 in 1:51.5). What a difference a year had made! At last his training was beginning to pay off. He had kicked at 250 metres out and looked easy, with his usual little wave at the finish. On the same afternoon, Tony won the 10,000 metres so between them they'd helped to put Britain into the Europa Cup final.

A fortnight later Steve went to the Philips Games in Gateshead, and stuck his neck out rather a long way by running in the 5000 metres. He'd run one before, in Ireland, in a little club race earlier that season, for 13:53.4, but here he was up against the one man who but for the African boycott would have threatened Viren in Montreal – Miruts Yifter of Ethiopia. In 1977 he was probably the number one in the world. It was a tough way to find out about 5000 metres running. Josh Kimeto led for most of the first nine laps, with Yifter, Bernie Ford and Steve in close touch. Steve was nicely positioned and looking comfortable, but he said afterwards that he found the race boring in the middle stages. Ford took the lead at 4000 metres, followed by Yifter, Black, Kimeto and Steve, and at the bell Steve was well in contention. But then, 250 metres out and with Steve poised in second place, Yifter kicked with staggering power and he was gone, leaving a 30-metre gap in his wake. It was astonishing to see Steve for once unable to respond, and afterwards he said it had just felt hopeless. Steve commented, 'What a beauty to pick for my first 5000. I didn't have any legs at the finish and felt as I did in that Stockholm mile the previous year.'

He'd never been in the position before of wanting to go

where his legs couldn't take him. Yifter's time was 13:20.6; Steve's in second was 13:25.0. He had run a 59-second last lap, for the eighth fastest-ever UK time. He lay on the track afterwards and I knew what would be going through his mind: 'What's wrong with me?' But there was nothing wrong with him. He didn't have the endurance in his legs that Yifter had. A man of indeterminate age, Yifter obviously possesses great natural ability. When he kicks he is technically a sprinter. I understand that many years ago he ran in the Ethiopian 4 × 400 metres team. For a 10,000 metres man, that's quite an asset, isn't it?

It wouldn't have made any difference had I been there, which I wasn't. Steve did everything he should or could have done. I was watching the race on a portable TV set in Nottingham because I'd started coaching a girl called Josephine White the previous winter, and I'd gone to watch her race that afternoon. As a coach you go where you think you can be of most use, and that day Jo broke the UK junior record for the 1500 metres with 4:16.8. She was quite an extraordinary athlete: tall, tough and aggressive. That summer, having previously never heard of the European junior championships, she won a bronze medal in them, coming down from 2:11 to 2:02 for 800 metres. But then she broke her ankle, and I think we tried to push her back into racing too soon. It was probably my fault. She's at college now, in the States, but she possesses the greatest potential of any girl I've seen in Britain. This was my biggest disappointment as a coach, and I sincerely hope that her college coach will help her to realize this potential.

Steve had a fine time at Bideford on 4 August, where he helped the local Lions Club in a charity fund-raising meeting. In one afternoon on a grass track he ran 1:58.1 for the 800 metres, 3:50.0 for 1500 metres and 8:22.2 for 3000 metres. The crowd enjoyed it and it was a very useful training session. Then came the Europa Cup final in Helsinki on 13 August. Helsinki is an athlete's paradise. The stadium, the atmosphere, the track, the

Finnish people themselves with their love and knowledge of track and field, and even the newspapermen, are a treat. The press ask sensible questions and can actually hold a conversation on running. The accommodation there is on the edge of a forest, with a big lake around which to train. If it weren't for the mosquitoes it would be just perfect. Steve seems to relish the very hard beds they give you.

The first day, he won the 1500 metres. It was a strange race. Jurgen Straub of the GDR led the first two laps at a real crawl (62.2, 2:07.0) and then local hero Ari Paunonen took over at 900 metres. Steve was about sixth or seventh – going so slowly it didn't make much difference where you were – but then Paunonen raised the pace. With 300 metres to go, Steve was still sixth, and in the final straight it was Paunonen from Thomas Wessinghage of West Germany and Steve in third place. Suddenly, with about 120 metres to go, Steve swung out, passed both men and won in 3:44.9 from Wessinghage, who recorded a time of 3:45.4. His last 400 metres had taken just 52.6, which is possible after a long crawl when you have so much in reserve.

That evening I'd taken Tony out for a drink to cheer him up after a disastrous 10,000 metres, and we ran into a bunch of European selectors. One of them, a talkative Czech who had had a few drinks and assured me he was very influential, said, 'We're hoping Ovett will be doing the 800 metres here tomorrow.'

'He won't,' I said, 'because he's already done the 1500 metres.'

'In that case we hope he'll run in the World Cup 800 metres, as we'd like to see Plachy in the 1500 there.'

'Steve wants to do the 1500 in the World Cup, and as he's the best in the world at 1500,' I said, 'he surely deserves to be picked.' Fortunately Arthur Gold turned up at this point to put a stop to this fellow's persuasions, but the incident gave me a new insight into the politics of selection. In any case, selectors should seek the advice of event specialists.

Next day, Britain had someone else representing them: Sebastian Coe, a newcomer. He'd won the European indoor championships the previous year and he had run very well, so he was selected for the 800 metres here. I was event coach looking after them, and I asked Steve to warm up with the lad, as he was new to the team. Steve was at great pains to point out that whatever happened Seb should aim to be clear by the time they reached the last 100 metres, because he wouldn't want to be involved in any last-minute struggle. Unfortunately in the race itself this proved timely advice, because just as Seb was in a position to challenge; three or four runners bumped each other and the biggest and strongest of the lot, Willi Wulbeck, gave Seb a dig that sent him staggering across the track to finish fourth.

Steve was supposed to be running in the Highland Games in Edinburgh shortly after, but there was an air-traffic controllers' strike and he couldn't get a flight out of Gatwick. So he climbed in the car with Matt and off they went to Dartford, where Matt and some of Steve's Brighton and Hove clubmates were running in a half-marathon. At a loose end, Steve asked the organizers if they'd mind him joining in, as he'd like to do a spot of distance running with the lads and could drop out when he'd had enough. He was so jocular about the whole affair that he'd given his racing shoes to Matt and was wearing clodhoppers. When the race got under way, Steve found that he enjoyed it. In fact he enjoyed it so much, that after being warned by Barry Watson, a 1976 Olympic marathon runner, that he was going too fast and not taking it seriously enough, he ran out the winner quite comfortably in 65:38, with a bit of stiffness the day after but otherwise no ill effects. I'd gone to Italy with an England team that week and I read about it in the papers coming home. Somebody on the plane asked me if I'd known Steve was going to do it. I said no, and neither did Steve. Of course this exploit brought out some spicy press comments, such as, 'What a stupid thing to do,' 'He must be mad to do this before the World Cup.' And one even queried, 'Is he thinking of doing the marathon?'

All year he'd been looking forward to the World Cup, in Düsseldorf. He was favourite to win the 1500 metres, yet going into the race his best mark for 1977 was 3:37.5, compared with Walker's 3:32.7, Scott's 3:36.1, Morsli of Algeria with 3:36.3 and Wessinghage with 3:37.0. The World Cup is a strange championship, if indeed it can be called such, comprising eight teams, including two 'best teams' from Europe (effectively Russia and East Germany) and a team from the 'rest' of Europe, of which Steve was a member. Except for the relays, they weren't really teams at all.

Mel Watman of *Athletics Weekly* captioned the Düsseldorf 1500 metres, 'Ovett runs the perfect race'. Geoff Dyson, when he saw Steve's run, said he thought it should be kept on film in athletics archives as a work of art and an object lesson in middle-distance running. The stadium in West Germany was packed, which undoubtedly stirred something in the bosom of Thomas Wessinghage. He had been outsprinted by Steve in the Europa Cup and here was his chance to avenge himself by running the legs off ziss Britisher. Away went Wessinghage like a bullet from the gun, leading through 400 metres in 56.5 seconds. John Walker, though, evidently didn't think this was fast enough. Moving to the front, the New Zealander led through 800 metres in 1:55, a stride in front of Wessinghage and with Steve a close third with 1:55.5. The third lap dropped off slightly as Canadian Dave Hill took up the running after 1000 metres and led past the bell, but at the 1200-metre mark it was still 2:54.9, much faster than Steve had ever run before. I must tell you that I was watching all this on television at home, pacing up and down and upsetting the dog, because I was more nervous than I'd ever been in my life. Not because I doubted that Steve would win, but because I was doing some mental arithmetic: 2:54.9 plus the last-lap battle to come between Steve and Walker, would undoubtedly add up to something very special. Steve looked composed, his breathing easy, as though he were saving himself. I could hardly bear to watch. Walker moved into the lead and then, just after 200 metres out, Steve started to drive. It was spectacular, like watching an action replay of Susanj destroying the field in Rome. By the time he was halfway down the finishing straight, the race was over and Steve was giving his victory wave. The only disappointment was to see John Walker step off the track shortly after Steve had passed him; I think he hit the kerb, but John himself couldn't explain it – it was just one of those lapses in a runner's concentration.

There was a huge gap behind Steve. Wessinghage was second in 3:36 dead and Straub was third in 3:37.5. Amazingly, Steve had run the last 200 metres (including waves) in 25.1 seconds and the last lap in 54.5. He'd set a new UK record of 3:34.5, just outside Jean Wadoux's European best of 3:34 dead, though really that didn't matter. It was a full 3 seconds inside Steve's previous best and 2.3 inside Mike Kearn's pending British record. Here he was, in his first season as a 1500 metres runner, racing against men of this calibre and beating them with room to spare, positioning beautifully, sprinting at just the right time, and making the whole thing look so good. To all intents and purposes, this was indeed the perfect race. Steve said afterwards, 'If anything, it felt easier than running 3:37/3:38. For the first time everything was clicking in one race. I felt really good all the way and stronger towards the finish.'

He was disappointed not to have had a bigger battle with Walker, but paid tribute to John's greatness as an athlete and said that what happened that day didn't in any way diminish his record. It was a rather different approach from that of the New Zealand runners them-selves, earlier in the year, who'd said some pretty nasty things about Steve. Personally I don't think there's ever been any point in athletes running each other down, because on the day they all do their best, and some days are better than others. Walker's record speaks for itself: on quantity of races alone he must rank as one of the greatest runners of all time. Even in seasons when he starts badly and you think, 'John's not going to make it this year' – he does. He has come back time after time, from serious injuries, and he won't give in. He has a very tough streak and he's a fierce competitor. In 1976 some critics said he was lucky Bayi didn't run in the Olympics: I don't agree. He'd pulled himself into shape by the games, and getting knocked out in the first round of the 800 metres was the best thing that could have happened to him.

Earlier in 1977, Frank Taylor of the *Mirror* had invited Walker and New Zealand's 5000 metres world record holder Dick Quax to challenge 'boy wonder' Ovett for allegedly pulling out of the AAA 800 metres (in fact he never entered). He quoted Walker as saying, 'It seems to me Steve doesn't give a damn, but runs when he feels like it.... You can't keep ducking out like this. Maybe Steve will grow out of his present attitude but he won't be a real champion until he does,' and so on. I've never understood the New Zealander's propensity for criticizing Steve over here because they know it's meat and drink to the press. The funny part is that on the two or three occasions when they've let slip a few of these quotes, they'll see Steve and myself training down at Crystal Palace and the first thing they'll do is to come over and tell us, 'Oh, don't take any notice of what the papers say. We didn't say this, and it wasn't as bad as that.'

Just for the record, what *actually* happened over that AAA 800 metres title defence was that Steve had won the UK championship mile and he was getting ready for the Europa Cup on 16 July, so the AAA 800 metres didn't enter into his plans, as he had informed the AAA months beforehand. Steve has never criticized Walker, or Quax, or Dixon, over *their* race plans: each athlete must do as he thinks fit. As to the question of Steve 'ducking' anybody – well, who was there for him to duck? He'd gone out of his way to run against Walker at his strongest distance, which was 1500 metres, at which Steve himself was supposedly a novice.

After Steve's World Cup 1500, he was asked why he'd chosen to run in the Dartford half-marathon just before Düsseldorf. 'No reason,' said Steve. 'Sheer madness.' He was also asked how fast he *could* have gone in the 1500. 'If pushed, perhaps another two or three seconds. I don't run for time: I just run to win.' I'd say his estimate was conservative. He could have run very close to 3:30 that day. There *are* days in athletics when everything about an athlete looks right, when everything 'clicks', as Steve put it. On these 100 per cent days a runner feels tuned, physically and mentally, and it's difficult to set any limit on what might be achieved. Sometimes you sense a few days beforehand that such a peak is coming. A coach looks at the athlete in training and thinks, 'I'd like to wrap this person up now in cotton wool and put him in a drawer.' He has extraordinary speed, he is at ease, he recovers quickly, he looks superb. You know the performance is already there. There may be a little doubt with some people as to how they will perform on the day, but with a runner like Steve you can guarantee it. If he looks like that in training, he has the intelligence and that streak of ruthlessness in him that make him a racing certainty. On these occasions, seeing Steve train I'll tell him, 'It's a real pleasure to watch you run now.' And it is: one is actually privileged to be on a training session like that, seeing what most people would pay a lot of money to see, like a *tour de force* in the theatre by a great actor.

Steve's magnanimous references to John Walker after Düsseldorf were typical of his nature, as was to be seen again after the Moscow Olympics. Despite his sometimes mickeytaking humour he is invariably gracious and generous towards people when it really matters, and always remembers when somebody has helped him. When he came back from the World Cup, for example, he had nothing but praise for Denis Watts, who had been European team coach there. He said, 'Denis was just what I wanted: reassuring at the right time.' The trophy

Steve was given that day he quietly gave to Denis when he retired as national event coach a couple of years later.

Steve's season was drawing to a close: his next race was a mile in the International Athletes' Club Coca-Cola meeting, and his winning time of 3:56.6 nevertheless included a 54-second last lap. The pace had slackened at the bell to 3:01.9, with Steve boxed in, but this didn't prevent him from bursting away at the 200-from-home mark to pass second-placed Wessinghage, who clocked 3:57.5. The same night Jo White broke the British 1000 metres senior record with 2:28.6, quite remarkable for a sixteen-year-old girl. On 17 September, Steve ran a very fast leg in a cross-country relay – the Blackheath Harriers cross-country at Sparrows Den – and broke the course record by the enormous margin of 21 seconds. His next run was a 3000 metres in Wattenschied, Germany, which he won in spectacular style in 7:41.3, the second fastest time in the world after Foster's 7:35.2 record, and this despite being down by about 6 metres with 200 metres to go. Kenya's Henry Rono had led past 1000 metres in 2:37.9 and 2000 metres in 5:11.8, followed by Steve and Karl Fleschen, but then the German faded and Steve tucked in behind Rono waiting to kick. His winning margin was 4 metres. The following day he was beaten by Wessinghage in a 2000 metres event, by 5:04.3 to 5:04.7, in Hanover. The season went out with him running in a high-quality invitational cross-country race, won by an Ethiopian called Tura, at Crystal Palace. Steve finished sixth.

It was the end of probably his best season to date. He had run fourteen races at 1500 metres or a mile and he'd won all but his early-season duel at the tape with Steve Scott in Jamaica. In recognition of this, the British Milers' Club made him a presentation, a bracelet engraved 'World 1500m Champion 1977'. The club had been founded during a dearth of world-class British milers with the aim of pushing the UK to the fore again, and with Steve's success we felt that this had been achieved. He was the first British athlete to top the rankings at 1500 metres or the mile since Derek Ibbotson in 1957. I didn't make the presentation myself, although I was chairman that year; I asked Frank Horwill, the secretary, to do the honours. In his thankyou speech, Steve mischievously reminded us of that young athletes course at Crystal Palace, long ago that I've told you about, when as a junior he had demonstrated his 'lack of what it takes to be a champion' by blowing a raspberry during one of Frank's lectures.

Steve turned down *Daily Mail* and BBC Sports Personality of the Year invitations; it's difficult to see the value of comparing one sport's champion with another, especially as the judging is not particularly objective. But the British Athletics Writers' Association was obliged by objectivity to vote Steve Male Athlete of 1977. His best marks, over an astonishing range, stood at 21.7 seconds for 200 metres, 47.5 for 400 metres, 1:45.4 for 800 metres, 3:34.5 (a UK record) for 1500 metres, 3:54.7 (a UK record) for the mile, 7:41.3 for 3000 metres, 13:25.0 for 5000 metres and 1 hour 05:38 for the half-marathon.

As an experiment Steve had run hardly any 800 metres races during the year, because we were finding that it wasn't strictly necessary. We felt all the time that he could run a fast 800 metres if the occasion arose (as it did in an invitation race against West Germany). As long as the quality of his training remained high there might at the most be 2 per cent doubt in our minds about coming up with fast 800 metres races.

6

Prague Gold and Silver

Fairly early on in 1978 we decided it wasn't on the cards to enter both the Commonwealth Games and the European championships. The latter were obviously the most important, with far sterner opposition, and sinnce these championships were to be Steve's main objecctive for the track season of 1978, it seemed pointless to jeopardize his form by the hassle of travelling out to Edmonton shortly beforehand. We felt that Steve's established record in the European team should ensure him virtual automatic selection on reasonable form, and he wouldn't therefore have tto worry about either the AAA championship to qualify for Edmonton or the UK championships to gain selection for Europe – and I think the British Board accepted this early in the season. Steve had never been too happy aboout compcting in North America because of the jet lag and tedium of the journey.

The year got under way with Steve winning the Sussex championships by over a minute from Peter Standing at Lancing College, and winning a five-miler in Belfast a week later (the Belfast cross-country race) by 15 seconds from the Scot, Nat Muir. He felt pretty confident about the Inter-Counties at Derby on 21 January, over $7\frac{1}{2}$ miles, though it was a foul, frreezing afternoon. He said he felt comfortable all the way, apart from some trouble keeping his footing in the snow and black ice on the hills, and he was always with the leading group. Negotiating the hills strongly (after Stanmer Park training), with about a mile to go he broke away and won by 11 seconds from Steve Jones. Matt was seventy-second.

This win spurred Steve's ambitions: he stepped up his mileage and for about a month, until two weeks before the national cross-country championships in March, he was averaging 120 to 140 miles a week of steady-state running and good-quality repetition 1000 metres on the circuit at Crystal Palace. He was well keyed up for the National. The course, at Roundhay Park, Leeds, is very tough and very hilly and it should have been right up Steve's street, but unfortunately he got off to a pretty poor start, which is bad news in these big cross-country races with fields of 1400 or 1500. The other runners knew that Steve was really fit and that whatever happened they would have to be away from him well before the closing stages. Coaching Ian Stewart and Tony Simmons I was aware of the general plan to show Steve what 9-mile racing was all about.

After the first 3-mile lap Steve had had a tough fight to get up to sixth, and he dropped back to seventh on lap 2. The others were all belting along like mad to keep him at bay; his big effort had told on him and he lost several more places on the third lap, but with something like three-quarters of a mile to go he came to life again and hauled himself back up to finish fourth behind Bernie Ford, Ian Stewart and Tony Simmons.

Brendan Foster came over afterwards to say, 'There must be something wrong with Steve.' Because he'd come fourth in a 9-mile race! Being expected to win over his whole distance spectrum does weigh heavily on Steve at times. He was very crestfallen afterwards; it made no diffeence that the people in front of him were three of the world's top 10,000 metres runners, or that the people behind him included some very good long-distance men. On the strength of his performance he was selected for the 1978 International cross-country team, but Steve decided to turn this down. The National, which was about the fastest cross-country race I've ever watched, cost some of the runners dear: neither of the first two finishers, Bernie Ford nor Ian Stewart, recovered sufficiently to make much of an impact on the season afterwards.

The following week Steve ran in Italy. The Five Mills race is quite extraordinary. The competitors run in and out of five flour mills in a little village, bending almost double to duck underneath the doors and then running through people's gardens, over treacherous cobblestones and round the roads. It's good fun, but it's also very competitive. Henry Rono chose a bad place to drop out, running round a football pitch in front of all the spectators shouting '*Turisto!*'

Then, between the cross-country and track seasons, came the usual weekend at Merthyr Mawr. We met David Shaw down there, the newly appointed secretary of the BAAB, who was brave enough to step into the lions' den with a lot of middle-distance runners and ask if they had any criticisms of the Board. Ian Stewart and Steve did have a few, and between them they gave him a pretty rough time. Their argument was that middle-distance running in Britain is the biggest event both in terms of spectators and participants, yet the runners themselves get very little support from the Board. In summer they pull the crowds, and in winter they struggle to find the money to train abroad. Ian put forward the idea of the BAAB buying a modest villa in Portugal to save the staggering expense of hotel bills for everyone each year. The team could use it whenever they liked to train and the Board could sublet the property in the summer, so it would be a good investment and good publicity for a sponsor such as a building society. David Shaw expressed great interest in implementing the scheme, but since then the villa has failed to materialize.

Track season 1978

Steve's track season began with a 7:57.8 time for the 3000 metres in the Southern championships at Crystal Palace, guesting for Brighton and Hove AC on 3 May. As usual, he left the leading to others, and one of the people who tried to break away just before the finish was Julian Goater, whom I'd been coaching since 1976. Between 8 a.m. and 9 a.m. on the morning of the race, Steve had been for a five-mile run, and he'd done ten miles hard after lunch. When the 3000 metres was over he was still so full of beans that he did a whole series of 60-metre sprints on the track. 'You have to keep the old training going,' he told interested observers. There wasn't much wrong with him speedwise either, because three days later, at Copthall, he won a tactical 1500 metres followed by a 47.4-second leg in a relay. The same day, 6 May, Tony Simmons, who'd switched distances, won the AAA marathon in 2 hours 12:33, so he was going to the European Games with Steve.

There was another significant result on 14 May, in the Yorkshire championships at Cleckheaton. Seb Coe ran 1:45.6 for 800 metres*– very fast for early season. Added to his record and his win in the European indoor championships the previous season, this meant that Coe now presented a considerable threat. He would be given the respect normally accorded to a serious rival.

On 20 May, Steve won a 2000 metres invitational race in Milan in 5:10.6, but while he was there he had very bad toothache. Back home he took himself off to the dental hospital and was found to have an abscessed tooth. A couple of nights later was the Philips meeting, and he was dubious now about running in it. I think he would like to have pulled out, but there were a lot of people there wanting especially to see him run. Henry Rono had agreed to turn out for the 3000 metres against him and the clash had been given a big build-up. Steve had a penicillin injection for his septic tooth and said nothing about his discomfort. In the race, Henry ran splendidly, pushing off with several laps to go, and Steve nursed himself along until the last lap before coming through quite hard for second place in 7:48 dead, behind Henry's very impressive winning time of 7:43.8. Though Steve never complains or makes excuses once he steps on the track, a biographer must fill you

127

in, and he was really in great pain that night.

In Belfast two days later he won a pretty slow 800 metres, but by 3 June he was rolling again at Crystal Palace in the invitational 2000 metres. Brendan Foster's UK record stood at 5:02.9 – not very special, and it wanted beating. After a respectable start, Nick Brooks took up the running through 800 metres in 1:59.0 with Steve lying fourth in 1:59.6. Nick Rose led on laps 3 and 4 with Steve second, and then Steve waited until 240 metres out before coming through to win in 4:57.8, a new British record.

17 June was a busy night for Steve's rivals. In Oslo Henry Rono was setting a new world record for the 3000 metres of 7:32.1, and Frank Clement finished fourth in a mile race for 3:54.2, breaking Steve's UK record of 3:54.7. Then, on 15 July, in the UK championships Steve had skipped, Seb Coe won the 800 metres in 1:47.1 at Meadowbank stadium in Scotland, only to be disqualified at first for breaking lanes too early and then later reinstated. The referee, my friend Neta Sinclair, had made her decision after consulting two official judges. Steve himself hadn't made the European qualifying marks for either the 800 metres or the 1500 metres, which worried some officials, but he very quickly made amends on 26 July in Malmö, Sweden, running 3:37.6 for the 1500 in front of Steve Scott, with 3:41.3. The following night in Turkü, Finland, equalling his personal best for 800 metres with 1:45.4, he beat James Robinson of the USA, who clocked 1:46.8. He was therefore selected for the 1500 metres in Prague, with the possibility of an 800 metres place too: the first double since the inception of the European Games in 1934. The only problem was going to be whether he could manage five consecutive races, including heats.

Just before the Commonwealth Games opened, in Oslo Steve improved his personal best for the 1500 metres, with 3:35.8, again at the expense of Steve Scott in second place with 3:36.0, though even this wasn't good enough to put him on top of the British rankings. In the

Commonwealth Games, Moorcroft won the 1500 metres in 3:35.5 by a tenth from Bayi, and John Robson recorded 3:35.6 in the same race; so we had three strong 1500 metres contenders for Prague, with Steve, on paper, the slowest of the three. Then, two or three weeks before Prague, disaster struck. Steve came down with bronchitis. He wouldn't stop training, but found great difficulty in running fast. He could keep his steady runs going, but anything remotely intensive would start him coughing badly. He didn't really know what to do. He hadn't told anybody, apart from a few close friends. We thought it best to leave any decision about Prague until the Rotary Games on 23 August: he'd give the mile a go. On the day, Graham Williamson did a lot of the leading in the race and Steve stayed pretty well back for most of the way before bursting past at 200 metres out to cover the remaining distance in 24.4 seconds. He strode home waving as usual, but in the warm-down area he had another attack of coughing and felt pretty rotten. He decided to go along to the European championships and see how he felt before racing.

Prague

Once we arrived in Prague, Steve obviously fancied his chances in the 800 metres. The only person in front of him in the rankings was Sebastian, who'd run an astounding 1:44.3 in Brussels on 18 August. 'The way I looked at it,' says Steve, 'was that the 800 metres was something to keep me off the training track, because as I said to Harry, if I go over there and sit around all day and don't do anything, and then go in the evening and sit around watching the athletics, it won't be good for me mentally or physically.'*

Prague was warm and sunny when we arrived, but quickly changed to cold and miserable. It drizzled most days, and Prague is a sad, bleak place anyway. The

*Athletics Weekly, 7 April 1979.

athletes were billeted in grim university blocks with a strong military presence. The rooms weren't too uncomfortable but the stone corridors echoed with noise at night. Steve's parents were with a tourist group on the other side of the city and their accommodation was better. The food in the village wasn't very good but was much the same as for the rest of the country, so you just had to put up with it.

Before the events started, I called all the endurance runners together and told them that I was their event coach, and I was there to look after them. If anybody wanted me to do anything to help him, I'd gladly do it. We had three cars available and I would drive them anywhere they needed to go. Not many people wanted to use these cars, because we'd heard frightening tales of the penalties for traffic accidents in Czechoslovakia, so I'd usually jam seven or eight of the lads into one car and ferry them to the woods for training, then drive them back again. Admittedly I wasn't driving all that well; the indicators weren't working properly, and one day I turned right instead of left and was accused of trying to wipe out the whole team. Though the cars were available to everyone, they were always borrowed under the watchful supervision of an ex-squadron leader, Norman Cobb. I did not, as was suggested in a recent book by Sebastian Coe and David Miller, commandeer a car for Steve: it was there for the whole team to use, as Coe well knew because he was at the meeting. I should like to refute certain other allegations in *Running Free* during the course of this book. According to Coe, I didn't give him much attention in Prague, particularly with regard to this car. But Sebastian never asked to be taken out in it. He never asked me for anything, because he was shepherded about by his father, Peter.

We never dreamed that Peter Coe was really called Percy (a name to be proud of as an athletics coach, cf. Percy Cerutty) and in fact his dual identity was to occasion some difficulty over his admittance credentials in Moscow. Steve has asked me to point out that in

Prague he was instrumental in getting Percy/Peter onto the warm-up track. 'I saw him wandering about one day and he asked, "How do I get in without a pass?" "Follow me," I told him, "I'll get you in."' And apparently he did.

My role as event coach in Prague was essentially to be on hand to give advice, to accompany members of the team to the warm-up track, analyse opponents (*foreign* opponents) and generally be of assistance as required. Some athletes are withdrawn; others are garrulous. You talk to the ones that want to talk and stay quiet with the others. As an event coach you know very little about the backgrounds of most of the runners in the team, seeing them perhaps three or four times a year, so it would scarcely be right to foist your opinions on them unless they are called for. I wouldn't think of telling a runner, 'You're going to beat everybody out of sight!' or anything so invasive, as we don't favour the American approach to psyching people up. Sebastian also mentions, in his book, a private conversation between myself and another athlete in which I confided that I didn't think there was any way in which Seb could beat Steve in the 800 metres. This was my honest opinion, and no more than Peter Coe would have said in reverse, had he been tackled on the subject. One is entitled to a private opinion. Aside from Steve and Seb, it was a tense situation for those members of the British team who had been to Edmonton and won medals in the Commonwealth Games. They were feeling jaded, yet they realized that Prague was a very different ball game, and they could well be wiped out in the heats. These athletes were apprehensive and tired. It was going to be a very tough championship.

Steve won his 800 metres heat very comfortably in 1:47.8. Olaf Beyer of East Germany won the second heat in 1:47.7, Andreas Busse of East Germany won the third in 1:49.1 and Seb the last in an easy 1:46.8. The semifinals were rough affairs, both of them. Neither Seb nor Steve, though, looked at all pressed. Seb won the first in 1:7.4 from Busse, who ran 1:47.6, and then Steve won the second in 1:46.5 from Beyer in 1:46.7. You couldn't help but conclude that the final ought to be decided between Seb and Steve. Compared with the others, 1:45 times or not, these two seemed so relaxed. Anyone who thought otherwise must certainly have had second sight. One unknown factor had been removed from the final: Wulbeck. A big destroyer who might have altered the eventual outcome, Willi came out of the tunnel as his heat began and he was disqualified.

While Steve was warming up for the 800 metres final, a friend of mine, senior coach Neville Taylor, remarked, 'Doesn't Steve look huge, Harry.' I looked across and sure enough, he did. When Steve is very fit and he's running and doing his strides, he *does* seem to tower over everybody else. He isn't physically taller than Wessinghage or these other characters, but because of this superb fitness there is a springy power and dynamism in his stride that give the impression of great height. And I've noticed this several times since that day.

The final was billed as the classic confrontation between the kicker (Steve) and the front-runner (Seb). There didn't logically seem to be any other way for Seb to run it than by leading from the gun. He had clocked fast times by front-running. On paper he had the .best speed; he knew that Steve liked slow races and was relatively untested in fast ones, and it seemed obvious that Seb should go out and set a very fast pace and try to burn everybody else off. Had I been his coach I wouldn't have advised him differently, although it did cross my mind on the eve of the race that he might suddenly do the unexpected and confound the lot of us. But I don't think it was a mistake for Seb to blaze it. Pace judgement is very critical on these occasions – maybe they'll hang on to you, maybe they won't, but if you are out in front there's always the chance that your opponents will get tangled up with each other, and Seb may have been influenced by the bump he received in the Europa Cup final the previous year. Steve's tactics were fairly simple: he was just going to sit in and run his normal middle-distance race. He wasn't apprehensive about rough stuff. He tends to let other people do the worrying about that.

The race set off more or less as expected, with Coe hitting the front and setting a cracking pace. I think the excitement of the occasion probably pushed him along, because nobody had quite anticipated 400 metres in 49.5 seconds (Coe himself had planned on 50.5), with Beyer on Seb's shoulder and Steve third in 49.9. I looked at my watch: the pace seemed rather extravagant. Steve hadn't done many 800s in the last two years; he would surely be feeling this by now. Just after the 400-metre mark Steve moved up into second and down the back straight I noticed Seb was beginning, almost imperceptibly, to slow. The splits showed 13.8 seconds for the sixth 100 metres, compared with 13.1 for the previous 100 and 12.2 for the first 100. Steve evidently wasn't having any difficulty hanging on and if anything he was closing in, sitting on Seb's shoulder. The 200-metre-from-home mark – and Seb appeared to be flagging. This ought to be the moment for Steve to go. Afterwards he told me he'd felt the same way, but he was concerned that in a race of this pace it might be too soon and he wouldn't be able to last if Seb had anything in reserve. So Steve held back.

I could understand his thinking – 'Don't set yourself up yet; wait a little longer.' The next 100 metres went just as slowly, in 13.8, and then, as they came off the final bend and into the straight, Steve went for the front. Seb fell back fairly quickly but suddenly, up on the outside of Steve, came the powerful, storming figure of Beyer the East German, who had been tracking him over that last 100 metres. Once Beyer was past there was to be no catching him, and home he went in the superb time of 1:43.9, a championship record. Steve hung on for the silver in a personal best and new UK record of 1:44.1. Seb took the bronze in 1:44.8. Beyer was a big, strong young runner, relatively untapped before these games, so it wasn't too surprising that he should have come good. Yet the 800 metres is a race of quick decisions and seizing

133

opportunities, and though it's easy for me to say afterwards that Steve should have gone at 200 out, I think Steve himself would agree. Opportunity rarely knocks twice, and it's astonishing that in a race you can nearly always pin down one precise point where you should have taken your chance and run. Everything clicks in your mind: Right, now! If you ignore it, nine times out of ten you're doomed. Steve explains, 'At 600 metres I thought Seb was easing down to kick again when really I think he was just feeling the effects of running fast for 600 and was slowing down. We slowed, giving Beyer the chance to catch us on the back straight. I think that was probably my big mistake. I waited on Seb round the final bend.'*

Steve was naturally disappointed, but almost the first thought through his mind afterwards was, 'This makes the 1500 a dead cert for me.' Having 1:44.1 pace at his disposal, better than ever before for 800 metres, he naturally felt very confident about his main event. Steve ran into Seb's father after the 800 final on his way back to the village and congratulated him on Seb's run, which was after all a pretty good effort. Steve was regaled by a flood of excuses and reasons for Seb not winning, but not the slightest recognition that Beyer and Steve had run well.

The 800 metres heats and final had taken up three consecutive days; the 1500 metres heats were the day after. There were only three, with the first three runners from each going through, along with the three fastest losers. Dave Moorcroft came second to Eamonn Coghlan in heat one, both in 3:40.0. Steve won the second comfortably in 3:42.9, and in the third, Loikkanen of Finland produced 3:39.7 ahead of John Robson, who ran 3;40. There was one day's rest. The rankings going into the final were: Wessinghage 3:35, Plachy (Czechoslovakia) 3:35.1, Moorcroft 3:35.5, Robson 3:35.6, Steve 3:35.8, Straub 3:36.1. On paper it looked a closeknit

*Athletics Weekly, 7 April 1979.

race. Yet for some reason the press were head over heels about the Finn, Loikkanen, saying everyone in Finland must be putting their money on him, he was their secret weapon and so forth; Ovett had been beaten in the 800 metres, he was vulnerable, so look out for Loikkanen, etc. etc. I thought the press were clutching at straws, but when I came back afterwards and played the video, even the BBC commentators seemed to place great faith in the Finn on the strength of his fast time in the heats, and even fancied Beyer's chances of doing the double. Steve, though, had no doubts in his mind. None at all. He was probably the most confident I've ever known him to be before a race. As well he might have been on his current form; he had beaten all his opponents.

The 1500 metres final got under way without further ado, and Beyer looked as though he would set the pace until Francis Gonzales, the Frenchman, took up the running and pushed it along at a lick, 57.5, with Steve lying sixth, but not far behind Gonzales, Wessinghage, Beyer, Coghlan and Moorcroft. Steve moved up to third as they approached 800 metres and it was still reasonably paced, at 1:57.7 with Steve two or three metres down at 1:58.1. So far the race was very tight, and as they came up to the bell with Straub leading, in 2:56.7, Steve edged back to sixth without losing much ground, running 2:57.1. There were now six runners within three metres of each other. As they turned into the back straight, lo and behold, this Loikkanen fellow hit the front, and for an instant some rather disquieting thoughts flashed through my mind: supposing the Finn had something after all? Loikkanen's glory, though, was shortlived; as soon as Steve saw him a switch fell in his brain and away he went, kicking harder than I'd ever seen before from just inside the 200-from-home mark. He was ten metres clear before anyone cottoned on; in fact the others appeared to be waiting for Steve and to have no other plan than to follow him in and pick up the crumbs. Some of them were apparently aiming for second place from the start. Thomas Wessinghage had said publicly that he was going for the silver, and I don't think he was the only one. So though Steve effectively had the race won with 150 or 160 metres to go and was able to relax and just stride towards the finish, there was a dire struggle going on behind him for second. The lucky man was Eamonn Coghlan, who managed to pip Dave Moorcroft on the line, and threw his arms in the air in the ecstasy of victory. 'First is first, and second is first.' Steve's time was 3:35.6, a championship record; Coghlan's was 3:36.6, Moorcroft's 3:36.7. It was good to see the European 1500 metres championship won in a respectable time for a change; it was the second fastest of Steve's career.

I think the race must rank equal with Düsseldorf as an exhibition of middle-distance running at its best; in a way it was better, because it had been preceded by three 800s and a 1500 heat, whereas Düsseldorf was a one-off. It always amazed Steve, and he often mentioned this, that the opposition never tried something different against him. There seemed almost an acceptance among his rivals that they would trundle round until 200 out and then rush vainly along in Steve's wake. Steve said shortly afterwards, 'My technique that season was to run from the 200-metre mark. I didn't try and surprise them with difficult tactics or anything like that. Everybody says, oh well, all you've got to do is stay with him and outkick him, but it's not as simple as that. That's the key, but you need the right person to turn the key and I don't think there is anybody. I'm running in the low 24s for the last 200 and that's easing down over the last 100, so if stretched I could maybe run maybe low 23s for the last 200. That means, to get past me, someone's got to run 22.9, 22.7, and I can't think of anybody. I can run, if trained for it, low 22s or under for 200 flat out, and I don't think there's anybody that can run 9 miles cross-country and couple that with that sort of speed.'*

Steve didn't attend the press conference, although he

* *Athletics Weekly*, 7 April 1979.

wished all the reporters an early Merry Christmas. But then this should have come as no surprise to anyone after three years, and if Sebastian thought it ill-mannered he was the first athlete ever to complain. I missed the victory ceremony myself as I was detailed to cover the last two miles of the marathon to let the lads know their positions, and it was sad to see Tony struggling along in thirteenth. I was quite concerned about our runners because when they reached the stadium they were moping around in a very distressed state, like most people after marathons, and wanting some words of comfort and advice, but the press kept coming up and pestering me to talk about Steve's victory. They couldn't see I was doing another very delicate job at the time and they said, 'Well you don't seem very pleased!' As soon as the marathon men were off the premises I went to look for Steve, and eventually found him still down in the underground clearing room trying to find enough pee to pass the drug test. It really gets quite distasteful at times because the various assays require a considerable volume, and it wasn't until after a lot of warm beer and much water on the wrists and whistling of happy tunes that Steve was able to oblige. 'OK,' they said at last, 'you can go home.' As you can imagine after all this, the night was no longer young.

We jogged back to the village, and I produced a bottle of champagne I'd managed to keep tucked away out of a number given to us as a hospitality gesture for official functions. I told Steve we would have a celebration, but unfortunately we couldn't find anybody much to celebrate with. The place was deserted but for the two masseurs as everybody else had gone off to eat. We drank the champagne and as we couldn't stand the thought of the village food, we went along to the Hilton in town. We'd been there earlier in the week with Steve's parents, and found the best food available was a hamburger, but by the time we arrived even hamburgers were off in the restaurant and we had to order them in the snack bar. That was our victory celebration – a hamburger and a beer in the snack bar of the Hilton. Not exactly the glamorous life referred to by Jimmy Green in his famous letter. We said hallo to Steve's parents, who were having a meal with a big party of people in the restaurant, and home we went.

Steve also felt that this race ranked alongside that of Düsseldorf. I suggested that it was his biggest win to date and he said, 'I suppose so, but it was what was expected of me.' Would that all our athletes did half what was expected of them!

The next day, an inquest was held by the British management on the team's performance in the games. The coaches had all been asked to submit confidential reports to John le Masurier. There had been some trouble in the village with athletes who had been knocked out early on making a racket in the corridors while other competitors were preparing for their events. One afternoon while Steve and Seb were each trying to get some sleep, there were fellows storming up and down yelling and hammering on the doors. 'Quiet' notices swiftly appeared, but at the meeting it was decided that in future we would take only those athletes along who in the phrase of my report could 'compete with distinction' in the games. To have people eliminated early and hanging around was neither good for them nor good for their fellow competitors. In these games Britain had collected only one gold medal, and when I spoke to some of the athletes afterwards they felt that they'd been over-ambitious attempting both the Commonwealth and European games. Brendan Foster and Mike McLeod were honest enough to say they had been greedy trying to win medals in both events. Britain had come away from Montreal with one bronze in 1976, and although we seemed to do well in Edmonton, we knew that the European Games were the premier competition of 1978; as the week went by it had seemed we wouldn't get a single gold there either – until Steve won the 1500 metres.

We arrived back at Gatwick to find the place congested with newspapermen. Nick Whitehead, the men's team manager, grabbed Steve and we forced a path through, with Nick giving some of the photographers a helping hand out of the way. Steve jumped into my car and I drove him to Gatwick station. I felt a pang of remorse leaving him there. One minute he'd been the European champion, the talk of the town, inundated with press-people, and the next here he was, standing all on his own on the platform with his bag, going home to an empty house because his family were still in Prague.

The following weekend was the Coca-Cola meeting at Crystal Palace. Steve didn't run at all for a couple of days on arriving home, as he was emotionally and physically pooped. He was due to run a 2-mile race against Henry Rono which was billed as a clash of the giants. Henry had recently cleaned up all the world records at the longer distances, and the new European 1500 metres champion was supposed to be tackling him on even terms at 2 miles. Rono had expressed interest in Foster's 1973 world 2 miles record of 8:13.7.

I met Steve at Crystal Palace on the Wednesday night. 'I just did about two miles' jogging with Harry,' said Steve, 'which is not exactly hard work, and I did a few strides just seeing how my legs could stretch out, and though I felt reasonable I didn't feel all that wonderful. He said there were going to be an awful lot of disappointed spectators turning up at the meet, as I was the only gold medallist and they'd like to see me whether I ran badly or not.'*

I tried to persuade him that once he was into the race, the concentration would overcome his tiredness. I was sure that once he got started he would put up a good show anyway. 'OK,' he said finally, 'I'll give it a go.'

He turned up on the Friday night of the race still moaning and groaning about being shattered and having all this responsibility on his shoulders. I told him not to worry too much about the pace.

*Athletics Weekly, 7 April 1979.

'I've *got* to worry about the pace,' he said, 'with Henry going after Foster's record.'

'But after the races you've been running, you may find this pace slow,' I suggested.

'Oh all right,' he said drearily. 'I'll go in there and see how many laps I can last.' It was a novel experience to hear Steve talking about lasting, rather than about winning. And it was even more astonishing that this race turned out to be probably the best of his career to date.

A good pace was set by Graeme Fell for three even laps, passing $\frac{1}{4}$ mile in 61.3 seconds, $\frac{1}{2}$ mile in 2:02.4 and $\frac{3}{4}$ mile in 3:04.3. Steve was lying third. The fourth lap dropped off to 64.5 with Malinowski leading, and whereas Foster had gone through in 4:05.4, Malinowski did so in 4:08.8, with Steve in second and Rono third. On lap 5 Rono took the lead, though without stepping up the pace (another 64.5), just ahead of Malinowski with Steve in third. There were now three laps to go. As though on cue, Rono put his head down and dug in very very hard: as we discovered afterwards he ran the last $\frac{3}{4}$ mile in a shade over 3 minutes, including some fast bursts and a 61 quarter. At the $1\frac{1}{2}$-mile stage it was Rono in the lead, in 6:14.3, from Steve at his shoulder in 6:14.4. They slowed slightly on the next, 63.1-second lap, so that at $1\frac{3}{4}$ miles they were 7:17.4 to 7:17.7. On the penultimate lap I was standing on the inside of the back straight, and as they came past Steve looked across at me and gave a little shrug, as much as to say, 'If this is the best Henry can do, no problem.' With 200 metres to go, no doubt realizing that this was Steve's normal place to kick, Henry started to push very hard and Steve stayed with him until just before the finishing straight. They were still rounding the turn when Steve moved out. He didn't sprint, but simply lengthened his stride and hauled past Rono down the straight, striding faster, opening a big gap before finally easing off to win, with a wave, by 8 metres in a new world best of 8:13.5, 0.2 sec inside Foster's record. He'd run 55.8 seconds for the last quarter. Steve says, 'It's not surprising that I was worried about this race. Having a cold and being exhausted after Prague wasn't the ideal sort of preparation for tackling Henry.'

It was a startling performance considering all the problems he'd had before the race, the sheer physical exertion, and the power he was able to generate on the last lap. It more than offset what had happened earlier in the evening, when Seb Coe had won the 800 metres in 1:44 dead to take Steve's UK record away from him, because although Seb assures us in his book that he doesn't carry his pacemakers around with him, he certainly carried one that night: Steve Scutt, a stablemate of Seb's under George Gandy. Scutt paced the first lap for him and then dropped out, leaving Seb well clear to run on his own. In *Running Free*, Peter Coe gloats over the fact that after the race he came up to me and said, 'Tell Steve that Seb and myself always considered the 800 metres record was only borrowed.' He doesn't quote my reply!

On 20 September, Steve went to Oslo. He had his eye on John Walker's world mile record, but the weather was so atrocious that night – windy, wet and 4 degrees Centigrade – that there weren't many people there. A local runner set a 55-second pace for the first lap but dropped out after 700 metres, and Steve was obliged to take the lead. Front-running was strange and uncongenial to him, and he was left to hammer it round as best he could for the rest of the race. In fact he ran the third lap quite speedily in 58.5 seconds and went through the bell in 2:53, the same as Walker during his 3:49.4 record. Then the appalling conditions and the pressures of front-running for so long on his own began to take their toll, and Steve only managed 59.8 seconds for the last quarter. According to reports, he finished while the second-placed man was still rounding the last bend, in a new British record of 3:52.8. Steve said 'Apart from shivering at the start, I found the track exceptionally hard, and with the pace-making going wrong so early there was no chance of a world record. After this experience I have no desire to run against the clock again. You had to be there really to appreciate how appalling the weather was and I regard this as one of my best efforts.'

He intended to finish the season there, but the IAAF pleaded with him to do the prestigiously sponsored Golden Mile in Tokyo. On paper the field looked quite strong, but most of the chaps had had enough of the season and weren't interested in fast times. There was a huge crowd of 60,000, and the race got under way with Henry Rono leading through two laps of 57.9 and 1:58. But then Henry dropped out, suffering from a mystery illness which debilitated him. Rod Dixon took over, with Steve lying second and Francis Gonzales third, but Dixon was weary too, and the pace dropped slowly down the drain. At 300 out Steve could wait no longer, and striding rather than sprinting towed a rapidly dis-integrating field home. He covered the last lap on about 80 per cent power, strolling in for 3:55.5. Gonzales was second in 3:57.3 and Graham Williamson, the second Briton in the race, was third in 3:59.2. It seemed a pretty strung-out affair and though the crowd obviously enjoyed themselves it was, as Steve said afterwards, a long way to go for a stroll.

7

AWOL in Nijmegen

Early in 1979, John Disley, the mountaineer and vice-chairman of the Sports Council, was awarded the CBE. In an interview which appeared in *Athletics Weekly*, on 3 March 1979, he was asked about his own athletic career as a steeplechaser and Olympic bronze-medallist in 1952, and how he thought athletes of yesteryear compared with those of today. He said, 'I think Ovett is the finest runner I have ever seen. I think he's the greatest runner that Britain has ever produced in terms of natural talent and range of ability. If I had to match some oldies against him it would be quite difficult. I would have to put Gordon Pirie there although if you look at the record book you won't find too much in Pirie's favour, apart from some very fast runs. Pirie was another Ovett, not perhaps so refined. It is that feeling of animal power Ovett has got. Herb Elliott had it, Pirie had it, Juantorena and Walker are in that bracket and Snell very close to it.'

Steve started 1979 ranked first in the UK both at 800 metres and the 1500 metres or mile, in recognition of which he had been voted BBC's Sports Personality of the Year that winter. He had had a fairly long rest after the European Games, so now he wasn't all that fit. There were just two small cross-country fixtures before the National, on 7 and 14 February, and in both races Matt won and Steve finished third. Matt is proud of the fact that to date he has more victories over Steve than Seb Coe. There are occasions when Steve wishes he could run a cross-country or road race just for enjoyment, drifting round like other runners without being expected to pull out all the stops, without being expected to win all the time. He does wish that occasionally.

The national cross-country championships were held at Luton on 3 March. For pretty well most of the nine miles, Steve and Tony were nip and tuck in seventh and eighth places, until Steve broke away just before the finish and passed Barry Smith with about 800 metres to go for sixth place. He finished 31 seconds behind the winner, Mike McLeod, though this was actually closer than the previous year, when he had come fourth. I think he was quite pleased with that run, because it had been achieved without the big build-up of the previous year and showed that perhaps results were obtainable without bulk mileage. He declined selection for the international championships in Limerick because he wasn't 100 per cent sure of his cross-country fitness, and on 1 April he ran in the Five Mills Race in Italy again and finished sixth behind Leon Schotts of Belgium. After a rough time in the middle stages when I thought he would drop back, he hung on to finish just 2 seconds behind Mike McLeod this time. He was improving. His next race was the Southern Road Relay, in which he ran, for Brighton and Hove AC, the fastest long stage, of $5\frac{1}{4}$ miles, in 23:47, making up 1:41 for his team despite his path being blocked at one stage by a crane.

Meanwhile the British Board had decided to form an elite squad of UK athletes, the better to help with their preparations for the Moscow Olympics, though the main objective appeared to be raising funds for them. Steve was dubious about belonging to this elite squad if by association it implied he was receiving Board sponsorship and he wanted it made clear to everyone that this was not the case. In fact the only advantage elite squad status would provide for Steve would be exemption from the Olympic Trials if he showed reasonable form prior to Moscow. As events were to demonstrate, it didn't exempt him from criticism for trying to prepare for the

Olympics in his own way.

Steve started the track season rather gently on 20 May by running in Eire in a place called Tullylease, where he won the 2000 metres in 5:20.8 from Frank Clement, two-tenths behind in second place. Next, Steve had a very leisurely 1500 metres win in the league race at Crystal Palace on 26 May, in 3:53.1. It was interesting from a training point of view that Bob Benn won the Inter-Counties 800 metres at Cwmbran a couple of days later with 1:51.4. He had moved up to 800 metres from 400, and he was obviously starting to show the benefits of running with Steve. By 9 June, Steve was feeling pretty fit himself. He ran in a league race at Enfield: it was a fine but gusty afternoon, and one of his Brighton team-mates, Barry Hawkins, wanted a fast time for the 1500 metres. Barry led the first lap and then Steve took over to finish with 3:40.8, a useful 1500 for so early in the season at a rather uninspiring meeting. Later the same afternoon he ran a 47.8-second leg in a 4 × 400 metres relay. Somebody else running fast early season was Sebastian. A week later, in the Northern championships at Stretford, Manchester, he clocked 1:46.3 for the 800 metres.

Much ado about Nijmegen

So far, the year had crept by without controversy. This happy state of affairs was to end on 23 June with a trip to Bremen, where Steve was to compete in a match against West Germany. Tony and I turned up at the airport around 11 a.m. Steve was already there, along with one or two other members of the team and Board treasurer, Marea Hartman. 'Where's everybody else?' we asked. It seemed the rest of the squad was at Crystal Palace. Because of the air-traffic controllers' dispute we weren't going to be able to get a flight out to Germany until late that afternoon. So there we were, stranded at Heathrow. Worse would be the mangling of all our travel arrangements in Germany; with no direct flights to Bremen we'd have to fly to Frankfurt or Düsseldorf and then make a long coach journey up to Bremen – an appalling prospect. Steve had an invitation to run in Nijmegen, Holland, on the Sunday, so he had a return air ticket from Heathrow to Holland. He approached Marea Hartman and asked if he might make his own way to Bremen via Holland on his air ticket. Then he could go back to Nijmegen, and come home on his own on Sunday or Monday. Marea thought it more sensible than hanging around Heathrow: at least it would mean one member of the team getting to bed at a reasonable hour. So off he went.

Eventually the rest of us arrived in Germany and after a horrendous four-hour journey by coach reached the hotel at about 1.30 in the morning. Steve had apparently already checked in and been asleep since around 9.30, so that was a relief. The rest of us, by the time we'd sorted out our rooms, turned in at 2 a.m. Next day was Steve's 1500 metres. It was a slow race; the first two laps, of 62.4 and 2:06.0, tried Thomas Wessinghage's patience and he took the lead for a 58 third lap, going through the bell in 3:04.2. Steve hung back a little way and with 300 metres to go he burst past, built up a big gap and strode home comfortably in 3:41.7, with a 52 last lap. Next morning Steve's mother, who was staying in an adjacent hotel, breakfasted with us and then Steve left for Nijmegen to run in this invitational 1500 metres. He won the race in the reasonable time of 3:37.7. Meanwhile, the rest of the team were running through the second day of the Bremen match before returning home.

I suspected all was not well on the Sunday, when every newsman in Bremen converged on me at the hotel. 'Where's Steve?' they growled ominously.

'He's gone to Nijmegen to run in the 1500 metres.'

'Why weren't we told?'

'He doesn't have to tell you his every move, surely.' They went away in a poisonous humour. They thought they had been done out of a record attempt or something and been hoodwinked into watching the second day of the Bremen match. Their imaginations fomented nastily. How come Ovett could go swanning off to Nijmegen? Did he have permission to go there? They contacted the board and somebody, presumably David Shaw, told then he would look into the matter very sternly, because he didn't think Steve *had* been given permission and therefore shouldn't have gone.

Returning home, we walked into the storm. David Shaw was talking in terms of banning Steve from competing in international races for some token period; it reached the stage of unpleasantness where Steve had to call in a solicitor. But really, when all the facts were examined, it was quite straightforward. Jos Hermans, the 10,000 metres runner, had organized a meeting in Nijmegen and had invited Steve to run. The board contacted me and said, 'We've had this invitation for Steve, but he's already agreed to run in Bremen. What do you think?' I referred them to Steve on the matter, and said he definitely intended to race in Bremen, and whether he wanted to do the Nijmegen meeting afterwards was up to him. Jos Hermans sent a letter to Steve's solicitor in which he explained that he'd consulted the board and was told Steve was committed to race in Bremen and probably wouldn't want to go to Holland, but that if he did, he could. Jos Hermans passed this information on to Steve and said that evidently it was OK for him to go if he wanted to. So Steve went. And when this had all been straightened out, David Shaw found himself in the unfortunate position of having to make a public apology to Steve through the newspapers, admitting that there had been a misunderstanding, that Steve hadn't transgressed at all and that no action would be taken against him.

The whole affair had dragged on for several days, and the threat of suspension hung over Steve like the sword of Damocles. He was due to run in Dublin on 10 July, but couldn't confirm with the organizers one way or the other because of this impending ban. It's pretty disconcerting when one moment you're told that you're part

147

of an elite squad that will smooth your path to Moscow and the next you're being treated like a miscreant for allegedly deserting the team to run in some unauthorized race. Yet at the very outset Steve had consulted Marea Hartman of the Board, and she seemed quite happy about the trip. I'm sure the whole affair was blown up out of all proportion by the press in their pique over missing Nijmegen. Steve felt that the whole affair was senseless and upon reflection realized that it was really a case of the media trying to tell the Board how to run its business.

One thing that niggled me personally was that the night before the Holland race, I sat up late talking to Tony, Steve's mother and Lynn Davies, the men's team manager, and Lynn had seemed very understanding about Steve's Nijmegen trip; he could see Steve was an individualist, going his own way in his racing plans, and looking back on his own days as an international athlete, Lynn was very sympathetic towards him. So you may imagine my astonishment to read, a few days later, that Lynn had apparently denounced Steve to the press for racing in Holland instead of supporting the team in Bremen on the second day. I have my doubts that Davies actually said these things on his own initiative; perhaps he was inveigled into making comments not entirely his own, but they certainly clashed with the views he expressed to us beforehand. There was no question of Steve 'deserting the team'. He had discharged his obligations by winning the 1500 metres for it. There was nothing else he could have done about other people's performances the following day. And as for *Seb Coe* criticizing him for deserting the lads – well, this invited the proverbial horse laugh. Coe wasn't even there, so he wasn't helping the team in any way whatsoever.

The Nijmegen row left a nasty taste in the mouth. Through no fault of his own, Steve had been threatened with suspension and had some pretty unsavoury things said about him. In the meantime, the team for the Europa Cup semifinal, in Mälmo, Sweden, had been selected; Steve had explained that he didn't wish to be considered for these cup fixtures in 1979. He wanted to train quietly in Britain, and not be involved in meetings lasting several days abroad. He was quite happy to do invitational races, travelling out one day and returning the next, but he wanted to avoid the Europa and World cups. The selectors picked Dave Moorcroft for the Europa Cup 1500 metres and he duly obliged, sprinting the last lap to win comfortably. Sebastian won the 800 metres in 1:46.7, lying back until the last 100 metres and then putting in a burst of acceleration. I came away thinking, 'He looks to have several seconds in hand. That's close to world record time if he goes flat out.' He was very, very fit.

On the second day Julian Goater ran in the 5000 metres and this was to give me another glimpse of behind-the-scenes wheeler-dealing in athletics. There had apparently been some serious discussion between the television outfit and certain members of the Board as to whether Julian should be asked to stand down for the 5000 metres, to give Dave Moorcroft the chance of a double. Julian had no intention of standing down: he was in good condition and he wanted to run. He came fourth in what turned out to be a tactical race, and I don't think anyone else would have placed higher. It seemed to us disquieting that television personnel, who are, after all, mere observers rather than authorities on athletics, should have attempted to persuade the Board to alter the composition of the team.

On 5 July in Oslo, Coe smashed the world 800 metres record with 1:42.33. It was a magnificent run. A Jamaican, Lennie Smith, set what seemed an extravagant pace to 400 metres before stepping off the track, and Coe forged on alone to break the record by a considerable margin. I couldn't understand why later, in his book, Seb should criticize Steve for having pacemakers in certain races and orchestrating his record attempts, when clearly many of Seb's record runs were paced – and this was a typical example. It was a superb run none the less and confirmed my suspicions in Mälmo. Shortly after this, an article appeared in the *Observer* by Chris Brasher, in which he suggested that Coe's rivals were frightened of him and moving up a distance to avoid Seb. Brasher quoted Peter Coe as saying, 'You can't go up a distance to get away from speed.... Bloody well go down and get yourself some speed!' The article didn't name Steve as one of these 'frightened rivals', but the implication was there.

A coach looks objectively at the requirements of an event–oxygen-debt tolerance, endurance, speed, tactical ability – and in order to be of best assistance to an athlete he may concentrate on one factor one year and another the next. (This is what I call my 'module system'!) But you can't isolate speed (or endurance or anything else) and say, 'This is the most important thing; we can neglect all the others.' As a coach you are trying to bring all these skills into coalescence, in one complete runner, irrespective of what his rivals may be doing at the time.

Steve's next race was in Dublin on 10 July. He ran a good 800 metres in 1:46.2, from Josef Plachy in second place, who ran 1:46.7. Steve took off with 200 metres to go and won quite easily. He decided at the last minute then to do the 1500 metres in the AAA championships at Crystal Place.

The heats went fairly smoothly on the Friday night, but the Saturday final was a strange business because Kevin Steere, better known as a 5000 metres cross-country runner, set off at an incredible rate, careering through the first lap in 56.5 seconds with a big gap behind him, and through lap two in 1:54.7 with an even bigger gap. At the end of lap 3 (in 2:55.8) he was starting to fade, but the crowd by this time were completely berserk at the prospect of either Steve moving through the field or this unknown 1500 metres runner hanging on to provide a major upset. In fact Kevin had shot his bolt on the early laps and towards the end he was pretty well legless, especially over the last 100 metres. Steve, who had been hanging behind Graham Williamson in third place, went to the front 200 metres from home and strode in quite comfortably to win in 3:39.1 from Williamson, in 3:39.3. Poor Kevin finished ninth in 3:45.2, a little slower than he'd managed in the heats. Steve waited for him to cross the line and immediately went over to put an arm round his shoulder and commiserate with him. They'd known each other since school cross-country championship days and Steve had a good idea what Kevin must be feeling: 'Here am I, with a chance to make a name for myself and what happens? I blow it on the last lousy couple of hundred metres.' Steve raised Kevin's arm in the air, as boxers do, to show Kevin was as much the winner that day as anybody: he was very brave in what he had attempted to do.

We were not exactly surprised next day, but somewhat bitter, to read press criticisms of Steve for allegedly belittling the efforts of the runners behind him. He had won very easily, while turning to look over his shoulder down the finishing straight. Nothing could have been further from Steve's mind than trying to belittle his rivals. It was more a case of the press trying to belittle Steve, nitpicking over his accomplishments, as usual. I'm sure Kevin Steere, had anyone taken the trouble to ask him, felt anything but 'infuriated' or 'belittled' by Steve that day. It goes without saying that Steve received little credit for winning the AAA 1500, though he had never failed to win a national title since 1970 (he won the 800 metres from 1974 to 1976 and in 1977 and 1978 he didn't compete).

Just before the AAA championship, Steve and I recorded a long interview on the track with the BBC. The Nijmegen affair was still festering in the backs of people's minds and the press seemed unable quite to give up the idea that Steve had in some way transgressed and deserved tough treatment. So Steve said, 'Come on, Harry, let's say something on television.' I rang David Coleman and asked if he could do an interview with Steve to uncover his side of the story. David did his job well and this was what Steve said on television:

I think it's only been my own sheer bloody-mindedness that's carried me through the past three weeks of arguing and bad organization of the governing bodies. Anyone else of, shall we say, lesser character, would have succumbed to the pressure put upon them a long time ago. In those three weeks I've done more political arguing than training, and that can't be good for an athlete.... I made my plans clear at the start of 1979: that I was low-keying the whole season. No big races. But the British press can't accept that.... The BAAB must understand that I've earned a break. I've run in four Europa Cup races and won all four, I've won the World Cup 1500 and the Golden Mile in Tokyo last year.... They must allow me to choose my own way of preparing for Moscow.... I don't like to have a loaded gun held up to my head and I will therefore be as bloody-minded as they are....

Steve did *not* say, as was reported afterwards, 'I'm an arrogant bastard! – he wouldn't dream of saying *that* on television. He said, 'If people think I'm arrogant for doing things my own way, then so be it, but I'll still do the same.' It was myself, not Steve, who said at the end, 'Don't forget, David, he's very patriotic. In fact if you go round to Harrington Villas and press the doorbell it rings Rule Britannia!' Apart from that, I didn't say very much; it was Steve's interview and I thought he put his point across rather well. It was absurd for the newspapers to suggest he'd received preferential treatment. He didn't deserve a reprimand because he hadn't done anything wrong. Some of the other lads had apparently raced abroad without permission, and they too were reprimanded by the Board only to have their reprimands withdrawn when it transpired that they had letters granting them official permission. So in fact the admin. came out of all this rather badly. It would have been far better had these matters been handled quietly between the administrators and the athletes themselves, without the intervention of the press, because this is the sort of material newsmen hunger for.

The ghost of Nijmegen evidently hadn't been quite laid to rest even after this, because *Athletics Weekly* then ran an article headlined, 'No Special Treatment for

Ovett' in which Jimmy Green again went maundering on about the subject, calling Steve's comments to David Coleman 'hogwash'. I don't know what the man wanted. Did he want Steve to be suspended for something he hadn't done? On the one hand there appeared to be the enlightened concept of an elite Olympic squad being encouraged to prepare for Moscow to their own best advantage, and on the other we were being warned, 'Fall into line! None of this individualist nonsense!' Jimmy Green referred to the threat of suspension hovering over Steve and said that he didn't understand how this put anybody under pressure. For a man who is supposed to be a senior coach to say this displays a singular lack of insight. If you tell a man he may lose his job, it puts him under pressure. If you tell a runner he may not be allowed to run, that he may lose the thing he loves, the thing he trains for, the mental and physical focus of all his efforts every day, it puts him under pressure. And anyone who doesn't understand this understands nothing about athletes.

Many readers wrote to *Athletics Weekly* complaining about Jimmy Green's article, and one who sprang to Steve's defence immediately was Matt Paterson. He wrote, 'I have been privileged to train with Steve Ovett for the past five years and I feel I know him better than most. Regardless of what the national press or your magazine say about Steve he is far from being arrogant and egotistical – in fact, in many ways, he is the complete opposite. . . . It seems to me that every person who writes an article for a paper or magazine seems to know exactly what to do when preparing for an Olympic Games – this is probably why we win very few gold medals! Leave Steve alone and let him prepare as he wants to.'

He had a fairly easy time in a league race at Hendon on 28 July: he ran 3:46.2 for 1500 metres and then a 47.3-second leg in a 4 × 400 metres relay. In the meantime the Europa Cup final had been held in Turin, and of course Seb was the star of the show, in great demand with the press and public and hounded

153

everywhere he went. As the team coach out there I reckon I did a good job keeping press people away from him; we had him warming up on an unobtrusive, shady spot, positioning ourselves between Seb and any photographers getting in the way and clearing the gents of cameramen whenever Seb wanted to go in there. So I don't think I showed any lack of attention towards Seb that day, and he won his 800 metres quite effortlessly in 1:47.3, beating Willi Wulbeck, the fellow who gave him such a shove in Helsinki in 1977.

On 15 August, a meeting began in Zürich in which Steve had been invited to run in the 1500 metres. A couple of days before the race, the promoter rang up to say Steve could no longer do the 1500. Sebastian had agreed to attempt a world record, but he wouldn't attempt it if Steve was in the race. He might not actually pull out, but he wouldn't go for the record. So the promoter wanted Steve out of the 1500, and he could either run in the 800 metres or the 5000 metres. Steve's response was, 'If I can't do what you invited me to do, I won't come at all.' So he didn't run in Zürich. On the night, things went perfectly for Seb and he broke the world record for 1500 metres with 3:32.1, his third world best of the season (after the 800 metres and the mile). I didn't see the race: I was playing in my team's annual cricket match in Watford.

Clock-watching

As for the Zürich 1500 metres, well, you might say, 'A race is a race. Why should Seb have objected to having Steve in the field? Surely the extra pressure would have made him go even faster.' But I know what Seb was thinking. A some stage the pace would give way and he would be left in front, pushing along after a world-record time, with Steve on his shoulder, perhaps, as he had been in Prague in the 800 metres; he would have come so close only to be passed by Steve at the finish and to have effectively set the pace for him instead. Generally speak-

ing, you go into a 1500 metres race either to win or to set
the record. It's very rare for the two to go together, the
tactics and the speed. Only in the ultimate races, the
finest races of all, does this ever happen. Now in reality it
may be unreasonable for a runner to take the attitude,
'I'm not going to make world-record pace for him,'
because in fact the best way for a front-runner *to* break
the record may be to make the running and burn the
others off. But it does seem to affect runners, this feeling
of resentment. Only an athlete who is 100 per cent sure of
himself, who knows beyond a doubt that he's faster than
anybody, is free from this fear of setting up the race for
somebody else.

I think Zürich was what triggered Steve off on his own
world-record bids. Anyone would be entitled to feel
aggrieved, after having been invited to do a specific race,
to be told, 'You can't do that, because so-and-so is doing
it. You'll have to do something else.' Steve wasn't exactly
a duffer at 1500 metres. With the crowds, and
performance-wise, he was still the equal of Seb, so why
should he be given this second-rate treatment? Quite
apart from the snub, a runner like Steve, for all his
prowess at outkicking his rivals, needs to know in his
own mind how he will handle a truly fast pace. Until he
does, there will always be a shadow of doubt. So rather
than leave it until Olympic year to find out, he felt that
despite what he's said about records, and racing against
the clock, he should go out and try his fitness now, and
see if he couldn't match some of these world times.

Steve ran a very fast 600 metres at Crystal Palace on
15 August, in 76 seconds. That's almost 50-second pace
for 400 metres all the way round. It showed he was in
good shape, and this was the start of a series of high-
intensity races such as he'd done before. Two days later
in Berlin he ran 3:54.1 for the mile, then came back to
Crystal Palace, where he had promised to run in a 4 ×
800 metres relay. It wasn't much of a race: Steve got
stuck in front and practically walked home in 1:49.8.
Immediately afterwards he went to Cologne, where he

ran a good 800 metres, beaten at the finish by James Robinson of the USA, who ran 1:44.8 to Steve's 1:45.0. He came back, did a few days' training and then, on 27 August, ran a fairly slow 800 metres at Crystal Palace, going at 200 out to win in 1:49.6; he followed this up with a fast leg in the 4 × 400 relay in 47 dead. Then, on 31 August in the Rotary Watches International Games, he had a go at the mile.

It was one of those rare evenings at Crystal Palace when the air was still. Pete Browne, Steve's 800 metres rival in the early days, did the pacemaking and romped through the first quarter in 55.9 seconds from Craig Masback, Wessinghage and Steve back in fourth. At 880 yards it was still Browne, pouring it on with 1:54.8 from Wessinghage and Steve in third place. Wessinghage took over now, and the pace slackened very slightly, the German still showing just ahead at the three-quarter mark in 2:52.7 but with Steve right on his shoulder. I thought Steve might have taken off at that point, but he waited until around 250 out then, without the usual distinct burst of acceleration in such a fast run, he hauled past the surging Wessinghage and ground it out down the straight for a winning time of 3:49.6. It was a new UK all-comers record, 0.6 outside the world record set by Coe in the Golden Mile. Wessinghage slogged in for 3:50.6 and second place. The race gave Steve the assurance he had sought – that he could indeed run a mile or 1500 metres at a consistently fast pace. His 1500 time was a personal best of 3:34. He hadn't lost a 1500 or mile race of any description, in fact, since May 1977. Only three men in history had broken 3:50 – Walker with 3:49.4, Seb with his world record 3:49, and now Steve. Ten men in the race broke 4 minutes, seven of them British. Steve was very proud of this race for, as he pointed out, the Crystal Palace track is notoriously slow, with a far from perfect surface. He agreed that he would have probably got the world record if he'd started his final drive a little earlier but he explained, 'In a race your first priority is to win, and at times you are reluctant to take the lead too soon in case the other kickers sit on you and you become the hunted instead of the hunter.'

Steve went to Brussels on 4 September for another out-and-out attempt on the clock, this time for the 1500 metres. Two local lads made the early pace, the first lap clipping by in 55.8 and the second faster still (1:53.0), with Steve running third with times of 55.9 and 1:53.1. At 800 metres the second hare dropped out and the powerful Wulbeck led through lap 3 for 2:50.7, though with the pace now slightly off the boil. At about the same point, 250 out, as earlier in the mile Steve struck out for home in a surging finish for 3:32.11. That was eight-hundredths of a second away from Seb's 3:32.03 record, and when you're as close as that to a world-record time, you know it's there for the taking. Steve said afterwards that he'd have liked the first two laps faster, and again there was a lull on lap 3, as there often is because the leaders are gathering themselves for the finish. Again Coe was an injured spectator, and did a lap of honour. Had Steve been just *one*-hundredth of a second faster, though, he would have been officially credited with 3:32.10 through rounding up, officially equalling the world record, Seb's 3:32.1. It's a matter of inches really: we're talking about running the last 200 metres maybe eight inches from the kerb compared with six inches. It's a fine line.

In spite of these record attempts, Steve still believed the most important thing was the battle of man against man on the track, the best man winning on the day. Because no matter who ran the fastest times for 800, or 1500, or the mile, the real race would be decided when the best runners met – and on the day, on the track, all that mattered would be who finished in front of whom. On these occasions runners are not worried about times; they are too busy trying to beat one another. Time, that abstract dimension, is of secondary importance. Steve was once asked, 'Are you not curious to find out whether you are the fastest miler who ever lived?' He replied, 'It doesn't really bother me. I know I'm good, but you can never say that because I run faster than Elliott or Ryun I'm a better miler than them. If I thought I was in the sport to be remembered I would probably go for these things but it doesn't worry me if everybody forgets about me in another two years. If I wanted to be remembered I would be on the image-building side of the sport, but I'm in the sport because I love running. It's what I do best – it's what I was born for.'*

I don't think I can sum it up better than that: it's what he does best, and really what results from it is very much secondary. A coach like myself, trying to produce satisfied athletes, finds with runners of this class that *knowing* is all-important. If an athlete knows, he is satisfied. Perhaps some unfortunate incident has occurred in the race, perhaps somebody tripped him up, perhaps he didn't pull out all the stops. But if he *knows* he could have gone faster, if he knows in his own mind that he could have beaten that fellow, he is satisfied. A coach doesn't have to reassure him. The athlete will usually come over and say, 'I could have won that,' or 'I could have gone faster.' I think a lot of runners are like Steve in that they seek this feeling of inner satisfaction. It can't, and shouldn't, be dragged out into the open.

A race is a reflection of many things: it reflects a runner's attitude and it reflects all the training *behind* that attitude, and all the hard work and agony that has honed the runner to his peak of fitness. The coach knows this, the runner knows it – and the press and public know nothing about it at all. The general public cannot possibly appreciate fully the excellence of a performance. We don't expect them to, because they haven't shared all the hassle and sweat that has gone into it. It isn't surprising that they don't understand the athlete's inner feelings about it. The press see themselves as mediators, trying to bridge the gap between the athlete's private feelings and the public. They nearly always ask the question of an athlete, 'What does it *feel* like?' They want

*Athletics Weekly, 14 April 1979.

to undergo the same experience that the successful runner undergoes. They want the public to share the experience. But it's impossible for them to do that. They can't get it on the cheap. You can't know what it's like unless you've gone through all the hardship beforehand. This is why athletes so often give inane answers, like 'over the moon'. What did it feel like to score that goal? What did it feel like when you breasted the tape? The classic answer, I suppose, must be, 'If you've got to ask, you'll never know.'

To understand the *in*significance sometimes of objective results, you could have been at Crystal Palace on 8 August. Steve was training there in the afternoon and he stayed on to watch the races in the Fire Brigade's Sports Meeting (they have invitational races; it isn't just for firemen). Steve asked if he might run in the 1000 metres and he won the first prize, which was a radio. That evening, in conjunction with the Fire Brigade meet there were some races for disabled people. Steve didn't want any publicity about it, and he was quite annoyed that it was turned into a 'story' later on, but he gave the radio to the slowest competitor in the 100 metres race for the blind. Steve had been given lots of prizes, and yet here was a fellow trying his hardest and finishing last. In Steve's eyes that was a far braver and more meritorious performance than his own in winning the 1000 metres. Shortly afterwards he was asked, how would he feel if he failed to win a medal in Moscow? 'I won't be bothered,' said Steve. 'I sometimes go to schools and see a lot of kids who can't run, can hardly walk, and, to me, to be blessed with the ability to run is enough. Olympic golds are secondary really. How can you worry about world records when some kids can't even walk? You can get too wrapped up in it, I think.'

Two days after Brussels, Steve went to Koblenz for what is virtually a local meeting of Thomas Wessinghage's club, and he set a new UK record of 2:16 for 1000 metres. Three days later he went up to Gateshead. He was very weary by this time and all he wanted was to go round the mile race and win it without being involved in any battles against the clock. He didn't respond much to the early pace, staying with a little group adrift of the leaders, and eventually Steve Cram took over the running and they reached the bell in 3:00.5. Cram was overtaken by Jim Espir, whom I'd been coaching since 1977, and Jim pressed on in front with around 250 to go, from Steve in second and McLeod at his shoulder. Just on the 200 mark, Steve eased past and did just enough down the finishing straight to beat Khalifa of the Sudan in 3:56.6. Poor Jim was tripped as they came off the last bend and missed his first sub-4-minute mile; Steve was simply relieved the race was over – he was pretty tired. Julian Goater won the 5000 metres that afternoon, outsprinting David Black – an amusing sight – and then Jo White, who'd been out for a year with a stress fracture of the ankle, won the mile emphatically in 4:34.3, second on the UK all-time list. Not a bad day.

Steve ended the season with a mile race in the Coca-Cola meeting at Crystal Palace, on 14 September. It was a typical Coke night – cold, very windy, and with scuds of rain coming across the track. Steve was to make one more attempt on the clock, though the conditions were against him and his opponents were tired. Pete Browne set the pace for the first quarter, in 55.8 seconds, and Graham Williamson, who'd just come home after winning the University Games in Mexico, was just behind in second with Steve third, in 56.1. Pete pushed it along on the second lap for 1:54.9, with Williamson on 1:55.3 and Steve 1:55.5, but now it was starting to look difficult, with Steve needing to run the second 880 yards in 1:53.5 to beat Seb's world record. Much depended on what Graham could do with the pace on the next lap. In fact he was shattered and having a job to keep going let alone scorch the earth, so just before the bell he gave way to Steve and dropped out ('My legs were dead'). Steve was left to run 450 to 500 metres on his own, and now the wind was howling and the rain bucketing down. He ended up with 3:55.3. Jim Espir, who'd fallen over at

Gateshead, got his sub-4-minutes: 3:58.0.

In November the elite squad was officially announced, and once again we stressed that Steve was receiving no Sports Aid Foundation grant. It was also announced that Steve and Seb were to be excused the Olympic trials, but that the others were not. The Board had effectively created an elite elite squad, because in the 1500 we had five 'elite' athletes with a good chance of making the Olympic final, and they couldn't very well *all* be excused. The other three, but not Seb and Steve, would have to run in the trials. In fact there was now an even tougher situation facing these people: with Steve and Seb already through for the 800 and 1500, there was only one place vacant.

So that was 1979: a year of consolidation, of cutting down mileage and running against the clock. Early on in the year, Steve had done an interesting interview with Mel Watman of *Athletics Weekly*, and Mel asked, 'How much time do you spend on average each day on training?' Steve said, 'Exactly the same as Matt, and you wouldn't say he was a full-time athlete, would you? About an hour and a half. I'm out at 7.30 a.m. and back at 8, and then I go out at night for another hour. That's all it is.' And in 1979, that's all it was. He also said, 'Harry's a great help, and a laugh. He sees me about once a month in the winter (now) and once a fortnight in the summer. If he sees me and says, "Oh God, you're looking a bit fat," or "You look as if you could do with some more speed work," then he's given me an objective viewpoint on certain things that maybe I've missed through training on my own with Matt. I talk races over with Harry and my parents and we generally discuss things. I'm trying to explain that there's nothing clear-cut with me; if anything I'm rather slap-happy about my sport.'*

In one respect his approach had become less casual. He'd shaved off his beard. In previous years he'd always

---

** *Athletics Weekly*, 14 April 1979.*

sported growths of different shapes and sizes, from a tiny tuft and pencil-line moustache to a bushy job with shoulder-length hair. To see some of those early shots of himself as the Bearded Wonder must make him cringe now. A beard, though, does mask that typically thin and drawn look of the runner. If you look at an athlete's features when he is very, very fit, there's not a spare ounce on him, and his face and neck become quite gaunt. In fact he doesn't look at all healthy. You'd never think he was eating prodigious meals and pushing back the frontiers of human ability.

8

Moscow

During the winter of 1979/80, a big training winter, there were new faces at our training sessions. Steve cut down on cross-country and Saturday races to step up his workload, and we were now meeting twice a week, with the added help and company of Bob Benn. On Wednesday nights we would get together at Crystal Palace and Bob and Steve would do a long, hard road run as well as some mobility exercises and sprinting indoors. On Saturday afternoons, after Steve's long morning run, we would all meet up, with perhaps Jim Espir along, and they would run 1000 metres repetitions on the grass circuit and do more sprints indoors. Another fresh face on these occasions was Rachel's. I first met her that winter: she would come to Crystal Palace and drink endless cups of tea while watching the swimmers, or watching us. I liked her immediately, not only because of the affection between her and Steve but because she wasn't overawed or silly and had a genuine respect for Steve's athletics and the part running played in his life. The pair of them had known each other for years before getting together; she was a model, having packed up high-jump and hurdling herself. It was mighty cold and miserable outside, but she would sit and watch the indoor sessions anyway.

Steve wasn't displeased to finish third in a cross-country race in Volpiano, Italy, on 12 January behind Nick Rose and Steve Kenyon (first and third finishers in the National 1980): all three were very fit. He ran the fastest short leg in the Southern Road Relay race on 12 April (14:52, 18 seconds inside the record) on Wimbledon Common. Meanwhile President Carter had urged the US Olympic Association to pull out of Moscow over Afghanistan, and Mrs Thatcher had advised the BOA to do likewise. On 15 March, though, the British Olympic Association announced that it would leave each event's personnel to decide for themselves. At the end of April Steve ran in a 4 × 400 metres relay for the Southern Counties at Crystal Palace, delaying his departure for a match in Texas to honour his commitment to the SCAAA. He ran 48.2, nothing special, but not bad on endurance training, and then he flew to Houston to run in a 3000 metres race on 3 May. He avoided heat prostration out there by hanging back and kicking on the last lap for 7:52.5, ahead of Steve Scott, who ran 7:53. Bob, who'd gone with Steve, ran 1:50.4 for 800 metres. Astonishingly, when this result appeared in *Athletics Weekly* it was followed elsewhere by a comment from Scott complaining Steve was 'ducking' him: 'He's very weird about who he runs against. He's just a talker.' Either an editorial oversight or else Scott was in some confusion himself.

Steve flew on to Kingston, Jamaica, next, but after a fifteen-hour hassle-filled journey he arrived shattered to find his 2000 metres had been cancelled. Feeling rather disgruntled he ran in the 1500; Bayi did most of the leading and Steve whipped past at 200 out for 3:38.7. Bayi finished in 3:39.5. Poor Bob, who was done in, ran 800 metres for 1:54. The following Wednesday at Crystal Palace I watched them both train hard to flush out their tiredness, and on the Saturday came Steve's first 800 metres of the year, in Cwmbran, Wales, in the England v. Hungary v. Netherlands v. Wales match. Steve, still jet-lagged, didn't do a great deal in the 800, waiting till about 50 out for his burst to finish in 1:49.2, which looks the way he felt. Second was the Hungarian, Paroczai, in 1:49.5. Steve ran a 400 metres in a relay afterwards but he was half asleep in that as well: some early nights

164

were called for.

Steve asked to run in the Bannister Mile on 21 May in the Philips Night of Athletics and he challenged Coe to race against him, which Coe refused to do. Seb ran in the 800 metres. I was amused to hear on the radio that Seb was asked, 'Does the name Steve Ovett crop up a lot in the Coe household?' To which he replied, 'Oh no, not at all; we never even discuss him.' Which is strange, because Seb's book is well larded with Steve's name. The Philips Night was pretty cold and there didn't seem much point in pushing too hard. Craig Masback led for much of the slow mile, reaching the bell in 3:05, and Steve waited until the final straight before kicking for 4:00.6 – a rare 4-minute-plus mile for him at Crystal Palace. His last lap was 55.2 seconds, though, and this was, counting heats, his fortieth consecutive mile/1500 metres victory in three years.

Three days later, Steve had a surprisingly hard run over 600 metres in Belfast, pushed almost to the last 50 metres by Paul Forbes of Scotland for 76.8 seconds. It promised 1:44 or 1:45 for 800 metres. Just as well, because on 26 May Seb ran 1:45.5 in the Inter-Counties at Birmingham. Steve's next run, on 4 June, was in Bergen, Norway along with Paul Forbes and Dave Warren in the 800 metres. Forbes led through 400 in 52.3 seconds but then faded, so Steve's winning time was 1:46.6, slower than we'd hoped. Coe the following night produced 1:45 dead for Loughborough v. the AAA, and on 7 June he won the Northern 800 metres championships in 1:44.7. The first of the Olympic trials, the UK championships, set the selectors some problems; Steve Cram fell over in the 1500 metres and Dave Moorcroft, who won the 1500 metres, was in two minds about doing 5000 or 1500 metres. Julian Goater *deserved* selection for a 5000 metres in 13.21:9 in Belgium. At the second Olympic trials in Edinburgh, though, Warren won his 800 metres place and Moorcroft, Nick Rose and Barry Smith were all chosen for the 5000 metres with times well off the standard, which had been set at 13:25.

Steve, denied the chance to race against Coe on the track, continued to do the next best thing and race against his times. On 27 June in the Talbot Games at Crystal Palace, he had a crack at the 1500 metres. It was quite cold and windy, but Steve was fit so it seemed worth trying. Bob would set the pace for a couple of laps, with Dave Warren having agreed to take over when Bob ran out of steam. Well, Bob did get up some steam certainly: 55 and 1:53, with Dave second and Steve running third (in 55.5 and 1:53.4) but when Dave took over, the pace billowed to 60, with Steve urging 'Faster!' Dave packed up at 1200 metres, after 2:53.6, and left Steve to front the wind himself for the last 300 metres, with Steve Cram, just nineteen, hanging on to him like grim death. A record was out of the question now, but Steve finished with a 3:53.3 – world record pace but for lap 3. Young Cram, who finished in 3:35.6, may have been led on by the press to venture that he thought Steve 'lacked zip' this year.

The Olympic team had been announced just before; Steve and Seb were both doubling up at 800 and 1500 metres. The British Olympic Association stressed that it would be a matter for the individual conscience whether the team members chose to go or not. The Thatcher administration were putting psychological pressure on them to withdraw, but almost everybody else was telling them, 'Go, and good luck to you!' Steve still had reservations. Like many of the lads he kept a wary eye out for events in Afghanistan and if there had been a bloody revolution like the one in Hungary, I'm sure they wouldn't have gone. Quite a few of them seriously considered Mrs Thatcher's boycott proposal, and were loath to be thought unpatriotic by flouting their Government's advice. On the other hand, as Steve and myself agreed, there was the Olympic movement itself to be considered. Just because it had been decided to stage these 1980 games in Moscow didn't alter the historic concept behind the Olympics, and no one had ever queried the moral credentials of the host countries before, or asked whether *their* regimes were cruel or oppressive.

About bloody time

Oslo is a fairly small town, tucked away on the Norwegian fjörds, but the Bislett Games are always very special, mainly because of the work of two promoters, Arne Haukvik and Svein Arne Hansen. These two, with Britain's Andy Norman, bring together a wealth of talent for their event in Bislett stadium. For days before the media are full of it, streamers flutter across the streets and everyone gets very excited. An hour or so before the start you can stand outside the stadium gates and see people queuing up to buy tickets from touts at inflated prices, as though it were the Cup Final. All over town the message goes out: 'The Bislett games are on!' If you've never been before, you're staggered because it's only a small stadium and the spectators in the front row can actually lean out and touch the runners on the outside lanes: the front barrier forms the outside of the track. There's a tremendous hubbub when you walk in, and this gets louder as Arne Haukvik goes out there to stir them up a bit more. There's usually a New Orleans jazz band playing, and it's a razzmatazz occasion.

The athletics themselves are high class. There have been forty world records set in this stadium since 1924, yet the track is quite worn, with bare patches here and there, and there are only six lanes. On 1 July, Steve was going to run the mile. Dave Warren said he would set the pace as a favour to Andy Norman, who'd found Dave a pacemaker for his personal best 1:46.2 800 metres in Porsgrunn just before. There was certainly no coercion, as has been suggested in Seb's book. The weather all day had been miserable, but this gave way to a super night, warm and calm. It began with Seb collecting his fourth world record, by breaking Rick Wohlhuter's six-year-old 1000 metres time. The early pacemaker was a chap called Mike Solomon, who shot through 400 in 50.1 with

Seb' lying third, in 51 seconds. He dropped out and another American by the name of Casselman took over, giving way at last to Seb, who was chased home hard by Wulbeck for a world record of 2:13.4. So the crowd were already buzzing; Bislett was living up to its reputation.

There's a little warm-up track just behind the stadium, a curved cinder path about 150 metres long, and all you can do is jog on it to avoid bumping into other people. As soon as the athletes set foot in the arena the crowd go wild, and when Steve popped his head out, they were in tumult. They were ready, Steve was ready, Dave Warren was ready, so off they went. Dave made perfect 55.5-second pace for lap 1, with Steve tucked behind in second and Cram and Williamson running fourth and fifth, bent on the one remaining Olympic place. Warren took them through lap 2 in 1:53.5, with Steve on 1:53.8 and the rest dropping back including Cram, in unknown country with 1:54.2. At 800 metres Steve was comfortably inside Coe's world record pace with 1:55.3, and with Dave starting to fade just after the bell, Steve decided to move. At 900 metres, all alone in his tatty Russian vest, he struck out for the long haul home. He reached the $\frac{3}{4}$ mile in 2:51, 2.4 seconds inside Coe's pace, covering the traditionally slow third quarter in 57.2, pushing harder than normal to ensure his time on this lap didn't let him down. But there was still a hell of a way to go. The crowd by this time were quite demented, banging with their fists on the metal advertising signs and clapping to the cadence of his stride; Steve plugged on and on, his legs wobbling slightly, past the 1500 metres mark in 3:32.7 (inside Coe's 3:32.8), his legs going, through the 200 from home, clap clap, bang bang, wobble wobble, pounding down the straight, to breast the tape inside world-record time.

At least, I'd got my watch on it and it seemed to be inside. Supposing I was being optimistic! There was a quick message over the loudspeakers in Norwegian and they seemed to be saying Steve had *equalled* the record. 'Oh no,' I thought, 'spare us that.' But then, a few moments later, came the announcement. The electronic timing device had broken down; on three official digital watches the time was 3:48.63; 3:48.79; 3:48.81, giving (not very generously) 3:48.8! Uproar in the stadium. A new world record for the mile. Steve had knocked two-tenths off Coe's time, and though I may be biased I suspected that if there had been some opposition over the last two laps there were another couple of seconds there somewhere. Running on his own was not Steve's style at all, though I'm sure a lot of his fatigue on the last lap was due to pushing so hard on the third. Steve Cram was second a long way behind, with a superb 3:53.8, which virtually clinched his Olympic place, and Graham Williamson, not himself that night, pulled his act together on the last lap for 3:56.4. Steve's splits, for the record, were 55.7, 1:53.8, 2:51 dead, 3:48.8 (55.7, 58.1, 57.2, 57.8 for the laps). He was quoted as saying, 'It tasted terrific!' He was also quoted as saying, 'About bloody time!' In fact Steve had said neither, but if writers are short of actual quotes then why not invent a couple? However it *was* about time he took this record as he had been capable of it for some time. He'd had a few goes by then, both at the end of the 1979 season and at Crystal Palace a few days before, and he was only the fifth Briton to hold the mile record, after Wooderson, Bannister, Ibbotson and Coe, because for a long period the mile wasn't very popular in Europe outside Scandinavia. Steve was still full of vim warming down on the cinder path; we did a few strides and he was running on air. His dad had come to Oslo to watch and he'd been sitting in the front row; it's not often he's able to see Steve race abroad and it was nice that he should have been there on this occasion. He was speechless at the finish.

Steve was pleased – in fact 'satisfied' would be a better word as this is what an athlete is striving for: to be satisfied with his performance. Once again he'd done what he'd set out to do and this is where his greatest satisfaction comes from – be it winning races or breaking world records. He also takes pride in running a whole series of high-level performances rather than the occasional fast time which punctuates a relatively low-key period. He thinks that maybe at times he races too often against high-quality opposition and his rivals know what to expect. Once Steve's season gets under way it's hard races all the time.

Steve followed up his mile record with a 1:48.2 800 metres in a meeting in the old traditional stadium at Gothenburg, just two days later. It was a very windy evening and I remember it clearly. It was pretty obvious that Steve wasn't going to push very hard into that wind, and he just waited until the last 100 metres and sprinted home ahead of Walker. That was 3 July. On 6 July he did a favour for me, and came to Gosling Stadium in Welwyn Garden City to help celebrate its twenty-fifth anniversary. He ran in the 3000 metres, striding gently through to dead-heat with Jim Espir in 8:24.6. The crowd enjoyed it enormously, just seeing him drift round. He stayed on afterwards with Rachel for a couple of hours, and the three of us wandered over to the nearby fairground where they had a couple of goes on the dive bomber. I gave up easily and left them to it; a fellow came over to me with a concerned expression and said, 'Is he allowed to do that sort of thing?' I said, 'He's human, isn't he?'

Steve was in good form, and the way to keep him so was to give him races. His training was going splendidly. Doing one of our speciality sessions at Crystal Palace – 300 metres fast, 30 seconds rest, then 200 metres fast, repeated four times with five-minute intervals – I thought what a pleasure it was to watch him moving so beautifully. Poor Bob was having a job to stay anywhere near him. Since he was in such good shape, it seemed logical to stage another world record attempt. He chose 1500 metres for the distance, and Bislett for the stadium. So on 15 July he was back in Oslo.

The atmosphere was good, the conditions were right and the field was strong, including several of the best men in the world who, because of national boycotts,

170

would not be running in the Olympics – Scott, Walker, Wessinghage and Lacey. If these fellows had anything to prove, here was their chance to prove it. Steve Scott in particular would have the opportunity to avenge himself on somebody who had allegedly been 'ducking' him continuously.

Chris Sly, from England, set 58.8 pace for the first 400 metres, which was a bit slow, and then Scott took over on the second lap for 1:53.6 at 800, which was just the opposite, with Steve in close attendance and Walker and Lacey just behind Steve. Scott, intent on winning rather than pacemaking, kept the lead on lap 3 and went through 1200 metres in 2:50.6, 1.1 seconds off Seb's world-record pace but within striking distance. Because this was a genuine race and Scott and the others were going to give him trouble if they could, Steve waited until the 200 from home mark, conserving his finish. Wessinghage in particular was going to challenge and, record or no record, Steve meant to beat these people. So at 200 out, away he went, a little late from the stopwatch point of view, and with his usual explosion of speed opened up a sizeable gap. Force of habit perhaps, but he then seemed to forget about running every step as though it were his last, and waved as he came easing down the last 50 metres. His time was 3:32.09, which rounded up to equal officially Coe's world record of 3:32.1. Steve said, 'I can go faster,' and he told David Barnes, 'It frightens me to death sometimes: it's unnerving to think that I equalled the world record and I was only jogging for two or three laps. I wasn't even trying. I could finish athletics without ever knowing what my real potential is, I'm so lazy!'. Steve Scott said nothing at all, having trailed home seventh; Thomas Wessinghage, who finished second in 3:33.16, said, 'Never have I seen running like that. Never. A year ago I felt we were starting to run close to Steve. I sensed he was human after all. Now I know I was wrong.' Perhaps poor Thomas thought he was a Martian.

171

The Moscow Olympics

I went out to the Olympic village in Moscow with the first official British party; Steve followed in the second a couple of days later. Thanks mainly to the enlightened approach of our new coaching director, Frank Dick, everything was very different from 1976, when I was *persona non grata*. Frank ensured, as common sense dictated, that the national event coaches would be appointed for the games, and also that personal coaches of certain members of the elite squad would be given full accreditation. As I wore both hats, Frank was good enough to let me choose my status, to decide either to concentrate on Steve or look after all the middle-distance lads. I said I'd be happy to do my normal job as event coach. We arrived in Moscow expecting the worst, but the village was a pleasant surprise and much better than that in Prague. The facilities were good and so were the restaurant and living conditions. We had a self-contained flat in the British block, with a room for Ron Holman (our long-distance event coach) and myself and a single room for Steve when he arrived. The weather was so nippy when we first got there that Ron and I snatched the blankets off Steve's bed, but by the time he turned up it was hot and humid.

We met Steve at the airport in the official bus, with photographers fighting hammer and tongs to get on board. Not content with this, and being warded off by the security staff, they then found it necessary to drive their cars alongside the bus and hang out of their car windows trying to take pictures of Steve sitting in the official vehicle as it went along. We reached the village without mishap, and Steve settled into our little flat very quickly. There were no problems with press people wandering in and out. If you wished, you could give interviews all day long, for the journalists would congregate on a patio outside the main gate, drinking coffee and grabbing passing athletes. We were staggered to read the occasional English newspaper report back

172

home, in which Moscow was described as the 'deserted city', because we thought the conditions on the whole were quite normal. There were obviously fellows in the village whose job it was to check passes, and if you didn't have a pass you didn't get in. If you *were* in, you didn't get out. But most of these officials were just young soldiers following instructions, so you accepted it. There was a little bus that did a circuit round the village, and if you moved away from the bus stop and leaned on the fence while you were waiting, a soldier would come up straight away and move you back again.

My first coaching event was the 800 metres; I was pleased to help Dave Warren before his races and then I went over to check that Seb had everything he needed, such as a list of starters. He said, 'My father's here, so I'm quite happy; I won't be bothering you at all.' I was surprised that he had agreed to a massive press reception: there must have been several hundred there. David Shaw thought these receptions would help the athletes and 'take a weight off their shoulders'. I thought just the opposite, and told him to forget about it as far as Steve was concerned. Steve kept a low profile in the village. As a matter of fact, he lurked about in a sunhat and dark glasses, but people still seemed to recognize the pair of us. Matt used to make the long journey out from his hotel in the middle of Moscow in order to meet Steve for his usual morning run, and it was really valuable for Steve to be able to keep to his normal routine.

The 800 metres heats went very easily. Steve won the first in 1:49.4, and he didn't have to do much because the first three in each heat plus the three fastest losers were going through – practically everybody. Seb won the fourth heat in 1:48.5, and Dave qualified in the last, second in 1:49.9 behind a dangerous-looking Marajo of France. Dave was to beat him in the semi. The semifinals themselves went swimmingly, considering Steve was ranked thirteenth coming into these games, behind Seb first and Dave seventh. Steve won his race, from world-ranked number two Busse of East Germany, in a comfortable 1:46.6. The other semi was won by Seb, in 1:46.7, striding along beside Wagenknecht, who finished with the same time, looking far less relaxed. The second semifinal was won by Kirov of the USSR in 1:46.6 with Dave Warren, who had the race of his life, second in 1:47.2. The European Champion Beyer placed fourth in 1:47.6 – he was knocked out. Steve and I had a long chat with Dave after the first round because Dave asked, 'What do I do now?' We suggested that he try to break away from the bell. 'Whatever you decide on,' said Steve, 'don't change your mind when you get there.' Dave didn't change his mind, did a lot of hard running just after the bell – and he got through.

During the heats and semis, Steve's routine had been to get up at around 10 a.m., go for an easy jog (it was very hot) round the roads for fifteen to twenty minutes, come back, shower, have breakfast around noon and then loaf about, play cards, lie down for a couple of hours' cat-nap, then get ready to go to the stadium. The late breakfast was a sort of brunch, so he wouldn't eat anything between then and the race in late afternoon, other than perhaps some biscuits with his tea. I don't think people realize what havoc major games play with an athlete's insides, because his stomach is churned up anyway, and then he has this rather disorderly eating routine.

The line-up for the 800 metres final was to be, from the inside, Nikolay Kirov (with a best of 1:45.6), Steve (1:44.1), Agberto Guimaraes (1:46.0), Detlef Wagenknecht (1:45.9), Dave Warren (1:46.2), Jose Marajo (1:43.9), Andreas Busse (1:44.8), and Seb (1:42.4). Though it was suggested that the East Germans might run as a team, I didn't believe it for a moment. The two younger boys, Wagenknecht and Busse, with whom you can always have a laugh and a joke, are quite different from Beyer; they're coached by a different man and they've always seemed much more westernized in their approach – whereas you could never speak to either Beyer or Straub. I couldn't see the two younger lads

174

running as a team, and I wouldn't be surprised if they were quite pleased to see Beyer knocked out. The lanes were a relief: a good draw, I thought, for all three Britons. Steve's lane 2 suited him because he was obviously going to play his waiting game and let the others make the pace before choosing his moment to kick. He could drop to the inside very quickly from lane 2. For Dave, 5 wasn't too bad either, and for Seb – who at least at the start would probably want to clear out and push the pace, perhaps tucking in a little later – lane 8 was a good draw as well. Maybe he wouldn't want to front-run it from the start as he had in the European, but he'd probably want to see himself out of trouble and ensure a fast pace before letting somebody else do the work.

The gun went – and the start was most peculiar. It appeared all eight had the same idea: 'I'm not taking the lead.' They broke after 130 metres, and if ever there was a case for having the whole race in lanes it was then, because all eight runners just piled up on top of one another, pushing and shoving, and anyone incapable of looking after himself was clearly going to end up flat on his face before the race was a quarter old. Guimaraes, from Brazil, was manhandled to the front, with Kirov following him. Steve said it was 'nearly a nightmare' here, because he took a knock and almost fell during the general hysteria. ('It was like a boxing match out there. Everyone was panicking because they weren't in the right position.') He seemed to be in the middle of a maelstrom of arms and legs and he decided, 'OK, I can't stay here,' and made an expedient exit. And for a little while he was in and out of position like that. Seb had started slower but steered clear of the mêlée by going to the rear and Steve, for all the pushing and shoving, ended up behind him.

It should really have helped Seb's cause, because he had had a smoother passage than Steve, who found himself seventh quite by accident, whereas Seb was probably running sixth by design. The pair of them were thereabouts for much of the race, though there were no more than three or four metres separating the field. About 40 metres from the bell, Steve was hemmed in again, so he tried to nip between the 6 feet 4 inch Wagenknecht and Kirov. The East German, who had run against Steve before, sensed his plan and closed the gap, so at the bell Steve still had problems. Guimaraes was still leading, poodling round in 54.55 from Warren and Wagenknecht. Dave had worked to the front because he was going to try the manoeuvre that worked for him in the semis, and the big East German was on his shoulder. Steve was sixth; Coe, unimpeded, was dead last. 'Right,' I thought. 'This is where Seb goes into action.'

But he didn't. Soon after the bell, Dave rushed to the front and tried to break away, but this was no semifinal and all the chips were down. Everybody went with him, with Kirov the foremost of them. Steve, sensing something afoot, followed Kirov. Seb still didn't move. 'He must be confident,' I thought. The race was three-quarters over. Just before the 600-metre mark, Kirov took the lead and Steve went with him. Dave was fading; Seb was still only fifth, 10 metres down and with a lot to do. Somewhere before the finishing straight, he was going to have to put in a burst, and that wouldn't leave him much for the last 50 metres. Seb might still have been OK had Kirov kept the lead and Steve waited, but approaching the final straight Steve drew level with Kirov, and then opened up very hard indeed. A big gap yawned and I turned my back because I simply couldn't watch: it was too good to be true that Steve should win an Olympic title so easily. 'Tell me when he's won,' I said to Ron Holman, and seconds later I heard, 'He's there.' I watched the immediate playback on the huge screen at the end of the stadium; from the side I could see Seb's desperate burst all the way down the straight, closing a few metres and then making no further impression, and I knew Steve was the better man on the day. Steve later said, 'Harry told me once I hit the front to keep running till I hit the wall at the end of the stadium.'

Steve's face, when he turned round, said it all. He'd waited since Montreal for this darned race, and he hadn't even had time to wave, so now he wrote in the air with his finger, 'I L Y'. It was a message to Rachel back home watching on television, and it didn't take too much imagination to work out what the letters stood for. The race had been won the way Steve likes to win; OK, it was a bit rough at times, but it had bursts, it had lulls, it had tactics, and everything to satisfy the 800 metres competitor in him. It even had intrigue. Afterwards, Dave Warren told me that while he was warming up he was approached by a well-known newspaper correspondent who said, 'I've heard rumours, Dave, that you and Steve may have come to an arrangement as to the way to run this race. If that's the case, I know somebody who would be particularly interested in making it worth *your* while to just run your normal race.' Dave was amazed, and also angry. 'You've got one hell of a nerve suggesting that I'm going to do anything *else* in an Olympic final!' he said. He was still quite upset when he told us the story.

I didn't see Steve for some time after the 800 metres final; he was in the dressing-room with towels over him and then he was swept away by the press and TV people – and this was one occasion when he couldn't really avoid them. He told Adrian Metcalfe on ITV, 'If anyone was guilty of doing more than their fair share of pushing, it was probably me, but I honestly believe that everyone ran a fair race. People were wearing half-inch spikes and if anyone gets close to you, you fend them off because they are dangerous.' It didn't immediately sink in that he was Olympic champion, but he told a reporter afterwards, 'The emotion came out of me in the dressing-room. I was burning up. I was so hot I had towels draped all over me.' The heat and humidity may have had something to do with it, but there was bound to be a reaction after four years of wanting to do this very thing. In fact he had won here in the same time as he'd recorded in fifth place in Montreal – 1:45.4 – so the wheel had come full circle.

Steve says that he sensed with 100 metres to go that he

was going to win, as he couldn't hear anyone breathing hard or see any movements out of the corner of his eye. Maybe this is why we never see the 800 metres replayed on TV, though we often see the finish of the 1500 metres – the close-up camera would have only one runner in the frame.

He went to see his parents at their hotel, and Ron and I jumped on the village bus and went back to our flat. A message arrived that Steve and his mum and dad had gone to a restaurant, and then Ron told me, 'You'd better have a look on your pillow, Harry.' I'll never forget what I saw. There on my pillow was a rough old scrap of paper, and on it Steve had written, 'Tiger! I hope you're as proud of me as I am of you. – Steve.' Ron looked at me and I looked at Ron, and both of us were pretty close to tears. Ron said, 'I hope somebody'll do that to me one day.' I couldn't speak, but really that little old bit of paper is probably the most valuable thing I've ever had out of athletics.

Steve was obviously having a little celebration with his parents, so Ron and I had a couple of beers and turned in early. We were woken up at 2 a.m. by a tall, exuberant person shouting, 'Wake up! Wake up! it's the Olympic champion come to say hallo!' So we had another celebratory drink, either very late or very early, and that's how we finished off the 800 metres final day.

We didn't see any of the newspaper reports till we got back to London. One or two columnists thought that Steve was a 'street-fighter', to use Ian Wooldridge's expression, and that he should have been disqualified for pushing – which simply shows how little these particular journalists know about 800 metres running. Seb sums it up succinctly in his book when he says that all the media people wanted him to win, because of Steve's refusal to cooperate with them. They must have been mighty sick to see the finish of the race, and they were clutching at straws even more desperately than usual to find fault with Steve. They couldn't simply say, 'A Briton has won us the Olympic 800 metres; what good news,' or anything like that. I really can't comment on what happened to Seb, who apparently said, 'It was a mental blackout. I chose this day of all days to run the worst race of my life, and I can't even explain why.' What did astound me, though, was that extraordinary outburst by Percy Coe in which he criticized Seb and called him stupid, adding, 'First is first, and second is nowhere.' I never understood it then, and I don't now.

What passes between a coach and his athlete is private (the more so, one would have thought, if they are father and son) and doesn't usually go via the press. The end doesn't justify the means. If in order to get an athlete to win, you have to leave scars on him afterwards, I don't think it's justified. I can understand the tremendous disappointment Seb's father must have felt, and he may have been led to comment in that frame of mind by the press; this is why it's always wiser to reserve comment immediately after a race. In his book, Seb surprises me somewhat when he says that on the podium he didn't know whether to shake hands with Steve or not, because normally you do it automatically. But then I suppose you do odd things in the flood of strange feelings after a race. That's why I think it's as well to get away and be private on these occasions, and Seb apparently broke down and wept outside the stadium.

After Seb's defeat in the 800 metres Chris Brasher and John Walker sent him a letter saying they were rooting for him in the 1500 metres, and dropping a few handy hints as to how he might win it. I can't imagine Brasher doing as much for Steve if Seb had won. It seemed as though the pair of them thought Steve winning both races would signal the end of British athletics. It wasn't right for Steve to win both – Seb must win one; so they were plotting ways and means of achieving this equitable outcome. At the same time there were all these statements coming from Seb's father, such as, 'If he loses this one they can bury him.' Ovett had won; life was at an end, people were being buried. It *had* come to a sorry pass!

While we were waiting at the warm-up track for the 1500 metres heats, Ron Holman and I had a chat with the two young East Germans, Andreas Busse and Detlef Wagenknecht, who congratulated me on Steve's 800 metres win. Busse said to us, 'Ovett is sportsman – he always talks to us and have ze joke. Coe is not sportsman. He is as you say, "stuck-up".' I thought to myself, how many of our pressmen, who are always on the lookout for quotes, would have printed this little gem?

The first round of the 1500 metres was four days later, and I think Steve would have much preferred to have continued his campaign while he was on a high note and Seb was obviously on a very low one. That respite allowed Seb to pull himself together and Steve to relax and go slightly off the boil about achieving the first double since Snell in Tokyo in 1964. There was bound to be an anticlimax anyway after fulfilling a four-year dream, and this was exacerbated by loafing about for four days in boiling heat. In my view, it was the first round of the 1500 metres that played the major part in ruining his chance of victory in the final. The first four finishers in the four heats plus two fastest losers would go through to the semis. Steve was drawn in heat 4, where the runners would know the preceding results and adjust their tactics accordingly, running desperado times and suchlike. It was Balcha, from Ethiopia, who took off and ran the first lap in around 56 and the 800 in 1:55. And when this happens in heat 4, because of the uncertainty over tactics everybody goes with the leader. Straub took over and pushed it along, and then Steve moved up on the last lap for 3:36.8 – very fast (the fastest in the whole competition and faster than even the final) and on a belting hot day. Afterwards Steve told me, 'Well, that's absolutely shattered me, that. I don't know how I'm going to recover'. He'd been expecting a fairly easy run with a fast finish. The preceding heats were quite different and indeed leisurely. Steve Cram got through heat 1 by the skin of his teeth as a fastest loser, and I gave him a lecture on concentration. Seb led most of the way in heat 3 and dead-heated with Fontanella of Italy in 3:40.1.

The next day, semifinal day, was slightly cooler. There was little pressure anyway because the first four and the fastest loser would all go through. Steve ran in the first semi, and the pace was sluggish. He took the lead rounding the last bend and produced a 52.9 final lap to win very comfortably in 3:43.1, including a wave. Steve Cram was fourth with 3:46.6. The second semi was faster. Seb led from a long way out and held off Straub down the straight, although they both clocked 3:39.4. The next day was the final. Steve saw no reason to change his usual tactics: sit in and go when you fancy. The heats and the semis hadn't given very much away. The two danger men were obviously going to be Seb and Straub. Steve had run against all the others without difficulty. We went down to the stadium on the bus, Steve, myself and Steve Cram. Seb had evidently gone in a car with his father. I had my doubts that Steve was 100 per cent ready for this: he said he felt very tired and in the dressing-room he was very conscious of the heat. But I still thought there would be enough left in him to win; I couldn't possibly have forecast the way the race would be run – a very strange race indeed.

It set off looking like a typical big games 1500 metres final: fairly slow, with everything counting on a fast last lap. The first lap seemed to play into Steve's hands. Coe and the formidable Jurgen Straub went out in front of a reluctant pack. They strolled along side by side, and at the end of lap 1 Straub had edged into the lead with 61.6. Steve was back in fifth place but only two-tenths off the pace, with the pack in concertina formation, though without the pushing and shoving of the 800 metres because of this leisurely pace. Then, even better for Steve, and even worse for the spectators, the second lap got slower still – 63.3, with Straub in front, a stride from Coe, and with Steve a close third. Straub had obviously gone into the race with a plan, and as they came to the last 800 metres, we saw what it was. Bowing his head,

Straub took off very, very hard at the start of the longest Olympic finishing sprint ever, bent on dropping Coe and Ovett.

Seb responded very quickly and went after him; Steve was obliged to extricate himself from a tangle, but tucked in behind Seb. At the end of the third lap the pace had picked up to 2:59.1, which meant Straub had rocketed through it in 54.2, a fair finishing speed. Steve was 0.6 adrift, in 2:59.7, so he had his work cut out on lap 4 to even get on terms with Straub, and the German was still going like the clappers round the back straight. It looked for an instant as though he might falter, but no, and by now you'd have said that with any normal opposition he'd have done enough to win. At 200 out he was four or five yards clear of Seb, with Steve another couple of yards down. It was starting to look difficult; ideally Steve would want to be on somebody's shoulder, so as to explode past and make his kick decisive, but here he would have to kick to close up, then kick again to get away. As they rounded the turn, Steve began the first burst, which immediately telegraphed to Seb to clear out. With a glance over his shoulder, Seb sized up the situation, drew level with Straub, and went for home – with the result that Steve narrowed the first gap only to find another opening out before him, and no rest in between. Certain journalists perceived what they thought was a 'double kick' from Coe. Runners don't think of it like that: you just go as hard as you can, and then you go a little bit harder. Eager athletics writers might be able to spot five or six kicks with a keen eye. Seb was away past Straub, and Steve, who had all his normal finish pulled out of him, couldn't quite close the gap on the German who'd never beaten him before. Coe won probably the finest race of his life in 3:38.4; Straub was second in 3:38.8, Steve third in 3:39.0.

He wandered about looking a bit lost at the end, but then quickly went over to congratulate Seb and Straub. Steve's attitude as they stood on the rostrum to receive their medals may have won him more friends than he ever made by running. He took the defeat marvellously well and he told David Barnes afterwards, 'I felt no despair. That's not for me. I'm proud of my bronze as I am of my gold because I did my best. It will be just as well displayed at home. I'm not bristling for revenge against Seb. If we keep trying to find out who is best, we'll lose the feeling for the sport. I never dreamed I'd be an Olympic champion so there should be no sadness. I'm not just putting on a brave face. There were a lot of athletes behind Seb and I who didn't get medals. To me they're not nobodies. I said Seb was a great runner after I'd beaten him in the 800 metres. Now he's proved it.' Steve was also quick to point out the part that Straub had played in the event and that his efforts had been largely missed by the press. Not only had he determined the way the final was run but he had also been largely responsible for the very fast pace in Steve's heat. Steve was satisfied; he had, as he said, done his best. There was no single reason why he lost: fatigue after the first heat may have been very important; there was the slight lack of motivation, the extra pressure of the double, and a small error of judgement in his positioning on the third lap. Any one of those he could probably have got away with, but added together, they were too much.

Steve's comment about his lack of motivation was, 'I'd climbed Everest once, had come down, and then was required to go back up again. It just didn't have the same importance the second time. Don't forget the 1500 metres was athletics life or death for Seb – I was already Olympic champion.' No doubt Seb raced like a man running for his life ... and his actions immediately after the race were like those of a man possessed. He quickly forgot his often-expressed dislike of any extravagant gestures of pleasure at winning.

Steve put his arm round Seb's shoulder and there were mutual compliments, but there will never be that much socializing between too such close rivals. Steve wishes we could be more like the Finns here ('they would love us both for different reasons') but you can't expect *bonhomie*

183

between the two of them, not in a contact sport like middle-distance running. However much respect they may have for each other's ability, they still want most of all to beat each other; they are still looking for weaknesses. And I think, particularly on Steve's side, there will always be a natural resentment at the way he has been cast by the press as a foil for Seb's shining virtue – the baddie set against the goodie. The courteous, co-operative, exemplary Seb and the surly, self-opinionated, 'street-fighting' Ovett; week in, week out, the story does begin to pall. Even the pictures seemed to be carefully chosen to highlight the smiling of the one, and the snarling and teeth-gritting of the other. It must have come as a shock to everyone concerned, to think the villain of the piece could behave so graciously in Prague and Moscow (whilst the hero was less than generous in defeat) and that perhaps Steve was natural and thoughtful and decent after all..

The media, in particular TV, seem to feel that they must present a certain image of a prominent sportsman to the public. This may appeal to some sportsmen and they'll go to extraordinary lengths to foster the image. However, if in order to become a goodie Steve has to avoid saying what he thinks, if he has to go out of his way to please people that he may have little respect for, if he hardly dares break wind in case it may spoil his image, then I for one hope he remains a baddie. I shall have more to say on the subject of images later on.

I felt very sad and sorry for Steve after the race. People never know what to say when you've lost, and in their embarrassment they will either avoid you completely or make some inane remark. It's the same *before* a big race, on the warm-up track; it must really get on an athlete's nerves, because person after person comes over to him with what they think is the magic one-liner that will solve all his problems: anything from 'Sock it to them kid!' to 'This is your chance!' Frank Dick has a different approach. He doesn't say anything; he just comes over with his hand outstretched and his eyes narrowed, and nods, and that conveys all the one-liners put together. But most people half-ignore you after a defeat. I was walking back through the tunnel when I met Steve, and his first words were, 'I'm sorry,' – as though he'd done something wrong. I thought he'd run himself more or less to a standstill; I knew there was nothing left in his legs at the finish. We sat on the bus together and any gloom quickly lifted. Steve doesn't stay down for long; if you do, you get counted out.

There was a party that night at one of the hotels, and we were going to that, come what may. On the way we called in to a little bar in the village, and Wagenknecht and Busse were in there, well through a big bottle of champagne and none too despondent, passing the time of day with us as usual. No sooner had we gone to the bar and sat down when we were approached by the Irish boxing team. The first member to speak, who was sporting a black eye, announced, 'We'd be greatly honoured, surely, if the Olympic champion would be after taking a glass of champagne with us.' Steve thanked him very much. There was a pause, and then up came another one, with a swollen nose, and made exactly the same speech, and this went on through the various weights until one of their boxers, the bronze medallist, came over and we were surrounded by these fellows, all in various states of damage, drinking champagne with us. The party at the hotel was a humdinger, the highlight of which was an Italian, absurdly nicknamed the Pope, dancing on the table wearing only an Italian flag. Goodness knows how many bottles of champers we sank, but we got back and woke poor Ron up at some ungodly hour, reeling ripe, and Ron sobered us up by reminding us that we had just four hours till our flight home. Steve responded to this news by plonking down on his bed with all his clothes on and going to sleep immediately. Four hours later I awoke with a most fearful hangover; what made me feel ten times worse was the sight of Steve, stomping about bright and cheerful as ever, saying how wonderful he truly felt.

185

We made our flight, and arrived back at Heathrow to find hundreds of newspapermen straining at the barriers. A kindly policeman smuggled the pair of us out of a side door, and there was Bob Benn waiting to whisk us quietly away in his car. Bob just strolled up to Steve and said, 'Well done, mate' – a typical thoughtful gesture from a real friend.

9

Records Come and Go

It was only the end of July when we came back from Moscow, and it seemed a shame to waste Steve's fitness. Andy Norman and I had the same thought: get him some races. On 8 August, at Crystal Palace, was the Coke meeting. Steve chose the 5000 metres because it wasn't his own event: there was no pressure, and he wanted to take things a bit steadily because he had a cold. The field was strong enough to extend him, but he strode round quite comfortably until about 120 to go, then put in a little burst and took the lead. John Treacy of Ireland gritted his teeth, and *he* put in a burst to catch up with Steve. So Steve thought, 'Hallo, I've got to get rid of this fellow,' and rather reluctantly put in another little burst with 30 to go; he thought that would be enough to take him through, and just before the finish he eased up and more or less walked over the line thinking 'That's it now.' But he'd reckoned without the determination of this chap Treacy. He had *also* done a second little burst as he approached the line, and instead of walking over like Steve, dipped very hard at the tape. They both clocked 13:27.9. Steve came over laughing and said, 'Do you think I've done it?' In fact he hadn't. The photo finish showed Treacy had won by a whisker. It was a very enjoyable race, and just what Steve needed after the Olympics. Everyone, including Steve, found it amusing that Ovett had been caught out at last with this habit of sauntering in.

On 15 August there was a meeting in Lausanne, and

187

Steve ran in the 1500 metres. Richard Harris of the USA set the pace alight to 800 with 1:49.8, then suddenly dropped out to leave Steve with an unscheduled solitary haul to the finish. It was a cold, wet, blustery evening and he finished with 3:35.4, some 40 yards in front of the next man. On 22 August there was a brave run in the mile in Brussels at the Van Damme Memorial Meeting. Again, the pace was a trifle fast, and at the halfway mark it was Omer Khalifa from Harris and Steve. Again, Steve was left with 600 to 660 metres to do on his own, and though he pushed as best he could, he finished with 3:51.6, 8 metres clear of Walker and Scott in a battle between themselves for second, which they dead-heated for 3:52.7.

Three days later came the Golden Mile, at Crystal Palace. Both Steve and John Walker had insisted before this race that the IAAF take a lead in their own event and test the first half-dozen finishers for drugs, and there were some notable absentees. The mile got under way with Richard Harris again the pacesetter, covering the first quarter in 55.7 from Craig Masback and Steve in third place on 56.5. Harris went through 880 yards in 1:56.2, well clear of Bayi, with Steve running fifth in 1:58.2. This was a genuine race, and Walker and Wessinghage, to name but two, would hope to mar any plans of Steve's to win in record time. When the pacemaker faded, Coghlan took over on the third lap. Strangely, Bayi made no move, though he couldn't hope to outkick this class of opposition. Coghlan reached the $\frac{3}{4}$-mile stage in a slow 2:58.5, with Steve in third in 2:58.8. Along the back straight Bayi and Coghlan began to push it along; then, just before 200 out, both Steve and Scott accelerated together, with Steve on the preferred inside lane. As they came off the turn, Steve, if you like, kicked again (there are a few of these double kicks about) and pulled away, easing down the straight for 3:52.8, from Scott close behind in second place in 3:52.9. Steve covered the last 200 metres in 26.3.

He wasn't finished with 1980 yet. His next run was

a 1500 metres in Koblenz just two days later: it was Thomas Wessinghage's club meeting, and with a quality field it was usually rather special. Garry Cook kindly agreed to set the pace and he did it superbly, taking them through 400 metres in 55.5 and 800 metres in 1:53, with Wessinghage and Steve set fair behind him. Steve told me later, 'I was feeling so good by then, I just knew a world record was on tap.' Wessinghage, who was racing on his own account, passed Steve at the 800 metres mark. Thomas knew that his best chance was either to drop Steve or to try and run the finish out of him, as Straub had done in the Moscow games. So the pace didn't falter, and with 2:50.7 at 1200 metres it seemed certain that the world record would go, *provided* Steve didn't pause too long. I was sitting at home, watching on television. Well. Sitting — I was pacing up and down, actually, and I wasn't watching, either, not at this stage. My mother was commentating for me, trying to calm me down: 'It's OK, yes, he's all right still,' and I was saying, 'Go now, Steve. Go *now*, Steve. Has he gone yet?' He seemed to be cutting it a bit fine because here was Thomas, motoring furiously all round the last lap. 200 out, no kick. Into the turn, still nothing. Then at *last*, at the start of the finishing straight, Steve opened the throttle and poured himself down the straight, striding long and hard, chased every inch of the way by Wessinghage. The West German crowd were rooting for Thomas, the local lad, and also Harald Hudak, close by in third, and they'd seen a race, all right. They had also seen something else. First, Steve Ovett, 3:31.36, the fastest 1500 metres of all time. Second, Thomas Wessinghage, 3:31.58, the second-fastest 1500 of all time. Third, Harald Hudak, 3:31.96, the third-fastest 1500 of all time.

Steve had obviously acquired a taste for this records business now: he probably had begun to tire of the old sit-in-and-kick-at-200 routine. It was a new challenge. He ran one more race in 1980, winning the AAA Mile at Crystal Palace in the modest time of 4:04.4 from John

Walker. When I saw him afterwards he said, 'Well, that's it, isn't it? It's a shame I've run out of races.' He genuinely felt he could have done more that season.

One thing we'd been promising ourselves for two or three years now was to walk along the Pennine Way. So in September off we went, Steve, Bob Benn and myself. We drove to Denis Watts' retirement home on the edge of the Lake District and he drove us to our starting point, a place called Malham, and said, 'OK then, I'll pick you up in a week's time in Appleby, Westmoreland.' I'd rung up little hotels and boarding houses along the way and Steve and Bob were the navigators; Rachel had made a big slab of fruit cake, which I thought really ought to be jettisoned as we were already travelling heavy, but it turned out to be valued sustenance to us. It was one of the most satisfying weeks any of us ever had. We would go for whole days without seeing a soul, through sun and rain, mud and meadow, and through a bog that the two of them led me into that nearly swallowed up my shoes and me as well. We walked altogether about 105 miles, reaching a little haven each night.

Steve had quite a long time off from running, almost till Christmas, but just at the beginning of December we went to Chailey Heritage, which is a home for severely handicapped children at Lewes in Sussex. Steve pays regular visits there chatting to the kids, and on this occasion they'd brought several schools for the disabled together to hold 'mini-Olympics'. We watched some of these extraordinary races, with children on crutches trying to stagger their way over 30 or 40 metres, and then wheelchair races – Steve took part in one of those and came last – and at the end of it all he presented the medals. It was a most moving experience to see these youngsters really trying their utmost to win. If some of those on crutches fell over, the others would shout for them to get up quickly, not a bit sorry for them or for themselves: get up, and try to beat the one in front. To see them trying so hard did us the world of good. I've already explained the feelings of Steve and myself about how lucky we are to be fit.

1980 rounded off wonderfully for me, because a friend of mine, Sue Gough, threw a party for all the people I'd ever coached. I was staggered when I arrived there that Saturday night: there must have been seventy or eighty athletes of varying ages and fortunes, with nothing in common except me, all chatting athletics together; some of them I hadn't seen for years. It was very touching, and marvellous for my mother to be able to meet the voices on the phone.

1981 – A sad start

1981 began rather sadly with the untimely death of Geoff Dyson, who had such a great influence on me in my coaching career. I hadn't seen him for a year or two, but I have many fond memories of the man, and I shall never forget his response to Steve's performance in Düsseldorf in 1977. Geoff wrote to me, 'I wish all athletes could express themselves as wonderfully as Ovett.'

Steve's own life was undergoing changes. He didn't start training until well on into the year, partly because he was busy shifting his headquarters from his parents' home to a flat in Brighton not all that far away, and close enough to Matt for the two of them to be able to continue their morning runs together. The time had come for Steve to come out from under the home umbrella and develop his own life. It's almost inevitable in a household of strong personalities that friction develops and it seemed sensible for Steve to set up on his own. In the spring Steve ran and won some fairly low-key road races, one in Italy and a couple in Norway; then in April he and Rachel went to Portugal, where Steve intended to start training in warm, sunny conditions. They might have known from our experience at South Lake Tahoe that the weather wouldn't be any good until I arrived a week later and sure enough, it was cold, wet and miserable; into the bargain Steve had a touch of tendonitis in the arch of one foot, so he was in a rather bad way. Of course when I got there the weather brightened up immediately: it wasn't exactly hot for Portugal but we could at least sunbathe and get some fairly fast running done. There was still the problem of Steve's foot, though.

We went along to a health clinic in Vilamora and, as luck would have it, the doctor who saw us turned out to be an Englishman, Dr Stephen Fevrier. He was a godsend. 'How many times a day can you come round for treatment?' he asked Steve. 'Well I'll come as many times as you want me to,' said Steve. 'Right,' said the doctor, 'come round three times a day, then you won't have to stop training.' So with the help of this treatment Steve was able to train twice a day, staying on for a little while after Rachel had flown home. In England, Steve would have been hard pressed to find anyone willing to treat him once a day, let alone three times, and we were accordingly expecting a pretty hefty bill at the end of it, but Dr Fevrier said, 'Forget it. It's been a pleasure to keep you running.' Really nice of him.

Steve was beginning to get back in shape. We went to Merthyr Mawr a week after arriving home for what was probably the best (i.e. most horrible) weekend we've ever had down there. Not only were there lots of youngsters pushing Steve hard on the fast circuits, but with good-class athletes like Julian Goater and Dave Clark on hand as well there was no let-up on the long circuits either. Julian had won the National cross-country championship a few weeks before by the biggest margin in history, which gives you some idea of his condition. So Merthyr Mawr was even worse torture than usual. During the winter, Steve was asked to guest at the opening of a new all-weather track in Brighton. The opening ceremony itself, including sponsored runs, had raised a large sum towards improving the facilities there, and this Brighton track was to prove a great help in Steve's training build-up for the 1981 season. There were going to be a couple of England matches in the first week of June: it was now the end of May. Steve felt that he'd really like a race somewhere as a pipe-opener for these international matches. There was a local meeting on in Brighton; he might run in that, but then it occurred to him that there was a better alternative. Mary Peters had just made a plea on television for last-minute entries to the UK championships over in Antrim – which many athletes had evidently avoided, perhaps because they were worried about the Irish Troubles. The UK championships hadn't figured in Steve's plans originally, but hearing about the parlous plight of these games, he contacted Andy Norman, who was by now a member of the British Board, and asked Andy to arrange a race for him in Antrim. This done, Steve took the first available flight, and arrived for the 1500 metres in Antrim Forum.

The heats went very comfortably, but when the final came up on the next day, 25 May, he could hardly warm up for being sick. A doctor he consulted told him he might have appendicitis, which put the wind up Steve straight away, but whatever it was (and it did seem afterwards to have been a stomach bug) he really did feel ill before the 1500 metres final. In the race, he stayed back in a bunched field behind leaders Frank Clement, Steve Anders, Keith Rothwell and Mike Downes. About 250 yards from home Steve put in his usual burst, hotly pursued by Clement, to stride clear at the finish for 3:42.80. (Times were officially to hundredths in 1981.) Steve really enjoyed the warm reception he received from the crowd and he spent nearly an hour signing autographs after the race. It was a good run to have under his belt; he was thankful to have been able to race at the last minute, when so many athletes had turned the meeting down. He told reporters at the press conference afterwards (yes, he even talked to the press), 'I wouldn't like to see the championships disintegrate, especially as they are taking place in Northern Ireland. I think if you come and run in a meeting like this, a meeting for the people, you lose yourself and forget your worries.' *He* was pleased, the Irish officials were pleased, and the local crowd were overjoyed to see him.

Next day, what did we find in the newspaper reports

but a comment from David Shaw to the effect that he was 'discontented' about Steve's late entry and wished these people would get in touch with him before they decided to race in the meeting. Yet Steve had consulted Andy Norman, a Board member, and Andy had notified the local Irish officials, so it was all 'above board' and Steve had gone through all the right channels. He couldn't win, even when he won. It was the usual story. Even going along to a meeting in these circumstances, and giving pleasure to a lot of kids in a torn country, he still ran into criticism. It was even suggested that there must have been some shady deal to induce him to compete, so he evidently couldn't do anything without some ulterior motive being attached to it. Asked about David Shaw, Steve replied, 'The last time I had a conversation with David was when the Board tried to ban me after competing in Nijmegen.'

Steve had a new club, now, called Phoenix AC. Matt, in addition to running with Steve, had also been coaching a lot of youngsters at his local club, and they were having problems. Matt didn't think the club was giving them much encouragement or backing, so he decided they'd be better off forming a new Brighton club of their own. Steve was very grateful for all Matt's help in his training and as Brighton and Hove AC hadn't really supported him much over the last couple of years, he felt that his loyalties should lie with Matt. This was how it came about that Steve joined Phoenix AC as a founder member and sported a different vest at the Antrim meeting.

The Philips Night of Athletics, at Crystal Palace, began with Sebastian winning the 800 metres in a front-running 1:44.06. The heavens had opened soon after the meeting started, and it bucketed down so hard that competitors couldn't warm up outside and had to use a tiny little indoor area. Steve's race was the 3000 metres. He wasn't really concerned with fast times yet, which was just as well because his stomach trouble refused to clear up and he now had a sore throat to crown

194

it. Craig Virgin, who had run so well in that year's International cross-country race, did most of the leading, with Nick Rose pushing it along at one stage, and Steve took over with 150 metres to go, opened a big gap almost immediately and then eased down over the last 50 or 60 metres to win in the relatively good time of 7:54.11, from Emil Puttemans, second in 7:54.92. Steve covered the last 200 in 26.8 and the final lap in 56.4. A reasonable start to the season.

If any confirmation were needed that Steve couldn't do anything right at all, it came when a minor controversy blew up over whether or not he had given his Olympic medals away as a publicity stunt. Steve had gone to visit a small boy in a Brighton hospital who loved athletics, and he had lent his medals to the lad to cheer him up. Hearing of the controversy, Mrs R. Smith wrote in to *Athletics Weekly* to say that Steve had shown great kindness and didn't deserve criticism. 'He left the ward as quietly as he arrived after promising to wave as he was running at Crystal Palace the same evening. I am the mother of the boy concerned. If the world had a lot more Steve Ovetts, the world would be a far nicer and happier place to live in.'

A virulent strain

On 7 June the Citizen International Match took place at Gateshead. Coe, originally down for the 800 metres, ran in a 4 × 400 relay, and Steve was to do the mile. He had been feeling rotten at the last couple of meetings and at Gateshead if anything he felt worse. He was in two minds about competing at all, and consulted a doctor who was with the England team, Bob Steele, himself a former 800 metres runner of some repute. He examined Steve and told him that there was nothing seriously wrong but that it was a case of identifying this rather stubborn virus freeloading on the Ovett anatomy. It was a typically windy day at Gateshead, though this in itself may have had nothing whatever to do with the fact that the band couldn't find the right national anthem to play for the Ethiopian competitors. After two wrong renditions, the Ethiopian team threatened to walk out. Andy Norman managed to pacify them by suggesting that they sing it themselves, whereupon the entire Ethiopian team marched out in front of the grandstand and gave a rendering of their national anthem, thereby averting an international crisis.

The mile race passed off without incident. Mindful of Steve's illness, Bob Benn had the good sense not to lead off like a bat out of hell, and they followed him round at a fairly leisurely pace, covering the first lap in 59.5 (Steve was fourth in 59.9). At the halfway mark Bob was just inside 2 minutes, with Steve just outside, and on the third the pace dropped to 3:02.3. Steve left it fairly late before pushing off with 100 metres to go, chased by Jim Espir, and I thought, 'Hallo, I'm going to have a first and second here,' until an Italian called Patrignani pipped Jim at the post. The result was: first, Steve and virus, 3:57.92; second Patrignani, 3:59.18; third Jim, 3:59.20. The virus had evidently taken up residence, but Steve needn't have worried about it because as soon as he arrived back in Brighton there was a phone call from Bob Steele telling him the name of a specialist to see at the hospital. Steve went along right away, and was put on a course of antibiotics that quickly did the trick.

Three days later, in Florence on 10 June, Seb set a new world record for 800 metres with 1:41.72. Whatever the conditions were like for him there, in Venice where Steve ran a 1000 metres on 17 June, they were appalling. Steve described the occasion to me when he came back, having run into yet another air-traffic controllers' dispute on the way out. A little group of athletes had gone to run in an incredible meeting on a sort of island in the Venetian lagoon. The event was about half an hour old when they were suddenly overtaken by hurricane force winds ('I've never known winds like it,' said Steve), and part of the temporary seating arrangements blew over in the torrential rain. What had promised to be quite a fast 1000 metres ended with Steve and the others pushing quite hard to avoid going backwards in the teeth of the gale. Bob did his best as pacemaker and in fact he finished third, but the wind was against fast times and Steve finished with 2:21.84. It was a pity because he was in reasonable shape now and looking for form.

Steve went into the Bislett Games 1500 metres on 26 June without the confidence of a hard and fast race behind him and with everyone clamouring for another world record, especially as this was Oslo, where records were about par for the course. I sensed that Steve wasn't confident enough; he usually looks to have one or two quality races tucked away before he goes after a world time. Another factor was going to be the size of the 1500 metres field. On a six-lane track there were somewhere between seventeen and twenty people hustling and crowding around the start line. They set off and the track could hardly accommodate them, so it was a kind of staggered start in rows. Pacemaking plans went west as Tom Byers of the USA shot off like a startled hare over the first 100 metres, followed by a lone Ethiopian rejoicing in the name of Wodhjo Bulti, with the rest of the field queuing quietly some distance back, waiting for the race to open. They included Scott, Cram, Wessinghage, Walker and Hudak, as well as Steve. Byers ticked off the first lap in 57.52, 15 metres up on the others. In case there wasn't enough muddle already with Byers thundering away from a star-packed field, an official contrived to add a touch more confusion by calling out Byers' lap time to the others as they passed. They naturally assumed the timekeeper was calling their own times. Steve, who'd felt the pace was a bit slow, heard '57.52!' and thought, 'Well that's funny; the fellow at the front must be clocking 53, 54.' Byers was still pulling away, completing the second lap in 57.31 (1:54.83 over the 800 metres) and now 50 metres clear of the pack. '1:54.83!' shouted the official as they trotted by oblivious in around 2:02.

Halfway through the third lap Steve had realized what was happening, but by then all he could see of Byers was a dot on the horizon. Anyone who went after him now would immediately set himself up as a hare to the rest of the pack. Through 1200 metres went Byers in 2:53.09 and as he entered the last lap, Steve went after him. The margin at the bell had been 70 metres and entering the straight Byers was still some 30 metres clear. Steve piled on a 52.3 last lap and 200 in 24.5, but in a lost cause. The American won in 3:39.01, from Steve who was second in 3:39.53. Afterwards everybody was very upset and some of the runners were in flames at this timekeeper, who seemed to disappear very quickly. I'm not sure myself that the timekeeping was wholly to blame. It may have been part of the problem, but I think that with such a big field at the opening of the season, there was bound to be some circumspection as they sized each other up. It would have been a cagey affair in any case. Steve came over to me at the finish and said, 'Well, I won *my* race.'

With all due respect to Byers, who ranked fifth in the world with 3:36.35, Steve was confident that he could take him on any day of the week. The people he was worried about – Walker, Scott, Wessinghage etc. – he'd beaten *them*.

That evening as we sat in the hotel talking over the race I said, 'If it took place again tomorrow and Byers and the others did exactly the same, I bet you still wouldn't go after him.'

'No,' said Steve, 'I probably wouldn't.'

He didn't feel too badly about it. That strange, abiding insecurity among athletes that I've told you about, that fear of setting the race up for somebody else, had combined with the early-season circumspection they all felt about each other's form to let this one get away. In a sense it didn't much matter what some comparatively unknown runner might be doing out in front. They were too busy eyeing each other to care. I'd always known this would happen one day, and here it was. Steve summed up his feelings about it when he said, 'We all ran like a load of hacks.' The race didn't turn Byers into a world-beater, as he hasn't won many since. And I still thought it was a little early in Steve's season for the promoters to be looking for a world record from him.

The European Cup semifinal began on 4 July. Steve likes Helsinki usually, but this time he had toothache. He couldn't train because if he ran it sent shooting pains up through his head. Once or twice in the past he's had this trouble with his teeth and I think dental problems must be stress-related. He didn't stay on in Helsinki after his race but came straight back to a London dental hospital for treatment. The day before he ran he was given a painkiller, but had very little sleep. 'The slower it is,' said Steve, 'the better it'll be for me.' He was mighty relieved that the 1500 metres was indeed rather leisurely, with 800 metres coming up in 2:07.2. Steve waited until 150 to go before pulling away from Markku Laine of Finland to finish in a casual 3:46.47 (Laine ran 3:47.13). Because of his dental trouble, he wasn't there to whoop it up next day with the rest of the team when Britain won the semi for the first time ever. It was a superb effort, and you have to go back a long way to find the UK beating the USSR in a major competition. I was pleased that both Steve and Julian helped with the points: apart from Steve's 1500 metres win, Julian came in at very short notice and ran second in the 10,000 metres.

Shortly before the Olso Games in Bislett Stadium, there was a strange coincidence. On 7 July, Coe ran a 1500 metres in Stockholm, recording 3:31.95 and falling short of Steve's world record time of 3:31.36. The following night in Milan Steve also ran in a 1500 metres, with Bob setting the pace for the first two laps (800/1:52.68); however the third dropping off, affording Steve a finishing time of 3:31.95 – exactly the same as Seb. So then it was off to Bislett stadium once more, on 11 July. Coe opened the proceedings with yet another world record, breaking his own 1980 mark for 1000 metres with 2:12.18. The haulage firm on this occasion consisted of James King and Rob Harrison, but Seb was on his own from 500 metres.

The finest mile seen

This was followed by what *Athletics Weekly* later described as perhaps 'the finest mile race ever seen'. Despite assurances to the contrary beforehand, the field was rather large, with virtually all the people who'd run in the earlier Bislett Games 1500 metres turning up here for the Oslo mile. It was a classy field, though, and promised a classy race. Steve's teeth were in order now, and he couldn't wait to get them into it. At the gun, Bob Benn set what I considered to be near perfect pace, through 440 yards in 56.7 (Steve in 57.0) and through 880 yards in 1:55.2, with Steve right on his shoulder. At the halfway mark, a buzz went through the stadium: Tom Byers, hero of the Bislett Games, hit the front. Was he about to break away again? Instead of a gap opening this time though, everybody bore down on him, and despite the fast pace, by the end of the third lap Byers was hauled in. Steve Scott, physically primed for this, took the lead halfway down the straight and drove off very hard indeed. At the ¾-mile mark it was Scott (in 2:53.4) from Steve, just a fraction of a second back with 2:53.5. Steve sounded him out at the start of the back straight, and Scott fought him off fiercely. He clearly meant to go all out for this one. I sensed what was going on in Steve's mind, as he weighed whether to take Scott or take his time. Any indecision was cleared up very quickly, because out of the corner of his eye, Steve caught sight of the menacing figure of Thomas Wessinghage coming up like a rocket on the outside of him and bidding fair for the race. So Steve struck out for home. With 200 to go he accelerated with fantastic power, laying a big gap behind him like a train. This done, he glanced over his shoulder and then strode through to the finish.

When the list of times went up on the board, nobody

had ever seen anything like it before. Behind Steve's 3:49.25 (440 splits: 57.0, 58.3, 58.2, 55.8), the third fastest mile in history, came a whole string of sub-3:51 miles. Second was Gonzales of Spain in 3:49.67, third Scott in 3:49.68; fourth was Walker (3:50.26), fifth Harbour (3:50.34), sixth Cram (3:50.38), seventh Wessinghage, (3:50.91). It was not surprising that this became known as 'the dream mile'.

'I think the pace was slow from the word go really,' said Steve, 'but it wasn't a time trial, it was a race: a super race, one of the greatest I have ever been in.' Once the pace had been set, everybody was trying to win, no matter what time it cost. There was no quarter given; Scott and Wessinghage threatened throughout, and Steve said he felt a real thrill to have been in such a fast race. It was his third sub-3:50 mile; no one else had *ever* run more than one. John Walker summed up his feelings by saying, 'That has to be the greatest mile race of all. At my age I should know. I seem to have run in most of them!'

On 14 July there was another very fast mile, and yet another sub-3:50 time for Steve, in Lausanne, where he won in 3:49.66. He now possessed four of the six fastest miles of all time. This time Bob Benn, perhaps mindful of Steve's complaint in Oslo that the pace had been too slow, dropped the hammer on the first two laps and went off at the fastest early pace of Steve's career (440 yards in 53.8; 880 yards in 1:57.1), though Bob still managed to finish the race. You'll notice in this chapter how often Bob Benn crops up as a pacemaker and there's no doubt that his assistance has been vital on many occasions. 'It's a measure of our friendship,' said Steve, 'that on several occasions Bob has sacrificed his own athletic aspirations to help me and although I've never really made it public, Bob knows my gratitude is there.' Thomas Wessinghage was going to take over on lap 3, but it wasn't one of Thomas's nights and he said afterwards, 'There was no way I could have helped Steve. The pace was much too fast for me and I had enough troubles of my own.' Steve was left to go it alone for almost two whole laps, through the ¾-mile mark in 2:50.4 and falling just shy of the required record pace of 58.3 on the final lap. He explained, 'I just couldn't concentrate out there on my own. I'm not the sort of guy who can relax when he's far out in front. I much prefer to be in the pack hustling.'

He put in a couple of weeks' decent training after Lausanne and had an easy 800 metres up at Gateshead on 26 July, beating Garry Cook 1:47.96 to 1:48.68. But then came a cracking 1500 metres in Budapest three days later, just outside his own world record and the second-fastest time ever. Bob Benn led through 400 metres in 55.8 and 800 metres in 1:52.2; Walker took over on lap 3 for 2:50.7 at the 1200 mark, but then Steve held back a little too long, finishing with 3:31.57. He said, 'Everything was perfect: the track, the conditions and the pace. It was my mistake. I should have gone at the bell instead of 300 out.' Yet he now owned five of the nine fastest 1500 metres ever, to go with his four out of the six best miles. Two days later he ran in the Talbot Games at Crystal Palace, recording a fairly sedate 1000 metres win in 2:20.67, ahead of Steve Cram. Then came a 1500 metres in Fana near Bergen on 3 August, where the wind put paid to record attempts and Steve rolled home in 3:34.63, again ahead of Steve Cram.

Things had been going rather too smoothly lately; just after the Bergen race, Steve noticed something the matter with his hamstring muscle. It didn't feel right. He said it was OK during steady-state runs but that if he wanted to pull out all the stops it felt as though something would break down. So he withdrew from the AAA championships at Crystal Palace and sadly missed the Europa Cup final in Zagreb on 15–16 August, where Britain finished overall third, her best result ever. While Steve was nursing his injury, Coe was at it again breaking records – this time in Zürich in the Weltklasse meeting on 19 August, with 3:48.53 for the mile. He had also hoped to break Steve's 1500 metres record of 3:31.36

en route, but in this he didn't succeed. He said after the race, 'I still believe the mile and 1500 records can go simultaneously, but it's mental, not physical.' I would think personally the chances are against it. If you're going for the mile, you can nearly always raise a little extra pace over the last 100 metres, whereas if you're after the 1500 metres record, you extend yourself from 1400 to 1500 metres. It's a hell of a long way between 1500 and the mile mark when you're tired, and that difference is crucial. Still, we shall have to wait and see. I'd say the barrier is physical rather than mental.

Steve tried out his hamstring in Berlin with a comfortable mile on 21 August, and the little lay-off seemed to have done him good. He was happy with his fitness again and raring to go. Naturally he wanted his mile record back. So 26 August found him in Koblenz asking the organizers to put on a special mile race for him, though he had been scheduled to run a 1500 metres. They were happy to oblige, but there wasn't a very strong line-up as a number of people in the 1500 metres had decided not to switch. That race was won by Steve Scott in 3:31.96, a US record, with Boit and Wessinghage in the field. Steve's comparatively lacklustre field for the mile was led off by Bob over the first two laps; he clocked off the first in 55.63 from James Robinson of the USA, with Steve lying third, and he held on until almost the end of lap 2, when Robinson, the USA 800 metres champion, took over. Robinson passed 800 metres in 1:53.59, with Steve 2 metres back in second place (running 880 yards in 1:54.5), but the American couldn't quite keep up the pace on lap 3 and sagged slightly before the bell. There was nothing for it but for Steve to go the long haul alone, much against his instincts.

Away he went in his faded red vest, pushing as hard as he could and needing a 1:54 for the second half of the race – a tall order for a man of Steve's pack-loving nature. This time, though, he seemed to be hitting his straps: through 1200 in 2:50.62 (Coe made 2:51.68 in

Zürich) and through ¾ mile in around 2:51.5; he needed a 57 last quarter and just got it to finish with 3:48.40, thirteen-hundredths inside Seb's week-old world record. The next finisher, Masback, recorded 3:54.14, some 6 seconds away, which gives you some idea of the quality of the field. On that last lap, Steve didn't exactly feel as though he was pursued by tigers and there was very little sense of urgency in his running. Still, he'd got his mile back and he was fit again. He said, 'It was such a nice change to run at a meeting where it wasn't raining, blowing or doing something to stop me. Everything was ideal. I couldn't waste the chance that gave me.' He added, 'When I went to the front I knew I had the record. It can go further.' Prophetic words, because two nights later Seb snatched it back again in Brussels. Acknowledging a pull from Byers and a push from Boit, he came up trumps with a well-orchestrated 3:47.33 – and that, as I write, is how it stands at the moment. In 1982, the lads may be a little more circumspect, building up for the European Games and so on. We shall just have to wait and see. The press have contrived to suggest that Steve's Koblenz time of 3:48.40 won't be ratified because the race was impromptu. Well, IAAF Secretary-General John Holt told the *Daily Telegraph*, 'The fact that the race was arranged too late to be included in an already printed programme is a technicality.... We would lose all credibility if we disqualified this record.'

After that, Steve had a couple of 800s close together, one in Ardal in Norway in 1:47 dead and quite a nice run on 31 August at Crystal Palace in the Amoco Games against Poland and Switzerland, in which he seemed almost to stride round for 1:46.40. That was pleasing, considering he hadn't run very fast for 800 metres that season. Without much rest but in a good frame of mind, he went off to the World Cup in Rome, feeling confident about his 1500 metres.

I thought Steve ran a super race there. It was competitive, and it was fast. Before the start Mike Boit and

Sydney Maree, the black South African now running for the USA, had apparently put their heads together and decided that the only way to deal with Ovett was to burn him off. Consequently Maree pushed it along for much of the way, and then Boit took over the torch with about 600 to go. Try as he might, he couldn't get rid of Steve, who simply steamed past at the start of the final straight to win with something in reserve in 3:34.95. Boit faded rather badly and John Walker ducked in for second place; Sydney Maree, surprisingly, finished a long way back in fifth place with 3:36.56. Immediately afterwards, Steve had to fly back to England to hustle through certain domestic preparations, as an event was coming up on 18 September that he didn't want to miss. He had a lot of arranging to do.

Rushing back home wasn't the best possible preparation for his next race, in Rieti on 9 September, but he flew back to Italy anyway and this time he was really caught out rather badly, because Maree outsprinted him in the mile. Maree had the lead just before the final 200 metres and as Steve moved up to take him, Maree pushed away to win fairly comfortably in 3:48.83. Steve was second in 3:50.23. It was no excuse that Steve was tired; it was his own choice to fly home and then fly back to Italy instead of staying there for the race. But he paid tribute to Maree's performance, saying he was obviously in superb shape. The race made Sydney the third fastest athlete in history over the mile, after Seb and Steve. Two years previously while Steve was in America, he watched their national championships and when he came back I asked him what he'd thought of the 1500 metres opposition over there. 'I didn't rate any of them much,' said Steve. He felt that far and away the best runner he'd seen out there was the fellow who'd won the 5000 metres, a chap called Sydney Maree, though at the time nobody thought of him as the coming miler. I like to think Steve can spot a bit of talent, as well as run himself.

Fading fast

Two days after Rieti, there was the Coke meeting at Crystal Palace. Not only was Steve fagged out by then, but he was running out of fitness. I think he won the 2-mile race that night first on his strength of character, and second on Eamonn Coghlan's lack of confidence. Richard Callan did most of the leading, taking over from Steve Cram, who wasn't going terribly fast. Callan stepped up the pace, and if you watched carefully you could see Steve breathing very, very hard to hang on. I was just hoping somebody wasn't about to burst away, because Steve's lungs were already labouring like blacksmith's bellows. Coghlan went into the lead at about 200 out, and Steve waited and waited; then just at the beginning of the finishing straight he gathered himself and hauled past Coghlan. At which point, Eamonn seemed to give it away, as though he were thinking, 'Oh here comes Steve, as per usual; I'd better get out of the way.' Well, Eamonn should have fought him all the way, because Steve wasn't in any great shape and it was a pretty tough race for him: he shouldn't really have won that night at all. It's always nice, of course.

Though he wasn't exactly match sharp, he didn't do any training between then and 18 September, and it served him right that on that day he was completely outshone by somebody. Her name was Rachel. Wedding days are really for women, and Rachel looked so stunning that all eyes were very much on her rather than on the blushing groom. All the press people surged to get a look at her and even tried to break into the reception, so for once Steve Ovett was quite eclipsed. He didn't mind, though. Asked why he'd taken so long to pop the question, he replied that he'd been a bit shy. He *is* very shy with women and though he'd had a good relationship going with Rachel for a long while, it was rather like an athlete doing his training, you see. He prepares and prepares, but doubts still linger in his mind and only when the moment is exactly right does

206

he make his bid for the race. Steve had to sit in for quite some time before seeing his opening there. But it was a lovely wedding and a smashing day, and everybody enjoyed it.

What with yet another virus complaint and the excitement of getting married and setting up home in their flat, Steve missed the inaugural race on the roads of New York, the Fifth Avenue Mile, which was won by Sydney Maree in the extremely fast time of 3:47.52. Steve wound up the season in Australia. Rachel went with him and he had four fairly easy wins in different races over there. I'd managed to arrange to do a week's schools coaching course in Brisbane, and luckily they agreed to switch the dates to coincide with these races of Steve's. So I was able to see one of them and then came home, while Rachel and Steve went off to Bali in Indonesia for their honeymoon. Certainly the end of the season didn't come any too soon for Steve, because in the Coke meeting and in all these races in Australia he was running more from memory than training. The only training session we did down under was on the young athletes' course, and those kids, sensing their chance, pushed Steve mighty hard. He was puffing and blowing, and really quite glad when that session was over.

At the end of 1981 he was a satisfied athlete, certainly: he'd got a world record, he'd run some very fast times, and he'd won a whole series of tough races on very little training. With the long rest he'd had the previous winter, the toothache and injuries, he must have missed something like 50 per cent of his preparation, yet he still managed to produce the results. As his coach, I was naturally rubbing my hands together thinking, 'If he can do that on the training he's had, what will he do on a full winter's work?' Towards the close of the year, Steve was paid a fitting compliment by fellow athlete John Robson. John was asked by *Athletics Weekly*, 'Who do you consider the hardest competitor you have run against?' Robson, who has run against most of them, track and cross-country, replied, 'Ovett! He can run any type of race. It could be dead slow and he has that finishing kick, and he can run a fast race as well because he's so strong. He has probably got everything.'

10

Thinking Ahead

A black Christmas

Steve started running again in the middle of November
1981, gently at first then gathering speed. By mid-
December he was telling me that for the first time he
really felt as though he was flying along. That was when
it happened. One evening as he was out running with
Matt around Brighton, they were passing the precincts of
a local church and Steve was pelting along so hard that
he didn't notice where he was going. There was a
sickening thud as Steve's thigh crashed against an iron
railing. He hit the thing so hard that although it didn't
break the skin, the muscle sheath just above the knee was
ruptured. When he bent his knee, a big bulge appeared.
Steve was annoyed, because just at that moment he was
getting up terrific speed. 'I was really going it, and that
was probably why it happened.'

We waited in vain for the bulge to go down and after a
few days we realized something pretty serious had
happened: it wasn't just your average bruise or bump.
Steve went to a doctor and within a day of consulting Dr
Peter Sperrin he was in the West Middlesex Hospital
undergoing surgery. Dr David Archibald, a surgeon
attached to the British board, made a long incision six
inches above the knee, replaced the muscle in its sheath,
and stitched everything back together again. Dr Archibald said there was no doubt that with the correct
rehabilitation, the muscle would be as good as new.
Steve was in plaster for three weeks, and as I write he

is about to begin a course of physiotherapy before he can actually start running again. He's naturally longing to be back on his feet; it's the first time he's been completely disabled since he had glandular fever. He couldn't do anything then and he couldn't do anything now, however much he might want to. But Steve is a sensible young man, and I know he won't stupidly try to make a premature comeback like so many athletes who lack confidence in themselves and rush back into the fray before their injuries are properly healed. The accident happened at the worst possible time, just before Christmas – runners tend to get out of condition anyway over the festive season as they eat, drink and make merry. If an athlete is lying around in a plaster cast all day long and not doing any exercise at all, Christmas can leave him in about the same shape as a turkey, but Steve seems to be coping quite well, imposing strict discipline on himself. The new Mrs Ovett is a good cook, you see, poised with the slabs of delicious fruit cake and so on, and I've no doubt she sees it as her duty to ensure that the Olympic champion eats properly.

Steve will get over his accident all right. It may well reinforce his resolve and his physical conditioning, because rehabilitation work includes strengthening exercises in areas comparatively neglected. So the plaster coming off on 1 January may prove an auspicious start to 1982. It already promises well with an MBE in the New Year Honours List.

I suppose the single biggest worry of most coaches and athletes in the UK is precisely this business of getting treatment for injuries, and your biggest headache as a coach is finding somewhere in an emergency to take the injured athlete for expert attention. We're in a very difficult position here at the moment. The Board has a small panel of doctors, but there ought to be centres throughout the country where athletes can go for emergency treatment for injuries. There are few of these, and very few doctors skilled in the matter of sports injuries: those that are seem to be scattered around in clinics distributed arbitrarily across the country and often hundreds of miles from the accident, with all the time and expense of travelling that this implies. What a pleasant change it was for Steve to find a doctor in the small Portuguese village of Vilamora able to give him physiotherapy three times a day. Time and again, athletes are injured in Britain and have to go foraging after diagnosis and treatment.

I quite appreciate that in a country as impecunious as this one there would be objections to spending money on sports medicine when general hospitals are crying out for cash, but the sport of athletics is not ailing financially and might well look after its own golden geese a little better. The same applies to sports physiology. We're not actually getting anywhere on this front in the UK, although there are pockets of enlightenment and little experiments being set up here and there. What we need is for such outposts of knowledge to be centralized under the umbrella of the British Association of Sports Medicine, with standardized physiological tests capable of gaining credibility with coaches and athletes throughout the country. Centres could then be set up, adopting uniform procedures instead of the hotchpotch we have at the moment. Now, you can go to one place and get one set of results, and to another and get a quite different set, because they are operating from different perspectives. Until British sports medicine and testing facilities are standardized, athletes and coaches are always going to be dubious about their value. And there is the same urgent need for efficiency over the question of drug abuse.

The drug problem that we have in athletics is largely the fault of the sport's governing bodies here and abroad: it is up to each country's athletics association to take a stand, show clearly that they regard drug abuse as abhorrent and stamp it out. Until we get this initiative, there will continue to be grey areas in the minds of athletes themselves. They'll continue to think, 'Oh yes, we know the law, but in such-and-such a country they get round it by so-and-so.' We have to ensure the

211

penalties are made so severe that these offending administrations themselves crack down. This might be achieved fairly easily by disqualifying not only the athlete found guilty of drug offences, but also his country from the competition in which he was taking part. In that way, any prestige attaching to the athlete's success would be lost, and his country would be implicated in his guilt. Certainly it would be better than the ludicrous state of affairs we have at the moment, whereby American discus-thrower Ben Plucknett, who had been disqualified for taking anabolic steroids, was voted American Athlete of the Year by his association on the grounds that he had broken the world record. How can a country lay claim to abhor drug abuse when it condones such discrepancies as this? Many field event meetings in the USA take place without proper testing facilities, where results would simply not be accepted in the UK.

Another problem is derisory penalties. If some poor devil can be banned for life for accepting a couple of pounds to run in some little professional meeting years before, why should there be less severe consequences for athletes who do what most of us regard as utterly repugnant? Ban the drug-takers and ban them for life, not just halfheartedly as we do at present. At the moment they get reinstated far too easily amid international wheeling and dealing, with governing bodies scratching each other's backs. Each country must fully accept the illegality of drug abuse in sport or we shall continue to have the present farcical setup whereby athletes who are in danger of disqualification simply steer clear of the countries and events where they suspect random tests may be carried out. Which is what seemed to happen when Steve and John Walker asked the IAAF to hold drug checks at one of its own meetings at Crystal Palace. In our view, there should be no rationalization or excuses, no broadminded references to the drug culture, no tolerance over the issue at all. If all coaches and governing bodies had shown their disapproval in the first place, the infection would never have spread. Tolerance has allowed it to seep into the atmosphere. One of the main reasons why substances are banned is that they have harmful side effects on the athletes who take them. Coaches who know this and yet continue to turn a blind eye are not being indulgent; they are being destructive. Of course it does all boil down to the honesty of each individual athlete, and Steve's approach is straightforward. 'When I retire I'll be able to say I did it all on my own natural ability – some others won't be able to say that.'

Insult to injury

Until Steve's injury is healed, he can't think about training, and until his training starts again he can't think about races at all in 1982. So much depends on the preparation he can fit in before the season starts. The press have given a great deal of space recently to a projected clash with Seb Coe, but Steve in his present condition is not going to be pushed into a confrontation with Seb or anyone else. (Sydney Maree and the others are not standing still, so it wouldn't just be Coe that Steve would have to face.) So I think it's pointless for newspapermen and pundits to build up speculation about some head-to-head showdown. Steve won't be taking part in any races at all until he is 100 per cent sure of his fitness. We have every confidence that he'll come back from his leg injury in good shape, just as he did from glandular fever. But fitness is the first priority. Knowing the difficulties we had in 1981 with Steve racing on a curtailed training programme, there's no danger of him rushing out challenges at the moment. He wants to be fully prepared.

I have a feeling, though, that those articles were written as much to get a rise out of Steve as for any other reason – to spur him into making some commitment about his racing programme. This is a penchant of the press. They invite athletes to make predictions and to put their heads in a noose before their event. A notable victim was poor Dave Bedford in Munich and Christchurch. He was drawn by the press into saying he would win, then lost and was summarily executed. They got hold of Dave Jenkins within moments of him finishing at Montreal, when the chap was heartbroken at probably the lowest point of his whole athletic career and obviously just wanted to be left alone, and they tried to get him to make comments for which he might be pilloried later on. They grabbed Seb Coe when he lost in Moscow, and when they didn't get what they wanted they grabbed his father. I don't know what impels such insensitive treatment, or what prompts the press to expose an athlete who has lost to cruel analysis and criticism. I think it may be that for some obscure reason they assume the athlete hasn't *tried*. I know very few instances of athletes who lose because they haven't tried, or who go to major games not intending to do their very best. There are one or two rare examples perhaps, but the overwhelming majority of athletes try very hard indeed. *Sometimes* they fail because they didn't prepare or train properly, but usually it's because they've been beaten by a better man on the day. That's something the press seem to find very hard to accept. Yet in an Olympic year, when everybody in the world has been preparing for years for the occasion, so-called 'unknowns' are bound to rise to the surface who have been kept under wraps in their own countries.

When there *is* a bad defeat, it's important that the coach and the athlete have a good working partnership. They may not want to conduct an immediate post mortem, but after a decent interval they want to find out what happened and why. I don't think you can just dismiss a bad result by saying, 'just one of those things', or 'I had a bad day'. You have to look into the reasons (which is quite different from looking for excuses). There's very rarely one simple reason why a runner has lost a race. It's usually a combination of causes and effects, and these will emerge given time. The press of course want to know straight away and to rake over the race while the feelings are still fresh in the athlete's mind. They want everyone to get a glimpse of the experience, and they want to expose where he went wrong. Well, nobody knows that better than the athlete, and nobody feels the defeat as keenly or regrets it as much as the athlete himself.

When runners are interrogated after a defeat, it's all in the interest of this sacred cow, the great Public Right to Know. I don't accept this principle at all. The public doesn't *have* a right to know an athlete's private hopes and fears about his races. It doesn't have a right to pry into his feelings of elation or grief afterwards. If some athletes volunteer this information, good luck to them, but Steve isn't that sort of person at all. He doesn't want to have his personal feelings examined under a microscope. One reason, as I've suggested before, is that the media are inveterate image-mongers.

They like to put over an image for the public delectation, and eventually the image replaces the person: it becomes a sort of caricature, a shorthand notation for him. Once this happens, woe betide the athlete if he pops his head out from behind it ever again, because the public, having nothing else to go on, believe in the image. When Seb broke his first world record, there were snide remarks of the type, 'You don't have to be a full-time athlete to break a record, ladies and gentlemen! Here we have, fresh from his studies at Loughborough, the new world record holder, Sebastian Coe, and what an affable young man he is, etc., not like that arrogant Ovett who runs all the hours that God sends, etc. etc.' (Which of course Steve didn't.) When Seb came along, the press must have got down on their knees and given thanks for him, because here was a white hat to go with the black hat they had created. Now they could have shootouts at the OK Corral. Everything you read in the newspapers *is* in black and white.

Television commentators are as much to blame in this image-mongering. If you're describing how a person runs a race is it *really* necessary to give the viewers a potted character study of him as well? Could we really not get by without such ridiculous expressions as 'Yifter the Shifter' every time the Ethiopian appears on the screen, or similar epigrams for the other competitors? Television people seem to be on a crusade to reduce sportsmen on the screen to images. I think it may be a sign of the times that athletics and sport in general are becoming more and more like showbusiness. If that's the case, I for one don't fancy the idea at all. The media really *will* be the message: they already appear to think they are more important than the people they are reporting on. This has far-reaching implications, and shows what influence newspaper and television personnel consider themselves to have with the public. Of course I appreciate that the press have a difficult job to do. Of course I realize that they have editors barking at their heels for interesting angles on their sports reports, and that if *they* don't invent images and epigrams, the caption-writer will do it for them. But everything depends on the way they go about it – and with Steve, particularly, they haven't been very clever or very fair at all. Obviously now they're stuck with the image they've made of him, much as Dr Frankenstein was stuck with his monster. They can't very well dismantle it, break the mould or say, 'Sorry, we'll read that again.' It must be rather embarrassing for them. Steve, too, considered himself stuck with the image once, though now it really doesn't get him down as much as it used to. As he told Mel Watman in *Athletics Weekly* of 14 April 1979:

You can see the race and you can write about the race; that's fair enough. But to try and understand me by, like yourself, coming down here for a couple of hours a year I think is ludicrous. My attitude to the press, though, has changed. I've reached this sort of Howard Hughes syndrome, where *not* talking to the press is doing more damage than talking to them, because people just regurgitate old comments, three or four years out of date. I *do* talk to the press; I talk to anybody who wants to come up and talk sensibly.... I'm trying to change this image that the press seem to be trying to perpetuate. I wouldn't like to think that kids coming through will think that's the attitude to have!' because it's false. This sort of 'kick 'em all in the backside and be objectionable all the time' – that's not me.

I'm probably the first athlete who hasn't given a lot of time to image-promotion. I don't constantly appear on television, I don't say the right things at the right time like a lot of other athletes, yet despite that and a lot of bad press coverage, when I've stepped out onto the track at Crystal Palace, the whole of the back straight have just stood up and applauded. It overwhelmed me.

People don't recognize me away from the track. When I go into shops and they ask me my name and I say Ovett, they say, 'You're not any relation to the runner are you?'

I just enjoy running, just enjoy ticking over. If I'm running well, then great: I enjoy it, that's what the sport's there for, it's not for putting yourself under intense pressure all the time, feeling sick all the time, coming home and being depressed, and all that. Good grief!

A wave of emotion

One thing the press have always found particularly irksome about Steve's happy-go-lucky approach to running is the famous Ovett wave at the finish of a race. Why does he do it?

'You think, great, that's over and done with, and you just run through the line. And of course, it's the old "Ovett waves his rivals goodbye," and things like this. Once or twice I have waved to my mum, letting her know that it's OK, but I'll probably stop if people don't like it. I get excited. I mean, I'm not the typical Englishman who wipes his brow, puts his tracksuit on and walks back for a cup of tea. I do get excited, and I show it occasionally. I cannot see why other people get so upset about it. It's not intended as arrogance. I just do it. I think, "Oh, great, that's over with." You know the old saying, you can never please all the people all of the time. If I weren't to wave, I'd upset some other people. They would think, "Why isn't he waving any more?" There's no malice intended towards other competitors.'

To give you some idea of the strength of feeling about Steve's waves, pro and con, here are a few extracts from letters written to *Athletics Weekly* about the matter in 1978. The first was a rather peculiar one complaining about Steve's antics, from a Mr Dave Ainsworth of Romford, Essex:*

Dear Sir,

Over the past year or so we have become accustomed to seeing track athletes giving the victory salute at various stages of the home straight. However at the 'Rotary Watches' meeting we saw such gestures being made even whilst one athlete was negotiating the final bend. How far back will this habit end? Could we perhaps witness the victory wave at 'the bell'?

What the practice does, as far as I'm concerned, is to indicate a high degree of conceit and arrogance by the few individuals concerned. They are not so much as letting everybody know how good they are in relation to the other competitors; but are in fact trying to show the vanquished up as scrubbers, deadlegs etc. To treat one's fellow participants with such contempt is an act which, in itself, is beyond contempt.

I work with a very respected athlete who, on the morning after the 'Rotary' meet, said that he longs for the day when Mr. Ovett will fall flat on his face whilst waving to the crowd anything up to 100 metres from the tape, instead of looking where he is going....

This provoked a number of replies, some of them complaining at the British tendency to carp against its own great athletes, some defending Steve's motives and others seeking to explain what these motives are. Frank Horwill wrote in saying:

I found Dave Ainsworth's letter hard to fathom. To show such venom over a great runner who displays a touch of gleeful arrogance when about to finish a race is symptomatic of a very

Athletics Weekly, 4 November 1978.

218

stuffy personality. Must all athletes conform to a stiff and starchy code of competition? Thank goodness for a little bit of individualism and confidence from a British athlete for a change.

Turning to another sport, boxing, it seems to me that Ali's 'arrogance' has enlivened the sport and who is to say that he is poor in character for his antics? Not many sportsmen would give away millions of dollars for good causes as he has done.

Steve Ovett IS a modest and unassuming man off the track and unlike many internationals I know, he doesn't virtually exclaim when he walks into a crowded room, 'I am here, Steve Ovett is here.'*

At this point, as Steve's confidant I thought it only fair to write to the magazine and clear up the matter. I took it upon myself, after due consultation with Steve, to disclose what had hitherto remained a secret known only to ourselves. We decided that it was in the best interests of the public, the press, D. Ainsworth and the sport of athletics to make the following revelation:

Dear Sir,

After reading Mr Ainsworth's letter re Steve Ovett's Victory Salute (hereafter VS) it's fairly obvious that this coach has not been aware of the phrase *Track Oscillation* (hereafter TO). This is not surprising as this phenomenon is, as yet, little understood and no organised research has been carried out to determine its cause and effect.

However those of us who are aware of TO realise that under *certain* circumstances, *certain* portions of *certain* all-weather tracks display all the symptoms of sympathetic oscillation in response to *certain* movements of *certain* athletes.

With Steve we are aware that the prospect of victory produces body vibrations which spread to produce violent movements in the lower extremities (foot twitch). TO can be produced as a result of these movements and this could cause serious unbalancing effects unless some form of counter action was introduced. So remembering Lewtons (or someone similar) Third Law on action and re-action Steve has introduced upper body movements (the VS) to counter TO.

Athletics Weekly, 2 December 1978.

A study of the video play-backs of several of Steve's races will reveal the varying forms of VS used to offset the varying type of TO. We have now started to look at the phenomenon in a more sophisticated way and by the use of pre-fix code letters are able to grade most tracks. Some examples are 'S' – Standard; 'E' – Eccentric; 'D' – Double and some consternation has been caused by grading Meadowbank – MMTO (macro and micro). I trust that this explanation clarifies the situation a little but I really do not think Mr Ainsworth knows Steve well enough to assume that he understands the motives for using the Victory Salute.

On a slightly more serious note, though, I would say to Mr Ainsworth and the athlete who keep wishing that Steve will fall over, 'wishing won't make it so'. If this athlete is going to beat Steve it's going to take a lot more than wishing.

In reality, matching Steve's 20,000 miles of steady state running, his score of hill sessions, the dozens of short recovery intervals, and his many, many sprinting sessions would have a more marked effect than wishing.

Harry Wilson,
Welwyn Garden City.

The year after these letters appeared in the magazine, I was at Crystal Palace one night, walking towards the middle of the back straight where special space is made for paraplegic spectators, when I heard somebody call me by name. It was a fellow in a wheelchair. I walked over to him and he said, 'You're Steve Ovett's coach aren't you?'

'Yes I am,' I said.

'I just wanted to tell you, Mr Wilson, that *I* know why Steve waves.'

'Well, please tell me,' I said, 'because I don't!'

And the man in the wheelchair replied, 'he's only doing what all of us would dearly like to do: he's doing the thing he loves, with the greatest of ease. If I were a runner and I could do things easily, I'd love to turn round afterwards and have a little wave to my friends.' I think that sums it up really. I can understand people objecting to displays of emotion such as we see on the football pitch, with players hugging, kissing and jumping on top of one another. I think that *is* distasteful. But I don't see anything wrong with somebody simply showing pleasure. You might as well prohibit laughing and grinning in sport, if that's the case. Stiff upper lip, hide your feelings – that sort of approach, which seems rather joyless.

To see why Steve waves, you have to consider the way most of his races are run. If you've had to grind away at the front, you're probably too shattered at the finish to feel much exuberance. But if you've spent the entire race lurking in the background watching and waiting, and then at *last* you can unleash all your pent-up energies in a burst of speed, the pleasure is quite spontaneous. One doesn't need a degree in psychology to understand that. After all, you have to be very singleminded to be a champion athlete, and you spend a great deal of your time channelling thought and energy and emotion towards a specific goal, through every training session, every race. Obviously, if you're out for a long easy run you can chat and joke, but in any intensive training session you have to be terribly single-minded, and the same applies when you race. You may be sitting in the dressing-room just before the start and you've got to be able to focus all your attention on the coming race, how you will run, and how you will win. You can't allow anything to impinge on that concentration. Inexperienced runners will tend to let the circumstances overwhelm them: the occasion, the surroundings, the opposition. I remember Steve Cram, after the 1500 metres heats in Moscow, telling me, 'I was on the last lap before I suddenly realized where I was.' An inexperienced athlete's mind just isn't sufficiently channelled for the big occasion. He doesn't have the necessary tunnel vision.

Steve Cram is learning very rapidly, and a runner has to learn, while he's warming up or waiting in the dressing-room, that singleminded recital of his aims: 'What am I here for? To run this race. What has all my training been leading up to? To run this race.' Herb

Elliott wouldn't shake hands with his fellow competitors before the start in case it interfered with that effort of concentration that great runners have to make. People like Zatopek might appear quite jocular before the start, but beneath that thin plating of humour there is a steel will and a ruthless clarity of purpose. You couldn't find a more ruthless fellow once a race got under way than Zatopek. He would put in bursts to leave his opponents staggering, without a backward glance. It shouldn't surprise anyone that when the race is run, and this effort of concentration is over, it causes a runner like Steve to show his joy and relief.

Character-building

It has often been said of athletics that like other sports it is character-building. Well, that's true for some of the participants; for others it's just the opposite. Sport shows up the dark side of their characters. I think the discipline and dedication involved in years of training *is* character-building and that an athlete gradually develops a philosophical outlook on life's ups and downs. The competition itself often brings out the worst in people, and sport has many a fleeting star who's here one day and gone the next, for whom the experience is likely to be anything but character-building. On the other hand, much that a runner does is on his own, struggling against his own weaknesses, arguing against the inner voice that says, 'You don't necessarily have to go out in this snow. Don't bother today. Don't push so hard.' That's where the character is built, not so much in the races themselves.

As a coach, I can't make anybody train. I can't make somebody do 6 × 1000 metres, or get people to push themselves. They themselves do the pushing. I can sow seeds, and put ideas in their heads. I can show them a sensible plan to follow so that they see clearly why they should be doing six 1000s, rather than three, or five. But I can't make them do it. Steve will work hard of his own

222

accord, and do his best of his own free will, because he knows this is the only way to get where he's going. I've known him come off the track after I've been thinking he's run very well, and say, 'I'm not too happy about that, Tiger,' even though he has won, because there was something in the race that he thought he might have done better. There's an inner mechanism, something like a conscience, telling him to live up to his full potential in every race.

I identify with Steve on the track. I don't know why, because I was never ever a runner of that quality, but I suppose a coach sees people training and he knows their level of fitness and what they're capable of, and hopes the race will be a fair reflection of this potential. A coach is very much involved during the race itself – at least I am. One abiding thought is 'I hope he doesn't get tripped up,' because then the race wouldn't reflect all the hard work that's gone into it. There can be few more frustrating experiences for a coach than to see his athlete, primed and fit and sharp as a tack, stumbling over perhaps through no fault of his own. Watching Steve in a race, there are times when I've actually known what's going through his mind. There are other times when I've thought, 'Well what is he doing?' – when I've almost felt like sending out a long pole with a hook on the end of it to move him into position. I do associate with the runners I coach, not only Steve but also several of the others: I more or less go through the races with them. I'm sure there are coaches who aren't very responsive, who can switch off when their job is done, but it would be totally alien to my nature not to feel these things during a race. Talking to Mel Watman during that interview in 1979, Steve said that he wouldn't care to stay in big-time athletics after he stops racing. 'I wouldn't like to go through again the situations I've been through already, even in a coaching capacity, worrying about big races and so on. Harry gets just as nervous sometimes as I do.' He told Mel that people look at him and think, 'He knows what he's doing; he'll be ready.' 'It's not me,'

223

said Steve. 'I panic, the same as everybody else.'

Steve does get nervous, but it's generally excitement rather than apprehension. He's keyed up. I get nervous, though other than when I'm watching a race on television at home, I don't think I show it very much. Yet no matter how good you are, or how hard you've worked, when it comes to the major races there will always be an element of doubt. A student may prepare for an exam and do all his revision, but at the last minute he still has that horrible feeling, 'Supposing the examiners pop in a couple of questions we haven't covered?' It's the same with an athlete. He may think that he's covered everything, but there's always that chink of uncertainty, and through the chink wells the nervousness in him, which starts the adrenalin flowing. Now with some runners it starts flowing too early – on the Wednesday, say, before a Saaturday race, and these people actually burn themselves out. Their pulse is high for three or four days in a row and by the time the race comes they've gone a little bit over the top. This is called 'peaking too early'. I like to see a runner a bit nervouus before the start of his race and in need of some reassurance, because this usually shows the adrenalin is charging him up properly. When somebody is blasé about a race and doesn't give a damn, or when he thinks he's gpt everything so taped that he's not even going to get worked up about it – that's when a coach starts to worry. A little apprehension is not a bad thing, provided it's not of disabling intensity.

As I've told you, I don't go in for psyching people up before a race. Whether other coaches in Britain do it or not, I don't know. My attitude has always been that race confidence is built up over a long history of training sessions, like the sstudent doing his swotting before an exam. The runner does his background work, his long intervals, his speed work, his mileage, and by then he's thinking, 'Well let's go: I'm ready.' The coach doesn't have to push him; he wants the races, he's dying to get into them so that he can prove himself. Of course, there are athletes who do all the preparatory work and then get

so nervous on race day that they don't do their best, and
when this happens it's a very tough problem to overcome. But Steve isn't like that at all. Provided he's been
able to do his training OK, he's happy – keyed up, but
happy. It's only when there have been gaps in his
training or the work hasn't been going too well that his
confidence sags. If Steve's done the build-up, he's not
going to forget *his* lines in the middle of the act or
anything like that.

So much for confidence *before* the race. What about
when the race gets under way? When a race is tactical,
you generally have a situation where somebody is setting
the pace and the others are sitting in. They're looking at
each other, deciding when to make their move. Now, the
one who breaks first is *usually* the one whose nerve has
gone, who hasn't the confidence to contain himself any
more: he daren't wait any longer. His nerve breaks, and
he breaks. So then he becomes the leader and the others
sit in on him. Of course, there is fine judgement in all
this. The runner has to strike a balance between losing
his nerve and making the equally dangerous error of
waiting too long. You can watch a pack sitting in on the
leader and see them playing this mental poker, bluffing,
holding back, and almost daring each other to make a
break. The leader makes himself vulnerable: he can be
picked off. If you're leading, all the other runners can
observe you and assess your speed, judging the most
opportune moment to take you. If a runner moves up on
you and he has explosive acceleration, there will also be
an element of surprise, because he may not only go past,
but open up an irretrievable gap. If you don't respond
immediately, you've had it. On the other hand, if you're
sitting in and you lose your nerve, you may go too soon
and not last the distance. Or you can leave it too long,
until the leader is beyond your grasp. Some runners like
to leave it late; I've seen people wait until the last ten
metres before making their move. If you do that and still
win, well, that's fabulous and everybody thinks how
clever you are, but there is a dividing line, a point

beyond which you've left it too late to show your finish. The rule is, 'The nearer the finish you make your break, the faster and fiercer your burst must be.'

In an interview Steve did with the *Sunday Telegraph* magazine in 1978, he described a strange feeling of detachment that comes over him sometimes when he's racing, even though the race at hand is his only concern. I think I know what Steve's referring to: it happens when he's so superbly fit that he feels the race is absolutely under control, and everything seems to more or less take care of itself. No matter what happens, he'll cope with it. On these occasions, there is a feeling of detachment, of remoteness from the actual business of running. The other competitors seem to move along like minor characters in the plot, with himself the pivotal point of the action. The others are there, but in a sense he is alone on the track. It's a strange experience, and difficult to describe to the uninitiated. It will only happen to Steve occasionally, in good-quality races, when he is sitting in. It won't occur when he's pushing so hard that it hurts. But when it does happen, I think it's because he's so very fit, and clear in his mind, that he's completely relaxed, poised for his cue to move up. As Steve said after Montreal, 'To get out of trouble, it's no good running with your eyeballs popping out. But if you're in control at speed, you can respond efficiently to any sudden moves.'

Half-open athletics

It's hard to say where athletics is going at the moment, or what the future holds. Everyone thought the whole question of professionalism and sponsorship would have been cleared up by now, but it obviously hasn't been. The IAAF doesn't seem to know which way to move on open athletics really and we are all in limbo at the moment, with certain sections of the British athletic administration voting to go open and other sections insisting they don't want anything to do with it. There are simply not enough people, either in Britain or internationally, who have thought this thing through; even if ground rules are agreed, there would have to be officials sufficiently knowledgeable and authoritative to implement them. In Britain as we stand at the moment, we couldn't implement an open athletics scheme because we don't have the professional people to do it. We would have a shabby, piecemeal situation, with an open race here and an open race there, and everything in between an utter shambles. Here, we're trying to make bricks without straw, building up an administrative body without the necessary expertise. So far as I can see, the only way ahead will be to call in outside help and professional guidance. There are bound to be problems and anomalies, even if and when it is decided to go open. What happens, for example, to the fellow who can command £1000 appearance money, when he runs for his country against East Germany? Will he simply get travelling expenses, or is he going to be paid? This has caused difficulties for professional tennis players when they agree to play in the Davis Cup; for a long while there were bitter wrangles between the players and the authorities about how a Davis Cup player should be recompensed for missing lucrative tournaments. Issues like this must be sorted out very clearly beforehand, or open athletics will be a one-way ticket to chaos, as has happened in other sports. Sponsorship will mean new responsibilities, with the professional athlete being paid to train as well as to race, whereas I always like to think a runner's first responsibility is to himself and his own potential.

But wherever athletics is going, Steve won't be standing still. Neither of us feel that he's anywhere near his peak yet. There's a lot more to come even at his present distances, and he hasn't even considered moving up to 5000 metres yet. Nobody can argue with that, because if he's getting faster each year and beating people, why should he switch? He's still exploring the planet he's on. This is why we wouldn't want to be drawn into making guesses and predictions as to what his ultimate speed may be at any distance. We don't know yet, do we? One thing is certain, though: if Steve does move up to 5000 metres – or down to 400 metres – at some time in the future, it won't be because he's been pushed into it; it will be entirely his own decision.

Statistics*

Steve Ovett's fastest marks

These statistics comprise, in order, mark, finishing place, venue and date.
+: during mile race; h: heat; i: indoor mark; m: manual timing; s: semifinal.

1500 metres

3:31.36	1	Koblenz	27 August 1980
3:31.57	1	Budapest	29 July 1981
3:31.95	1	Turin	8 July 1981
3:32.09	1	Oslo	15 July 1980
3:32.11	1	Brussels	4 September 1979
3:32.7 +	1	Oslo	1 July 1980
3:33.34+	1	Lausanne	14 July 1981
3:34.0 +	1	London	31 August 1979
3:34.1 +	1	Oslo	11 July 1981
3:34.45	1	Düsseldorf	3 September 1977
3:34.63	1	Bergen	3 August 1981
3:34.7 +	2	Rieti	9 September 1981
3:34.95	1	Rome	5 September 1981
3:35.26	1	London	27 June 1980
3:35.4	1	Lausanne	15 August 1980
3:35.57	1	Prague	3 September 1978
3:35.8	1	Oslo	3 August 1978
3:36.6	1	Gothenburg	7 August 1979
3:36.79h	1	Moscow	30 July 1980

Mile

3:48.4	1	Koblenz	26 August 1981
3:48.8 m	1	Oslo	1 July 1980
3:49.25	1	Oslo	11 July 1981

*Compiled by Dave Cocksedge.

229

3:49.57	1	London	31 August 1979
3:49.66	1	Lausanne	14 July 1981
3:50.23	2	Rieti	9 September 1981
3:51.56	1	Brussels	22 August 1980
3:52.8 m	1	Oslo-Stovner	20 September 1978
3:52.84	1	London	25 August 1980
3:54.1	1	Berlin	17 August 1979
3:54.69	1	London	26 June 1977
3:55.23	1	London	14 September 1979
3:55.5	1	Tokyo	25 September 1978
3:55.58	1	Berlin	21 August 1981
3:55.7 m	1	Dublin	11 July 1978
3:56.6	1	London	9 September 1977
3:56.6	1	Gateshead	9 September 1979
3:57.0	9	Stockholm	30 June 1975

800 metres

1:44.09	2	Prague	31 August 1978
1:44.91	2	Cologne	19 August 1979
1:45.38	1	Turku	27 July 1978
1:45.4	1	Moscow	26 July 1980
1:45.44	5	Montreal	25 July 1976
1:45.5	5	Zürich	18 August 1976
1:45.78	2	Rome	4 September 1974
1:46.1	1	London	2 August 1975
1:46.11s	2	Montreal	24 July 1976
1:46.1	2	Helsinki	10 August 1976
1:46.2	1	Dublin	10 July 1979
1:46.4	1	London	31 August 1981
1:46.5 s	1	Prague	30 August 1978
1:46.6	1	Nice	17 August 1975
1:46.6	1	Bergen	4 June 1980
1:46.61s	1	Moscow	25 July 1980
1:46.7	1	London	5 June 1976
1:46.7	1	London	3 July 1976
1:46.8	1	Warsaw	30 June 1974
1:46.9	1	London	13 July 1974
1:46.9	1	Edinburgh	6 August 1976

Steve's best marks: 22.3 (200 metres), 47.5 (400), 1:16.0 (600), 1:44.09 (800), 2:15.91 (1000), 3:31.36 (1500), 3:48.4 (mile), 4:57.82 (2000), 7:41.3 (3000), 8:13.51 (2 miles), 13:25.0 (5000). Half-marathon (road): 65:38.

230

The world's fastest miles: performers and performances

3:47.33	1	Sebastian Coe (UK)	Brussels	28 August 1981
3:48.40	1	Steven Ovett (UK)	Koblenz	26 August 1981
3:48.53	1	Coe	Zürich	19 August 1981
3:48.83	1	Sydney Maree (SA/USA)	Rieti	9 September 1981
3:48.8	m 1	Ovett	Oslo	1 July 1980
3:48.95	1	Coe	Oslo	17 July 1979
3:49.25	1	Ovett	Oslo	11 July 1981
3:49.45	2	Mike Boit (Kenya)	Brussels	28 August 1981
			(fastest losing mark)	
3:49.4	m 1	John Walker (NZ)	Gothenburg	12 August 1975
3:49.57	1	Ovett	London	31 August 1979
3:49.66	1	Ovett	Lausanne	14 July 1981
3:49.67	2	Jose-Luis Gonzales (Sp)	Oslo	11 July 1981
3:49.68	3	Steve Scott (USA)	Oslo	11 July 1981
			(fastest third place ever)	
3:49.74	2	Boit	Zürich	19 August 1981
3:49.93	1	Maree	Aichach	16 September 1981
3:49.95	3	Stephen Cram (UK)	Zürich	19 August 1981
3:50.12	4	Walker	Zürich	19 August 1981
			(fastest fourth place ever)	
3:50.23	2	Ovett	Rieti	9 September 1981
3:50.26	4	Walker	Oslo	11 July 1981
3:50.34	5	Todd Harbour (USA)	Oslo	11 July 1981
			(fastest fifth place ever)	
3:50.38	6	Cram	Oslo	11 July 1981
			(fastest sixth place ever)	
3:50.51	2	Boit	Aichach	16 September 1981
3:50.56	2	Thomas Wessinghage (GFR)	London	31 August 1979
3:50.58	1	Walker	Auckland	18 March 1981
3:50.6	m 1i	Eamonn Coghlan (RoI)	San Diego	20 February 1981